Grow~~ing At Risk~~
Medicinal Herbs
Cultivation, Conservation and Ecology

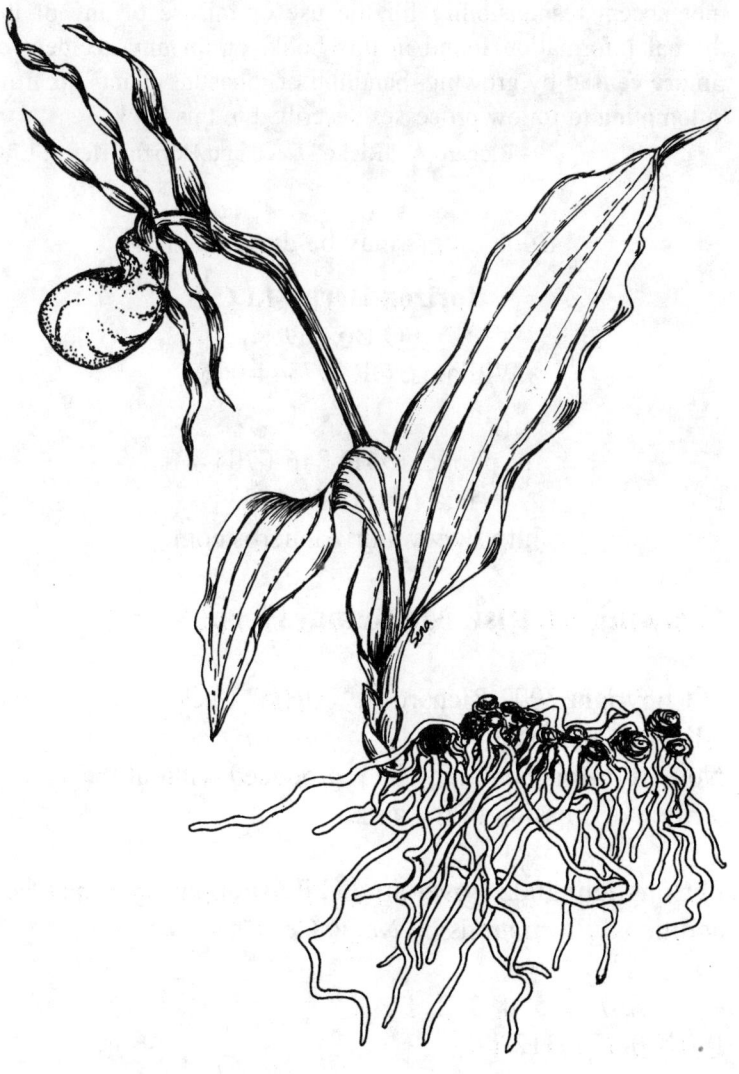

Disclaimer

Although all cultures on earth use plant-derived medicaments, we cannot recommend self-medication with plant products. Rather, we offer medicinal information in the context of historical usage and from personal experience, augmented by our studies of current research. Please seek the care and advice of a qualified healthcare practitioner for all medical problems. We do not accept responsibility for the use or misuse of any of the herbal information found in this book, or for any accident or injury caused by growing, handling or ingesting plants, or from attempting to follow processes described in this book.

—Richard A. "Richo" Cech and Horizon Herbs, LLC

Book orders may be directed to:

Horizon Herbs, LLC
PO Box 69
Williams, OR 97544-0069
USA

phone: (541) 846-6704
fax: (541) 846-6233
http://www.horizonherbs.com

Growing At-Risk Medicinal Herbs

10 9 8 7 6 5 4 3 2 1
ISBN 0-9700312-1-1

Growing At-Risk Medicinal Herbs

Cultivation, Conservation and Ecology

by Richo Cech
illustrated by Sena Cech

A Horizon Herbs Publication
Williams, Oregon
2002

By the Same Author

Making Plant Medicine

"An excellent overview of making medicinal tinctures, vinegars, glycerites, water-based preparations, syrups, salves, baths, poultices, etc. Clearly explains the methods for making everything from simple teas to professional quality, mixed-solvent tinctures equal to those in health food stores."

—J.L. Hudson, Seedsman

ISBN 0-9700312-0-3, 282 pages, cost $14.95 plus $4.95 s/h

Growing Your Garden Pharmacy

This is a book of stories by Richo, also including information on starting seedlings indoors, medicinal gardening in pots and the organic cultivation and harvesting of herbs for family medicine. 30 pages, cost $4.95 plus $3.45 s/h

Horizon Herbs Seed Catalog

Published twice yearly, this catalog provides access to organically grown live roots, plants and open-pollinated seed of over 600 species of medicinal plants from all over the world. Also included are Richo's growing guidelines for medicinal plants as well as specific medicinal, germination and gardening information for each herb.
96 pages, FREE

All publications available:
online at horizonherbs.com
by phone: (541) 846-6704
by fax: (541) 846-6233
or by writing: **Horizon Herbs, LLC**
                PO Box 69
                Williams, OR 97544-0069

This book is dedicated to my family.

Acknowledgments

A book of this sort is a little like a plant—it germinates and grows in accordance with the surrounding environment, nurtured not only by the gardener, but by the garden itself. Try as I might to generate this natural, garden-like atmosphere internally, the successful completion of this book required the cooperation of my family, friends and colleagues who were to me like the soil, the air, the rain and the sun. Thank you!

Rosemary Gladstar (heroine) requested that I write the book. It took longer than she expected, and it is much bigger than what she wanted. But Rosemary, when you plant a seed, do you always know how fast and how big the plant will grow? You are the best!

Sena Cech (younger daughter) illustrated this book, patiently working as the seasons progressed, sometimes even sketching a root at dormancy and finishing the drawing months later as the plant came into flower. While her classmates watched Saturday morning cartoons, she was delving into the intricacies of the rhizome and rootlets of the lady's slipper orchid. Amazing focus and perseverance!

Nadja Cech (elder daughter) also contributed some wonderful illustrations to this book, including the black cohosh plant and some of the seedling illustrations for blue cohosh, ginseng and goldenseal. Thank you, Sweetie!

Mayche Cech (wife) influenced this book in many positive ways—as the designer, the editor and the inspired critic. She also stemmed her native ebullience in order to give me space to write. I love you!

Robert and Annette Cech (parents) held from an early date the nascent table of contents for the book, following my progress as I wrote. They were solid supporters throughout, a cherished cheering section. Annette also read and edited the text!

Katarina Stuart (friend) was instrumental in applying an English teacher's expertise to the final editing of the text.

Tracy, Tressi and Nance (coworkers) kept the phone answered while I traipsed mentally through the hardwood forests of Appalachia. They even managed a round of applause when the last word hit the paper. Much appreciation!

The following individuals provided expert consultation: Rod Angeroth, Tane Datta, Norman Deno, Steven Foster, Joe Hollis, Howard Horne, Tom Kaye, Robyn Klein, Michael Moore, Charles Perry, Shawn Sigstedt, Paul Strauss and Greg Tilford.

Table of Contents

Foreword
by Michael Moore

I have wildcrafted medicinal plants for about a third of a century and taught folks about gathering plants for about a quarter of a century. I feel that you cannot know an herb unless you have met it where it lives, taken its measure . . . sat down for a chat, as it were. I have also watched the wild gardens diminish year after year. At the same time that I have defended wildcrafting, I have watched myself draw an ever tighter ring, showing fewer plants and increasingly learning and emphasizing naturalized plants and those native plants that like human beings.

I no longer take students to the Ozarks to show them goldenseal, black cohosh and the like (it's all been poached out) . . . I no longer drag folks up to the Great Basin for lomatium, or to the Panhandle to dig in large stands of *Echinacea angustifolia*. I have come to see the accumulative effects of this gathering.

I went to the Sand Hills of Nebraska, a place recommended by John Uri Lloyd as having some of the best echinacea on the planet. I found out that it had all been dug out in the 1930s (for the drug trade) and has never recovered. The same has happened to the limestone hills of western Oklahoma. I visited a state park in Missouri that was in turmoil. Poachers had come in several nights earlier and dug out the 4,000 giant yellow coneflowers *(Echinacea paradoxa* var. *paradoxa)*, the largest existing stand of this rare plant and one of the very reasons for the park's existence. The rural roads of southern Missouri were prowled by work gangs in the late 1980s and early 1990s and flatbed trucks took out many thousands of tons of *Echinacea pallida*. I am told it has not recovered very well.

I have many other such stories. Suffice it to say, I have become much more moderate in the plants I harvest and the plants I teach about.

The Romans prized a giant umbel, Cyrenaic silphium (an unknown species of *Ferula)* for its aphrodisiac and antifertility effects. By the second century it was more expensive than gold;

by the third century it was extinct. With this in mind, I have ceased using lady's slipper and false unicorn root completely. I explain to students that these plants simply do not exist for herbalists anymore; the same for wild American ginseng. Buying or gathering any of them is the moral equivalent of eating "bush-meat" derived from the mountain gorilla. Other plants can be used . . . MUST be used, instead of wild-gathered plants.

I have also begun to modify my concept of "wilderness." I have come to realize that North America has been shaped for millennia by human beings, and my romanticized concept of it as unspoiled is simply my Urban American Myth. Nowhere is without our footprint. While many plants are fading out, others are taking their place. Many of our old friends, those we once cultivated on ground that we prepared or burned off, whose seeds we spread, are diminishing.

There is less chia than formerly . . . no one is there to spread and nurture the seed. That peculiar kava-like clone sweet-flag that was once carefully spread by plains folks is diminishing without its former care. Saya *(Amoreuxia palmatifida)*, that delicious little Sonoran food plant is almost extinct. Even the Arizona variant of yerba mansa, once spread from seep to seep by Native Americans, in past ages, is almost gone. The great Pacific oak stands, trees with subtly "guided" large acorns that once fed millions are diminishing (Mediterranean grasses and suburbs are displacing them). Maca *(Lepidium peruvianum)* nearly became extinct in the Andes until its "worth" was reestablished by academics. Ancient diviner's sage clones almost disappeared from the earth until ethnobotanists and academic "stoners" found them worthy. The classic mound dwellers coaxed amaranth and *Chenopodium* into full-scale food plants along the Ohio River Valley (none have survived) and strains of flood-sown panic grass once fed thousands along the Colorado River Valley and the Rio Sonora. I have only seen a little annual datura growing in Northern New Mexico near old Anasazi ruins . . . nowhere else. In other words, those "wild places" have always borne the marks of humans. That's what we do.

Europeans came to North America and invented a completely novel concept of land use—Boom and Bust; use it up and move westward. We have done more harm to our environment in two centuries than the Greeks managed to do to theirs in three or four thousand years. We tilled every inch of prairie by 1875, drove nearly every large predator to extinction by 1900, and almost wiped out the most abundant ungulate the world had ever seen, the American bison. We completely wiped out the passenger pigeon, perhaps the most numerous flock bird that ever existed.

The earth does not exist for our benefit,
rather we are OF the earth.

Thank God for Richo and folks like him. I was born with a brown thumb (somewhat akin to a tin ear). I cannot grow things. I have come to realize that without growing and nurturing some of our plant allies, they are doomed. Richo views plants the same way I do, as life forms with quirks and needs, thrumming their green energy off in some alternate universe that I can only vaguely understand. Richo seems to understand their language rather well (at least for a human) and, like the older traditional humans, coaxes them and thrums at them in turn. I have always said that an herbalist needs a good brain and dirty fingernails. For me, the dirty fingernails come from digging up and garbling wild plants. Richo has gone much further in this book. For him, the dirty fingernails come from nurturing and coaxing plants to grow for themselves in a place that he has access to. This book is far more than it seems. Don't underestimate what Richo has accomplished. He has taken some of the most difficult plants imaginable, plants that sometimes find even the breath of humans to be anathema, and figured out what they need in order to grow near us and by our leave.

He has a good brain and dirty fingernails.

Michael Moore—SW School of Botanical Medicine
(hrbmoore@mindspring.com) http://www.swsbm.com
Teaching manuals, 2000+ images, classic herb, eclectic,
pharmacy and botany information are all on the school's web site.

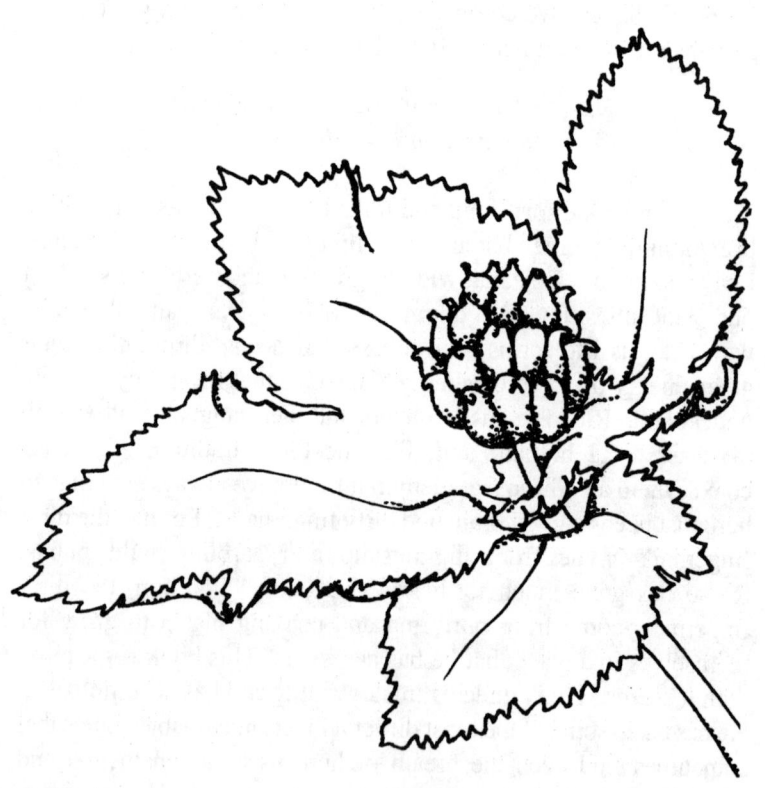

United Plant Savers
by Rosemary Gladstar

A nonprofit grass roots organization, United Plant Savers (UpS) is dedicated to preserving native medicinal plants and the land they grow on in order to ensure an abundant renewable supply of organically cultivated medicinal herbs for present and future generations. Formed in the spirit of hope, our membership reflects the great diversity of American herbalism and includes herbalists, botanists, health-care professionals, organic farmers, business owners, wildcrafters, seed savers, manufacturers and plant lovers from all walks of life.

To date UpS has initiated a number of replanting projects including our "plant give-aways" in which over 50,000 goldenseal roots and several thousand other at-risk plants including black cohosh, blue cohosh, bloodroot, slippery elm and white oak saplings have been distributed to members to plant on their land. UpS encourages the stewarding of existing wild medicinal plants by spreading their seed within the habitat and by weeding out non-native species. We also encourage gardeners to propagate at-risk medicinal plants in their backyards, gardens, farms and privately owned lands. By monitoring the status of these valuable plants from season to season we can gather information in order to help assure their continued survival. We feel that the most positive changes are often the results of thoughtful, committed citizens taking action. Though large planting projects and funded scientific research are an important part of plant conservation, equally important is individual participation by laypeople. Often it is those people out there "doing it," living and working with the plants for decades, that have the most expertise. We support the "grow your own medicine" mentality and encourage our members to plant medicinal herb gardens and to help reestablish nature's wild gardens on their land.

Our largest and most complex task has been to define and develop the medicinal plant "at-risk" and "watch" lists. These lists are continuously reviewed in order to identify those native medicinal plants that are of highest conservation priority. These lists have become a guide for the conscience of the herbal industry, the herbal community and the concerned public. We are choosing to promote the cultivation and conservation of these plants before they disappear from the native landscape forever.

With the generous support of our "green angels" Judy and Michael Funk, United Plant Savers established a 370-acre botanical sanctuary in Meigs County, Ohio. This land serves as a model farm for medicinal plant conservation, research and education, and as a seed repository for American medicinal plants. This beautiful farm is rich with native medicinals and has a number of research and educational projects under way. We have also established the "botanical sanctuary network," a program that helps members make their land into thriving botanical sanctuaries.

The book *Planting the Future*[1] is the collective effort of many concerned herbalists, including professional wildcrafters, practitioners, manufacturers and community herbalists. Each brings their personal knowledge and love of the plants and a great passion to ensure that these plants continue to flourish in their native landscape, remaining an intricate part of the great web of life. Richo's new book *Growing At-Risk Medicinal Herbs* picks up where *Planting the Future* left off, delving deeply into the nature of the at-risk plants, their habitat requirements, natural companions and the details of their cultivation and preparation.

Through these and other projects we are seeking solutions, and we are optimistic that our efforts are making a difference. Our mission is to ensure the perpetuation of important medicinal plants and their native habitat so that when future generations of plant lovers walk upon this planet, they, too, will know and appreciate the medicines of their ancestors and the healing power that grows from the heart of the earth.

---

[1] *Planting the Future* is available from Horizon Herbs, LLC
online: horizonherbs.com
phone: (541) 846-6704
fax: (541) 846-6233
or by writing: Horizon Herbs, PO Box 69, Williams, OR 97544-0069

The good news is that it is not too late; none of these important North American medicinal plants are extinct. Each of us has the opportunity and skills needed to make a difference. If we chose to use plants as our medicine, we then become accountable for the wild gardens, their health and their upkeep. We begin a cocreative partnership with the plants, giving back what we receive—health, nourishment, beauty and protection. We invite you to join in our efforts to help plant the future.

Frances Thompson, the English poet, once wrote that one could not pluck a flower without troubling a star. If we cannot pluck a flower without troubling a star, what then if we lose a species?
— Loren Israelson

To become a member of United Plant Savers contact:
United Plant Savers
PO Box 77
Guysville, OH 45735
phone: (740) 662-0041
fax: (740) 662-0247
www.plantsavers.org
e-mail: plants@frognet.net

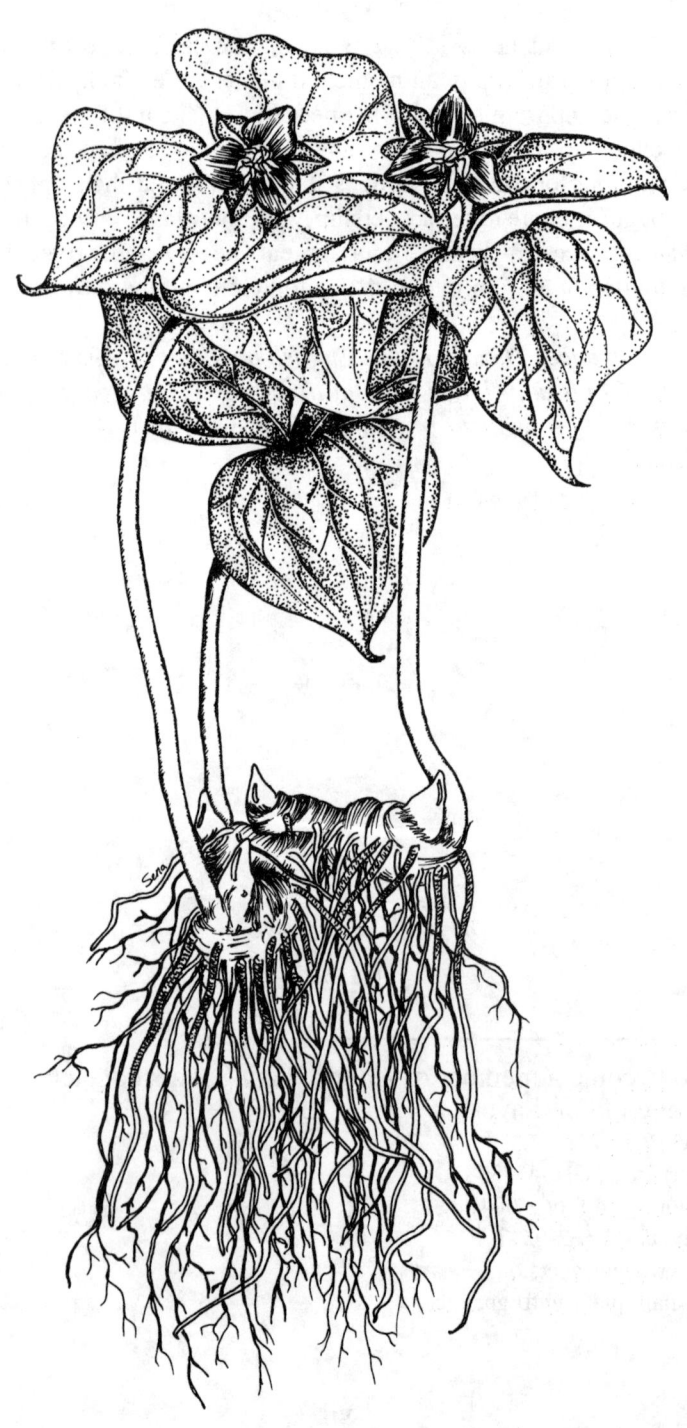

Why At-Risk?

Frozen fields, gray skies and fog on the mountain often characterize deep winter in southern Oregon. Seeking the solitude of a short hike along Munger's Creek, with its chiming water fed by cold rain and snowmelt on the high slopes, I retreated to the lower parts of our farm, footsteps muted by sodden maple leaves. Passing the trellised beds of dormant, woodland medicinals, I paused for a moment, then stooped to examine a spot where I had previously planted many goldenseal seeds. The seed should have germinated that spring, but despite my expectant lookout, the tiny spoon-shaped cotyledons had failed to emerge. On an impulse, I parted the partially frozen mulch of rotting leaves and dug a hand into the sandy bed, bringing up a large divot of soil. As the soil particles fell away, I began to observe many trailing golden sprouts. Creekside walk now forgotten, I produced my pocket magnifying glass and brought one of these nascent plants into trembling focus. The simple hair-like radicle, looming under the 10X, glowed berberine yellow, topped by a tiny bud of the same vibrant color. Undisturbed by the sudden, crass flapping of a blue jay in a nearby alder, I took a good breath, leaned back on my heels and mulled. Clearly, under certain conditions goldenseal is not a simple overwintering germinator, but can also be a two-phase germinator, producing during the first growing season a healthy root and bud, nourished solely by its energy reserves and by its relationship with the soil, perfectly healthy without the benefit of photosynthesis. The survival advantage of this would be to allow vigorous emergence of aerial portions from an already-established root system in the early spring when the woodland floor is sunny, and before other plants begin to compete for resources. I marveled at this adaptive strategy, and as I carefully pricked the seedlings back into place in the bed, firming the soil around them and returning the mulch over them, I smiled inwardly at the thought of the impulse which brought me to this little discovery. The seedlings had spoken to me as I passed, their tiny voices piping in my consciousness, begging me to investigate, to know

1

them better. Continuing my walk along the winter stream, I considered how on a worldwide basis the plants are clearly speaking to us, and gave thanks for the many folks of natural persuasion who are tuning their perception to recognize these healing voices.

Poised here at the beginning of the 21st century, herbalists are challenged to serve the burgeoning human population while at the same time the wild plant populations, the main source of our traditional materia medica, diminish at an alarming rate. Farnsworth and Soejarto reported that we are currently losing around one plant species per day. They suggest that by the year 2000 we will have already "driven to extinction medicinal plants worth $40 billion annually in the United States alone" (Farnsworth and Soejarto, 1985). Beyond concern over the economic losses caused by plant extinction, there is clearly a personal, cultural, scientific, medical and aesthetic value in maintaining the health of our wild places and in fostering our wild plants.

There are many similarities among the 20 plants that comprise the United Plant Savers (UpS) at-risk list. Most come from very distinct habitats, environments that are under siege by development, grazing and/or logging. In fact, native plant habitat in the United States is disappearing at the alarming rate of over 2,400 acres daily (Liebman, 1997). The at-risk plants have been traditionally utilized in medicine, with substantial historical or current trade that has led to overharvest in many cases, thereby challenging their sustainability in these wild environs. These plants are harvested mainly for their nonrenewable portions, either the entire plant or the roots, so that the harvest of the medicine usually spells the end of that individual. For the most part the roots of at-risk plants are quite small, and therefore it requires the harvest of many individuals to fill a given harvest quota. These are mainly long-lived, perennial plants that may not quickly or reliably reproduce in the wild once the adult, seed-bearing individuals are harvested. They are challenging to cultivate. In many cases, the cultivation methodologies have not been well-established because these plants require very specific germination and growth conditions. Often they are difficult to start from seed, and when started from seed may require many years to develop to harvestable size. Therefore, many people continue to harvest plants from wild populations, often the cheapest or the only source of raw material for the manufacture of certain herbal products.

Populations of wild annual or biennial plants that reproduce readily from seed are generally sustainable even in the face of wholesale harvest. There is usually an intact seed bank in the soil that produces ample regrowth the next year and seeds may even lie dormant in the soil for decades until the right germination conditions are encountered. However, the harvest of a long-lived perennial plant has much greater impact, because it can take many years for the plant to be replaced in nature. Older, seed-bearing individuals are the repositories for the genetic and regenerative potential of the population. Robyn Klein has done excellent work on compiling the age ranges of some of the plants on the at-risk list, reporting that American ginseng *(Panax quinquefolius)* can live for 50 to 60 years, *Echinacea angustifolia* 17 to 44 years, false unicorn *(Chamaelirium luteum)* 30 to 80 years, trillium *(Trillium ovatum)* 72 years and yellow lady's slipper orchid *(Cypripedium "calceolus")* 30 to 100 years (Klein, 1999; Kindscher and Klein, 2000). It gives one pause to consider that the plant being harvested for medicine may actually be older than the human it is destined to treat.

The historically dwindling supply of wild ginseng, goldenseal, lady's slipper orchid, peyote and Venus fly trap has resulted in their regulation in Appendix II of the Convention for International Trade in Endangered Species of Wild Fauna and Flora (CITES). Without further conservation and cultivation we are likely to see others of the at-risk herbs listed by CITES in the near future, with black cohosh and osha already under consideration. Although CITES listing tends to slow exportation of the herb (although only in the raw form), it has no power to limit domestic trade. We can only hope that these tighter regulations on trade will be augmented by more proactive efforts by government, industry, nonprofit and educational institutions. Monitoring wild populations, educating the public about the source of the herbs used to make their medicines and researching appropriate cultivation methodologies would more successfully protect these wild resources.

3

The tides of consumer demand strongly impact the sustainability of our wild medicinal plant populations. For instance, black cohosh has recently registered increased consumer demand resulting in "the largest gain for any single herb . . . rising 477% from the first eight months of 1999 compared to the same period in 1998: $586,469 to $3,385,393" (Brevoort, 1998). Even though the cultivation of black cohosh is relatively rapid and easy, American growers have not yet taken advantage of the rising demand for this herb. Cultivation efforts remain in the fledgling stage, and the vast majority of black cohosh used in manufacturing is therefore taken directly from the American forests.

The story really starts in the eastern hardwood forest biome, where Native Americans first introduced the settlers to ginseng, black cohosh, bloodroot, blue cohosh, goldenseal, false unicorn, lady's slipper orchid, trillium, Virginia snakeroot and wild yam. The ongoing utilization and sometimes exploitation of these plants is a matter of history, resulting eventually in their listing on the UpS at-risk list. Even as early as 1898 the eclectic physicians Felter and Lloyd wrote of goldenseal: "Once plentiful along the Ohio river banks, it is now found only in isolated spots, having suffered extermination as fast as the woodland yielded to the pioneer's axe" (Felter and Lloyd, 1898). So the fate of these plants is linked to the forest which nurtures them, and the plants are further threatened by massive harvest for use in domestic and foreign manufacturing. In 1997, Joy Welvey Bannerman reported that "the annual volume of goldenseal entering the United Kingdom [was] approximately 10 metric tons with an estimated value of U.S. $1.55 million. At a minimum of 200 roots to the pound, that 10-ton import amount for the U.K. alone suggests a staggering annual harvest . . ." (Bannerman, 2000). In fact, the yearly wild harvest of goldenseal plants from the American forests was computed by Joseph Brinkman and myself at between 45.4 and 68.1 million plants (Cech, 1997). And for wild ginseng, the situation is similar. According to John Lentz, during the 1997-1998 season in Ohio alone, over 8,000 pounds of dry, wild root was purchased and recorded. This equates to a minimum of 2,500,000 plants. The wild "roots have become so scarce that tiny juveniles are illegally dug and dried" (Lentz, 1988).

4

The slippery elm tree *(Ulmus rubra)* has also found its way onto the UpS at-risk list, mainly due to a concern over loss of trees to Dutch elm disease. The inner bark is a much-utilized demulcent, available at health food stores in bulk quantities. Slippery elm bark is also the main active constituent of several popular throat lozenges and an ingredient of the Essiac anticancer remedy.

Four plants found primarily in the southern United States that are also found on the UpS at-risk list are still in commercial demand. The light, grassy roots of true unicorn *(Aletris farinosa)* grow wild in the sandy soils of Florida and range across the southern states to Texas, also occuring sparsely in the midwest. This herb is rarely available due to its limited habitat, the paucity of wild populations and the lack of cultivated material.

Stillingia *(Stillingia sylvatica)* is a member of the *Euphorbiaceae* family, ranging from Maryland to the Gulf of Mexico and across to Mississippi and Louisiana. It grows in sandy soils near water features, including the ocean, the major desert river flood plains and the margins of the southern swamps. Populations have diminished hugely in the last century due to loss of habitat (the building of condominiums and the draining of the swamps) and excessive harvest pressure. The plant is an ingredient in the famous Hoxsey anticancer formula.

Venus fly trap *(Dionaea muscipula)* is found only in a few scattered bogs of North and South Carolina. Due to its popularity as a novelty plant, the wild populations were very early reduced at a rapid rate. More recently, as the anticancer effects became known, demand again increased. Although a certain amount of poaching still occurs, greenhouse cultivation methods are well understood and the majority of plants for the novelty and medicinal trade are now cultivated. Use of wild plants for any purpose is certainly a travesty, given their extremely limited distribution.

Peyote *(Lophophora williamsii)* was once abundant in its native Southwestern desert habitat, but has been increasingly challenged with overharvest over the last 30 years. Although cultivation is possible by seed and by cuttings, this cultivation is illegal. Therefore, in recent history the wild plants have been continually utilized.

According to Rabbi Matthew S. Kent of the Peyote Way Church of God:

> In recent years we have become alarmed that peyote is threatened with extinction in its native habitat in south Texas. Destruction of the peyote fields and incorrect harvesting techniques have created a serious shortage of holy plants in Texas, which also creates a serious threat to the existence of our church. The Mexican government listed peyote in 1991 as an endangered species, and permits harvesting for religious use. It is a fact that peyote has a wider range and grows more abundantly in Mexico than in Texas (Kent, 1996).

The elders of the Peyote Way Church of God approached United Plant Savers in 1996, requesting that the plant be included on the at-risk list. After reviewing the evidence, and given the frequent and widespread use of this cactus in healing ceremony, we responded by listing the plant. The elders then replied with the following words, "Thank you for your good works. Peyote is a sacrament and an endangered species. We hope you are not prejudiced against it because of the government's hostile position."

Crossing the Rocky Mountains into the western states, we find another group of popular native medicinal plants that UpS has determined are at-risk. These include *Echinacea angustifolia,* lomatium *(Lomatium dissectum)* and osha *(Ligusticum porteri* and other *Ligusticum* species). Though these plants are widely distributed and locally abundant, they are known to be slow to reproduce. For instance, even *E. angustifolia* (which reproduces rapidly in comparison to lomatium and osha) has been reported to take an average of 2 to 3 years in the wild to produce a mature flowering plant (Hurlburt, 1999). These species reproduce by seed, but they maintain their populations primarily because they are long-lived. Therefore, the harvest of too many adult individuals can seriously compromise the wild populations. In fact, a recent thesis on wild *E. angustifolia* suggests that in order to maintain the current range, wild populations can withstand a maximum yearly harvest of only 5% of the total population (Lantz, 1997).

The genus *Echinacea* consists of nine species, of which wild and cultivated *E. angustifolia* and *E. pallida* and cultivated *E. purpurea* are common in trade. An additional conservation concern arises when rare species such as *E. simulata, E. atrorubens, E. sanguinea, E. paradoxa* or the federally listed endangered species *E. laevigata* and *E. tennesseensis* are used in trade, or are found as adulterants to commercial shipments of roots of the more common species.

Echinacea is fairly easy to grow, and in reaction to a rising public outcry against use of wild roots, many manufacturers are now utilizing cultivated material, especially *E. purpurea.* Sales of echinacea products in American health food stores exceed $80 million annually (Lantz, 1997). However, there is still a major problem with poaching of wild echinacea species. Christopher Robbins of Traffic USA puts it mildly when he states of echinacea "collection in the wild in some cases may be greater than what the population can withstand."

The age of harvestable-sized plants of lomatium and osha has not yet been accurately determined, but it is clear from my own experiments in growing these plants that many years may pass before they achieve adequate size to produce seed. For instance, on the dry slopes where lomatium resides, it is very common to find a population consisting only of older individuals, without any seedlings present. Insects and other wildlife eat the seeds, and should they successfully disseminate and sprout, seedling mortality in these dry conditions is very high. Cultivation scenarios have been established for lomatium and osha, but we are far from producing the first commercial crop, and given the slow growth, it will be a long wait. I would also like to mention that echinacea, lomatium and osha are considered "big medicine" by many of the Native American tribespeople, who view them as cultural resources to be used only by initiates.

Another plant of the mountains of the West (which is more common in Alaska than in any other state), is sundew *(Drosera rotundifolia),* a tiny insectivorous plant found growing mainly in cold water bogs. These red-green, glistening plants are extremely delicate and are largely dependent on a distinct peatland ecosystem, which is good reason for inclusion on the UpS at-risk list.

7

The plants are sold as a curiosity for the nursery market, but the herb is also used medicinally. Given the rarity of sundew in the wild, it is imperative to use only cultivated plant material.

Crossing the Pacific Ocean to the island of Hawaii, we find kava kava *(Piper methysticum)*, a member of the pepper family. Kava root is traditionally used in island culture to make a relaxing, mildly psychoactive beverage. Kava has also long been utilized in European and now American phytomedicine as a sedative, muscle relaxant, treatment for menopausal symptoms and for treating anxiety.

Kava does not spread without human assistance, as it reproduces only from cuttings. Since it cannot reproduce sexually, the genetic diversity of existing strains is severely limited and the plant is therefore susceptible to systemic disease. Kava has within the last five years become extremely popular and remaining "wild populations" (patches of ancient plants, long ago planted, now forgotten) are threatened by rediscovery and wholesale harvest. These wild populations act as essential genetic reservoirs, can be nurtured to provide cuttings of new and useful strains of kava and will prove invaluable in the event that the cultivated fields are adversely affected by disease. UpS at-risk listing is meant to support efforts to preserve these ancient kava plants as a part of the island heritage.

This overview provides additional background and justification for the listing of plants found on the UpS at-risk list. These few plants represent a very obvious "tip of the iceberg" and should not be viewed as the only plant conservation challenge faced by modern herbalists. As was all-too-graphically demonstrated by the devastating loss of forest and plant habitat in the recent plague of fires affecting widespread areas in the mountains of the West, our wildlands and the life they hold cannot be viewed as a limitless or permanent resource. We are all responsible for maintaining the diverse ecosystems that serve as the original homes for the plants that provide our livelihood, our medicine and our inspiration. May we treat these places and plants with great respect, for in our interconnectedness, their fate becomes the fate of ourselves.

References

Bannerman, J.E. 2000. *Goldenseal in World Trade: Pressures and Potentials.* HerbalGram, No. 4, pp. 51-52.

Brevoort, P. 1998. *The Booming U.S. Botanical Market: a New Overview.* HerbalGram, No. 44, pp. 33-46.

Cech, R. 1977. *An Ecological Imperative: Growing a Future for Native Plant Medicinals.* United Plant Savers Newsletter, Vol. 1(2), pp. 1-5.

Farnsworth, N.R., and Soejarto, D.D. 1985. *Potential Consequences of Plant Extinction in the United States on the Current and Future Availability of Prescription Drugs.* Economic Botany, 39(3), pp. 231-240.

Felter, H. and J. Lloyd. 1898 (Reprinted 1985). *King's American Dispensatory.* Portland (OR): Eclectic Medical Publishing, Vol. 1 & 2, 743 pp.

Hurlburt, D. 1999. Thesis, Lawrence (KS): University of Kansas.

Kent, S. 1996. *Letter to US Congressman Jim Kolbe.* Sacred Record, Klondyke (AZ), Vol. 17(4).

Klein, R. 1999. *How Old are Our Medicines?* United Plant Savers Newsletter, Vol. 2(1), pp. 5-10.

Kindsher, K and R. Klein. 2000. Manuscript in preparation.

Lantz, G. 1997. *Coneflower's Popularity: Prescription for Trouble?* June/July. National Wildlife Magazine.

Lentz, J. 1988. *Wild Ginseng: Enforcement Update.* United Plant Savers Newsletter, Vol. 1(3), p. 18.

Liebman, Richard. 1997. *Planting the Future.* United Plant Savers Newsletter, Vol. 1 (2), pp. 6-8.

Black Cohosh
Cimicifuga racemosa
roots, rhizome, young
plant and seeds

Black Cohosh

Cimicifuga racemosa (L.) Nutt.

Family: *Ranunculaceae*

Black Cohosh is a long-lived and vigorous woodland herbaceous perennial. The rhizome is knotted, dark brown to black in color, bearing on its upper surface crater-like stem scars and peculiar, cone-shaped stumps. Numerous smooth, tapering rootlets, often reddish in color, extend down from the rhizome, also radiating out just beneath the soil surface. The rhizome and roots together are popularly termed "the root," which is the part used in herbal medicine. The plant is single-stemmed in young individuals, developing multiple stems as it matures. The smooth, furrowed stem rises up from the ground and divides into three, a characteristic that is helpful in field identification. The large, compound leaves are smooth, two- or three-lobed, opposite, double-serrated and sharply pointed. A single plant may produce several upright flowering, wand-shaped racemes. The buds are like round, white pills, opening out into white flowers bearing numerous showy stamens (see page 14). The fetid smell attracts gnats and flies to pollinate. The seed capsule is characteristic—an oval, ribbed follicle that splits on the ventral surface, revealing two stacked rows of brown seeds that loosen and scatter in the late summer to fall as the plant dries. When disturbed by wind, the flight of birds or the passage of mammals, the pods and seeds shake noisily, which long ago gave rise to one of the folk names for this plant, the "rattle pod."

Range. The current distribution of black cohosh stretches from the Appalachian Mountain Range across the eastern hardwood forest biome to the Ozark Plateau and north into the Great Lakes region (USDA, NRCS. 2001). According to historical accounts, the original center of distribution was the Ohio River Valley (Felter and Lloyd, 1898), and indeed, according to my observations, the states of Ohio and West Virginia still boast the largest remaining native stands.

11

Current Range of Black Cohosh in the U.S.

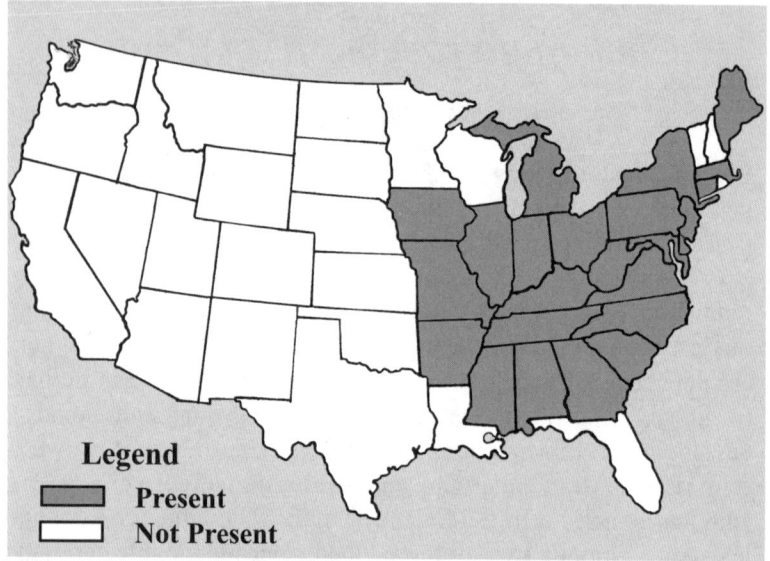

Legend
- ◼ Present
- ☐ Not Present

Hardiness and adaptability. Black cohosh demonstrates a strong winter dormancy and is not hindered by hard winters. The plant stores energy reserves during the growing season and when the tops die back in the autumn, the dormant root is perfectly happy to rest under a blanket of leaves covered by an insulating layer of snow until its reemergence the following spring. Furthermore, the seed must experience winter temperatures before germination is possible. This fact, coupled with a degree of dependency on forest soils and shade, delimits the periphery of its natural distribution—the South is too warm, and the Great Plains have insufficient forest cover.

Black cohosh thrives under cultivation in most areas of the United States including areas outside its natural distribution: the mountains of the West, the maritime regions and even the Southwestern states. If sowing from seed presents too much of a challenge to the gardener, the plant is easily propagated by root division. Black cohosh is tough and it likes people. The main requirements of partial shade, good fertility, occasional weeding and regular watering are readily supplied by most gardeners, and attention to these practices will produce plants of monumental proportions.

Ecology. Black cohosh prefers the partial shade of a mixed hardwood forest. Mature plants will also grow in full sunshine, but will not self-seed in full sunlight. It will grow at the edge of the forest where it receives full morning sun, but it will also prosper in areas that receive only dappled light such as wooded hillsides, riparian zones and the deep, dark hollows of Appalachia.

In nature, the plant lodges in a wide range of soil types, including loam, sand, shale and clay soils. Deep forest loam is preferred. Soils produced by hardwood trees are best, but the plant will also grow functionally in soils found under conifers. The ideal soil is slightly acid, ranging between pH 5 and 6. Sandy soils encourage the development of a profusion of thick rootlets in preference to rhizome development. Heavy clay soils are well-tolerated, as long as there is a good cover of organic mulch.

Adequate moisture is another prerequisite to healthy growth, flowering and root production. In a drought year the plants will struggle, and early dormancy often results. Conversely, a summer of plentiful water will speed development and keep the plants vibrant until frost.

Natural stands of black cohosh tend to disperse sporadically across the wooded hillside. In undisturbed stands, plants often occur singly or in groupings limited to several individuals, while dense patches are unusual. Is this growth pattern due to low seed germination, or is low seed germination a survival mechanism developed by the plant to produce the desired spatial distribution? Sparse distribution of plants decreases intraspecies competition, thereby increasing plant size and raising the percentage of seed-bearing individuals in the population. Large individuals, once established, are very effective contenders for woodland resources (e.g. nutrients, moisture, light and space). In my experience the seeds of black cohosh are very sensitive to fungal infection, the seedlings are sensitive to damping-off disease and the roots are subject to rotting—especially if plants are closely spaced. Therefore, it is not surprising that the plant may have developed mechanisms to keep individuals separate, and thereby improve the overall health of the local population.

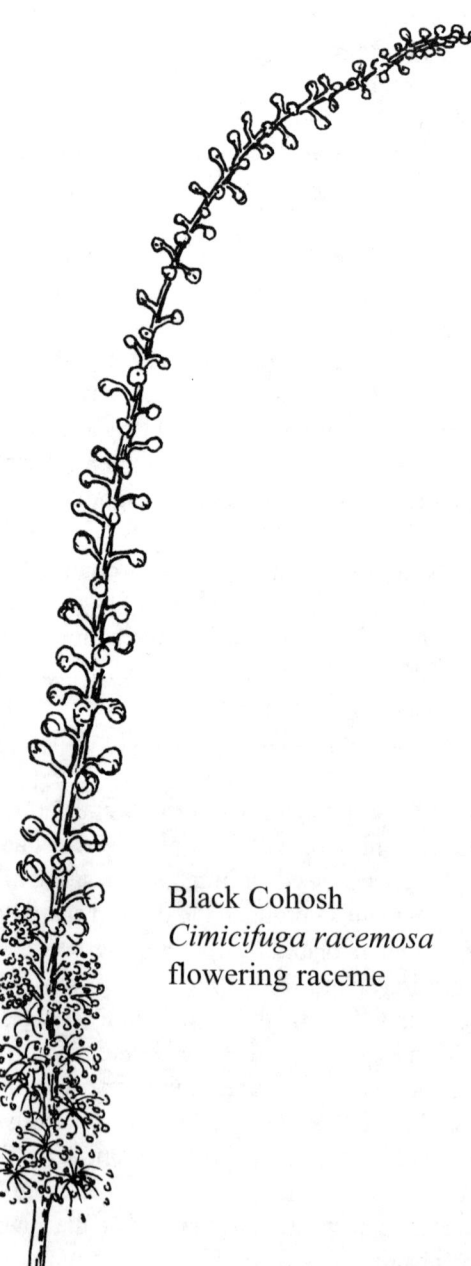

Black Cohosh
Cimicifuga racemosa
flowering raceme

Community. Examples of understory plants that are common associates of black cohosh in the mixed hardwood forests of the eastern states are American ginseng *(Panax quinquefolius),* bloodroot *(Sanguinaria canadensis),* goldenseal *(Hydrastis canadensis),* mayapple *(Podophyllum peltatum)*, trillium *(Trillium* spp.), white baneberry *(Actaea pachypoda)* and wild yam *(Dioscorea* spp.). Black cohosh itself is considered by some to be a "pointer plant" for wild ginseng (Perry, 2001). Spice bush *(Lindera benzoin)* and wahoo *(Euonymus atropurpureus)* are woody shrubs that often grow in close association with black cohosh. Finally, among the many tree species that make up the eastern mixed hardwood forest, tulip poplar *(Liriodendron tulipfera)* and pawpaw *(Asimina triloba)* are likely to shade black cohosh. If these plants and trees occur in the woods, it is likely that conditions are right for growing black cohosh.

In the West, ideal soils are found under mixed alder *(Alnus oregona)* and big leaf maple *(Acer macrophyllum)* forests. Understory plants that are good indicators for black cohosh in the West are false Solomon's seal *(Smilacina racemosa),* red baneberry *(Actaea rubra),* Oregon grape *(Mahonia nervosa)* and Trillium *(Trillium* spp.).

Black cohosh is known to hybridize. However, hybridization in nature relies on close genetic compatibility as well as synonymous flowering and pollination. Since flowering and pollination cycles for related bugbane *(Cimicifuga)* or baneberry *(Actaea)* species may differ, several closely related species are likely to occupy the same econiche without crossing. For example, I have often seen black cohosh grow in close proximity to white baneberry *(Actaea pachypoda)* without apparent hybridization. Still, it is probably not a good idea to cultivate black cohosh in close proximity to native stands of its many close relatives in the bugbane and baneberry genus.

In cultivation, it is preferable to mix the planting or at least alternate beds of black cohosh with other shade-dependent herbs in order to approximate the natural forest community of plants, thereby promoting balanced soil ecology while increasing resistance to disease and pests.

Life cycle. In nature, black cohosh flowers in the summer and is pollinated by gnats, flies and other insects that are attracted to the carrion-like smell. The plant slowly ripens its seeds in the late summer to early winter, scattering them to the ground where they are dispersed naturally by wind, water, snow, snowmelt and the activities of mammals and invertebrates. Although a profusion of seeds is produced by a single plant, only a few are destined to germinate, and of these only a very few actually survive to produce plants. Low germination rates are caused by a variety of factors including short seed life span, fungal infection in the follicle, fungal infection in the soil, late seed maturation and a complex stratification requirement (warm/cold/warm) (Deno, 1993). The plant spreads in nature only by seed, and it takes up to five years for a seedling to reach seed-bearing age.

Cultivation from seed. Cultivation of black cohosh from seed yields several advantages: genetic diversity is enhanced, hundreds of individuals may be propagated from a single parent plant, and in my experience seedlings are more disease resistant than plants grown from cuttings. Seeds are best sown about ¼ inch (~0.64 cm) deep in well-drained soil, tamped in and kept moist and shaded throughout their stratification and early growth. To sprout, the seed requires a short period (at least 2 weeks) of warm conditions (~70° F = ~21° C) followed by an extended period (at least 3 months) of cold conditions (~40° F = ~4° C). Black cohosh seed was sown on 1/23/01 at Horizon Herbs Seed Farm in outdoor conditions. The seeds emerged as vigorous seedlings on 4/8/02, a germination period of 440 days. If the warm stratification period doesn't do the trick, the seed may demonstrate double dormancy and germinate after a period of approximately 800 days. A recent study of germination characteristics of tall bugbane *(Cimicifuga elata)* demonstrated the same requirement of a warm/cold/warm cycle (Kaye, 1999).

These conditions may be provided naturally by sowing the recent seed in the late summer to early autumn in a shaded outdoor nursery bed or in shaded outdoor flats. Alternatively and usually with less success, the seed may be artificially stratified by mixing it in a barely moist medium (sand, potting soil, vermiculite or peat). The bag is then subjected to at least 2 weeks of warm temperatures, followed by 3 months of cold treatment. The mixture is then removed from the bag and planted in a warm greenhouse. Germination is epigeal (that is, the seed leaves emerge from the ground, as opposed to hypogeal germination where the first leaves to emerge are true leaves). Average cultivation success with black cohosh seed is about 25% and can range as high as 90%, but complete failures are not uncommon.

Seedlings may be grown at close spacing (~2 inches = ~5 cm) in the flat or nursery bed until they produce their second set of true leaves. At this point, they are best transplanted to individual gallon pots or to a wider spacing (6 inches = ~15 cm) in the nursery bed. During the first year of growth, the plants must be kept adequately shaded. I find that dappled forest shade is fine, and in controlled conditions (shadehouse or greenhouse) a 66% shade cloth has proven completely serviceable.

Potted plants may be transplanted after 1 or 2 years of growth, either in the fall or in the spring. Space the plants 2 feet (60 cm) or more apart. Bare-rooted transplants dug out of nursery beds are best transplanted in the fall, just after the aerial parts go dormant. If plants are to be placed in an unprotected woodland situation, care should be taken to intersperse them among existing features such as rocks, trees and different species of perennial plants and ferns in order to mix the ecology, not providing a monocrop lunch for visiting herbivores. The newly transplanted rhizomes will produce white, hair-like feeder roots in the cooling autumn soils. These rootlets help secure the plant, both physically and nutritionally, to survive the long winter dormancy in top form.

Cultivation from root cuttings. Black cohosh is easy to propagate by root division, and this is a very sure method to increase the plant in cultivation or in the wild. Divisions are best made from mature, seed-bearing individuals in the autumn, after the plant has set buds for the next year's growth and after the aerial parts have died back. Dig the roots and shake them free of dirt. Large, cultivated roots consist of a knotted rhizome with associated rootlets and numerous nascent buds that point upwards from the crown, curve upwards from the base of the rhizome or flank the base of the previous year's stem(s). Divide

17

the root with a sharp knife, a machete, a pair of snips or by manually breaking it apart. A good transplant consists of a piece of rhizome with associated rootlets and at least 1 nascent bud. Older, woody portions of the rhizome (lacking a nascent bud), tend to rot when transplanted, instead of producing new growth. A single mother plant may produce as few as 2 or as many as 6 or more divisions. Nestle the root cutting back into the soil, maintaining at least a 2 foot (60 cm) spacing between plants, orienting the cutting with the roots down and the bud pointing up toward the surface. Cover with mineral soil and then provide a generous layer of leaf mulch, bark mulch or rotted sawdust to improve water retention and to protect the transplant through the winter. A plant grown from a root cutting will usually reach harvestable size in 3 years.

General care. Once black cohosh grows past the early seedling stage, the plant will withstand a great deal of light. As long as the sun is not burning the leaves or crisping the flowers, more sun equates to faster growth. Locating the patch in an area where it receives morning sun and afternoon shade is ideal.

Although the plant requires only moderately good drainage, very poor drainage sets up conditions for a fungal disease that pioneering growers have unofficially dubbed "black cohosh root rot." This condition erodes the rootlets and reduces the rhizome to a necrotic, corky mass. Root rot has been known to wipe out large numbers of plants, especially during the sensitive transplant phase. To avoid root rot, the depth of planting is best altered in accordance with the drainage capacity of the soil. If the soil is poorly drained, transplants are set in shallowly. In well-drained soils, setting the roots in more deeply will increase wind resistance and yield.

Competition from weeds can be a problem, more so in open areas than in forest plantings. My suggestion is that instead of pulling weeds, they can be smothered, buried under applications of composted manure or forest-derived mulch.

Finally, black cohosh really needs regular watering to do well. If rains are not forthcoming, a weekly irrigation will keep them growing right along. Sufficient water in the late summer is particularly important, since lack of water at this time will cause premature dormancy and reduced yields.

Medicine. The fresh or dried black cohosh root (the root and rhizome) is the part traditionally used. The *fresh* root is preferred, as it loses much of its activity in the drying process. This is a good example of a situation where plant conservation is enhanced by good pharmacy, that is, choosing the method of extraction that optimizes the total yield of active constituents on a per-plant basis (Cech, 1999; Moore, 1993).

Michael Moore also suggests that the fresh, renewably harvested *leaves* of black cohosh may be used interchangeably with the root (Moore 1993). Although there is little historical evidence supporting the internal use of aerial portions of the plant, this is an area ripe for further study and evaluation (e.g. safety, chemistry and if appropriate, clinical trials).

Yield. In order to demonstrate the degree of individual variation in root size, and to illustrate the impact of environment on yield, I dug a block of 50 cultivated, unfertilized, forest-grown plants and a block of 50 cultivated, fertilized plants that were grown in the open garden, then compared the results.

Plants aged at 3 years, grown from root cuttings in the forest without fertilization, ranged in weight between 15 g and 500 g. The average fresh weight of these roots was 200 g (a little less than ½ pound each).

Plants aged at 3 years, grown from root cuttings in the open garden with fertilization and water, ranged between 400 g and 2,700 g each. The average fresh weight of these roots was 1,400 g (3.08 pounds) each. The largest individual weighed in at 6 pounds and boasted 87 nascent buds!

The main active constituents found in black cohosh roots are triterpene glycosides (Harnischfeger and Duker, 1985). Given the great difference in growth rate and yield between fertilized, field-grown roots and unfertilized, woods-grown roots, a comparative analysis is definitely needed. Based on taste tests, my subjective opinion is that both methods of cultivation yield medicinally active roots.

The average water content of fresh black cohosh roots ranges between 64% to 69%. This means that 10 pounds of fresh roots will dry down to about 3.35 pounds.

Harvest, processing and storage. Black cohosh is preferably dug in the autumn, after the plant has fixed primary and secondary constituents and when the root is at peak weight and medicinal activity.[1] Shake the roots free of dirt, and keep them together in a clean sack or other container. Keep them covered from the sun so they don't dry out. If the roots are to be stored in the fresh state for any period of time, do not wash them. The covering of dirt will help keep them from getting moldy in storage or in shipping. This is a real concern, as the fresh roots are truly susceptible to mold while under storage. Just prior to tincturing or dehydration, wash the roots with a pressure hose. You may have to chop up the larger crowns in order to free them completely from dirt and small stones. Once all the root pieces are clean, process them immediately in the fresh state or dry them.

Generally black cohosh is dried in the whole form, that is, not chopped into small pieces. This helps prevent undue oxidation and loss of medicinal activity. Dry the roots in a warm place with positive airflow, turning often. An herb dehydrator is very helpful in drying black cohosh. Dry for 1 day with low temperature (70° F = 21° C) and high air flow, then turn up the temperature to high (110° F = 43° C) and dry them until they snap, making certain that the larger pieces are dehydrated all the way through. Once they are thoroughly dry, the roots are best stored in plastic bags in lightproof sacks or drums, in a cool, dark and dry location. Stored in this manner, the roots retain useful potency for about 1 year.

Black cohosh seed is tan to dark brown in color, hemispherical (half-moon shaped) and flat or wedged, usually with a raised peripheral edge. The seed measures approximately 1.5 by 3 mm. There are approximately 450 seeds in 1 gram.

---

[1] In the forest garden, it makes sense to make a root cutting and replant into the same hole at harvest, but in the field it is probably best to fallow the ground after harvest and plant a cover crop. This will prevent disease problems that can stem from ongoing cultivation of root crops on the same farmland. This is not a problem in the forest, where the trees keep the soil healthy and balanced.

Seed collecting, cleaning, storage and longevity. The seed is best collected as soon as it rattles in the pod. This means that the seed is ripe, and that the follicle has begun to split, thereby allowing the seed to shake out. If the summer has been rainy and humid, there is likely to be damage from mold to some or all of the seed pods. Mold has a strong negative effect on germination, and therefore it is best to avoid taking seed from plants that are badly molded. This is rarely a problem in the West, where we do not really understand summer humidity like they understand it in the Midwest, the East and especially in the South.

Various black cohosh plants, even when growing in close association, will mature their seed at different intervals. In order to collect from a diverse representation of plants in a forested area or in the field, one must return several times, gleaning the seed as it ripens. Also, the seed at the base of a raceme may be ripe and ready to dehisce while the seed at the tip is still green.

A plastic bucket is probably the most useful tool ever invented for seed collecting. Purists may wish to experiment using a large calabash gourd, which is probably just as good, and a lot less plasticky. On a clear and dry day, the ripe raceme is upended directly into the bucket (or gourd) and shaken vigorously against the sides. Sometimes the raceme is too long to fit, and some of the seed scatters and goes back to nature. But much of the seed, including also associated bits of stem, pod and other chaff, will fall into the container. If the seed and chaff are at all moist, they must be laid out on screens and dried in the shade and stirred occasionally for several days before further processing. An herb dehydrator may be useful. Lay the seed on pieces of torn sheeting on the screens and stir frequently until they are dry. Be sure the temperature does not exceed 90° F (32° C).

Sometimes the seed, although not moldy, acts like it is "glued" inside the follicle and will not readily shake out. Perchance the follicle is fully developed but has not split sufficiently to release the ripe seeds. These conditions are usually caused by wet weather during maturation or collection, or by cool weather during seed maturation. In this case, either the collection must be postponed until the seeds are loose, or the capsules may be manually stripped from the stem and dried. In

21

order to remove the seeds from the follicle, small quantities of the dry pods are placed on a flat surface, such as a breadboard, and gently crushed with a tool such as a rolling pin. This technique is usefully employed for initial separation of various seeds that occur in pods (e.g. wild indigo, *Baptisia tinctoria)* but not without some regrettable aging of these useful tools. In fact, my occasional historical raiding of the kitchen in search of breadboard and rolling pin did not go unnoticed. My wife eventually amended this situation after a lucky find at a local garage sale. An unfamiliar and impressively tattered combination breadboard and rolling pin appeared predominantly on my workbench, with a large label that read "FOR SEEDS." Such is a woman's wit.

Once the seed and chaff are thoroughly dry, they can be further separated by using screens. A screen just large enough to let the seed fall through will separate out the pod and stem fragments, while a screen just small enough to hold the seed will separate out small fractions. In both cases, be sure not to throw the baby out with the bath water. Finally, the seed may be wind-winnowed, which will help separate the heavy, viable seed from empty seed coats and other light, seed-sized debris. However, after all this work, the seed will still not look very pure, and it won't be. This is the sad reality of cleaning black cohosh seed— it is never easy to attain very high purity due to the content of much dense chaff that approximates the size of the seeds. The best way to obtain high purity is to dump the sample on a smooth table and go at it the slow way, separating by hand (by finger) the chaff into one pile and seed into another.

Seed destined for storage must be cleaned to the highest possible purity. This improves air circulation in the stored seed and divests it of necrotic tissue that can carry mold spores and disease. The seed must also be thoroughly dry. The dried seed may be stored in sealed plastic bags in the freezer. Although best results are obtained by sowing the seed as soon as possible after harvest, the expected life span is at least one year.

Conservation status. Black cohosh is the next most likely herbal candidate for listing in CITES, Appendix II. Unlike goldenseal, which is sold mostly to domestic markets, much of the black cohosh now being harvested is used by foreign companies to produce phytopharmaceuticals. Wild harvest of black cohosh would be significantly diminished by a CITES listing, because these regulations specifically curtail foreign trade. Although black cohosh is still abundant in localized areas, it is my opinion that global trade in the wild-harvested root will eventually be regulated. The reasons for this are: efficacy of black cohosh in treating the widespread and quirky condition known as menopause; likelihood that the plant will remain one of the best treatments for this condition and that the number of women suffering from menopause will not soon decrease; consequential high volume of trade in raw black cohosh root; large existing domestic and foreign market for black cohosh root and products derived from black cohosh root; dependence of the wild plant on a specific woodland habitat; slow growth of the plant in the wilds; and ongoing deterioration of wild woodland habitat due to urbanization and logging. Finally, academics and government already have a concern for the sustainability of wild black cohosh and virtually every species of North American *Cimicifuga*.

In just the same way that widespread cultivation of ginseng once saved the remaining populations of wild ginseng, the cultivation of black cohosh will help preserve the last intact populations of black cohosh. And in the case of black cohosh as compared to ginseng, it will be a labor more easily achieved, because black cohosh is more productive and also more amenable to cultivation. It remains only for farmers to come up to speed.

Adulteration and nomenclature. Taxonomists have had a hard time with *Cimicifuga* and *Actaea,* deciding which is which. Black Cohosh itself was first assigned to the genus *Actaea* by Linnaeus, then reclassified by Thomas Nuttal (1786-1859) as belonging to *Cimicifuga*. Such taxonomic furniture moving is not too unusual. Currently investigators are thinking the plant really belongs back with *Actaea* (Compton, Culman, Gibbings and Jury, 1998). However, Michael Moore has a much more pragmatic way of looking at it: "If it has a pod, it's *Cimicifuga.* If it has a berry, it's *Actaea"* (Moore, 2002). In fact, this position makes so much sense to me that I have resisted pressure to reclassify the herb as *Actaea*, herein retaining the familiar Latin nomenclature *(Cimicifuga racemosa).*

Traditionally, diggers in the woods have also had a hard time differentiating *Actaea* and *Cimicifuga*. Both red and white baneberry are readily identified during flowering and fruiting phase. However once the plants die back in the autumn, leaving only a vestigial forked and blackened stem, they look almost identical to black cohosh. The root of baneberry is also similar in overall appearance and taste to that of black cohosh. Baneberry species are so widespread (see distribution map) and attracted to such similar habitat, that the two cohabit many areas. In 1898, Felter and Lloyd observed that "white cohosh" *(Actaea pachypoda)* "is frequently found as an adulterant among commercial lots of *Cimicifuga*," an error that continues to the present day. Felter and Lloyd went on to state that this adulteration was "not considered objectionable." However they also noted that large doses of baneberry produce "violent emeto-catharsis" and "grave irritation and gastrointestinal inflammation." I was taught that rare incidences of black cohosh toxicity or abortifacient activity may be attributed to admixture with baneberry roots. Cultivation of correctly identified black cohosh is a sure way to provide the right medicine.

Current Range of Baneberry Species in the U.S.

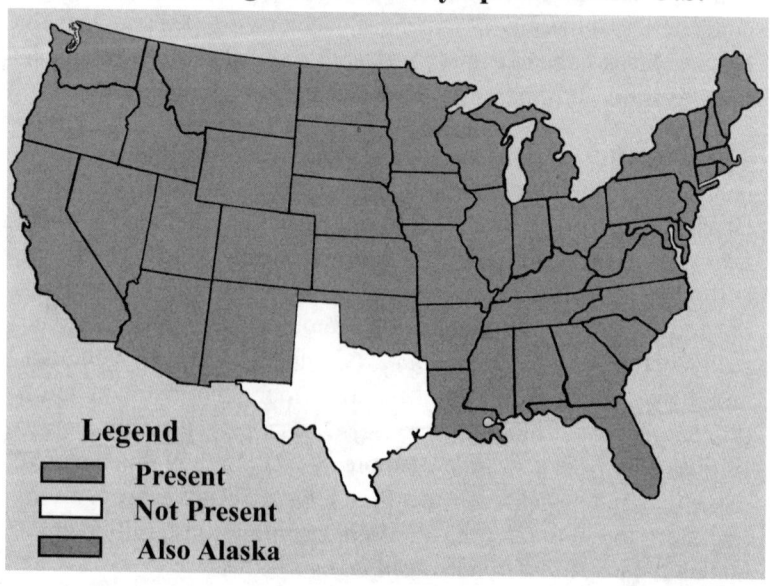

Legend
- Present
- Not Present
- Also Alaska

Other indigenous American species. There are two major species of baneberry occurring in the United States. They are white baneberry *(Actaea pachypoda)* of the eastern states, and red baneberry *(Actaea rubra)* of the northeastern, north-central and western states. Ethnographic accounts of internal and external use of baneberry by Native Americans are many (Moerman, 1986), but baneberry's potential toxicity is also mentioned (Steedman, 1928). Baneberry is also used, albeit rarely, by modern herbalists. According to Michael Moore, the activity is the same as black cohosh "with the exception of estrogenic" activity, which is apparently lacking in baneberry (Moore, 1993). Although Moore acknowledges the toxicity of baneberry fruits, he believes that low dosage of baneberry *root* is nontoxic.

Six species of bugbane are native to North America. Mountain bugbane *(Cimicifuga americana),* Appalachian bugbane *(C. rubifolia)* and our black cohosh *(C. racemosa)* are native to the eastern states, and are probably used interchangeably in herbal medicine as "black cohosh." These plants all appear on various state and federal conservation lists as at-risk species.

Arizona bugbane *(Cimicifuga arizonica),* tall bugbane *(C. elata)* and Mt. Hood bugbane *(C. laciniata)* are endemic species of the West. These three species are medicinally allied to black cohosh and have been used as substitutes for it (Moore, 1993). However, these western bugbanes are from fragile environments, they are not widely distributed and they have been given various federal and state designations identifying them as at-risk species (Phillips et. al., 1995; Kaye and Kirkland, 1999). For environmental reasons alone it makes sense to protect and augment the native stands of these interesting and stately plants, and maintain the native populations by encouraging cultivation and use of black cohosh itself, a safe and time-tested medicine.

References

Cech, R. 1999. *Balancing Conservation with Utilization: Restoring Populations of Commercially Valuable Medicinal Herbs in Forests and Agroforests.* Herbalgram No. 45, pp. 58-60.

Compton, Culham, Gibbings and Jury. 1998. *Phylogeny of Actaea Including Cimicifuga (Ranunculaceae) Inferred from nrDNA ITS Sequence Variation.* Biochem. Syst. and Ecology 26, pp. 185-197.

Deno, N. 1993. *Seed Germination Theory and Practice, Second Edition,* State College (PA): Pennsylvania State University.

Kaye, T. 1999. *Propagation and Population Reestablishment for Tall Bugbane (Cimicifuga elata) on the Salem District BLM.*

Kaye, T. and M. Kirkland. 1999. *Effect of Timber Harvest on Cimicifuga elata, a Rare Plant of Western Forests.* Northwest Science, 73, pp. 159-167.

Felter, H. and J. Lloyd. 1898 (Reprinted 1985). *King's American Dispensatory.* Portland (OR): Eclectic Medical Publishing, Vol. 1 & 2, 743 pp.

Moerman, D. 1986. *Medicinal Plants of Native America.* Ann Arbor (MI): University of Michigan Department of Anthropology, Vol. 1, 534 pp.

Moore, M. 1993. *Medicinal Plants of the Pacific West.* Santa Fe (NM): Red Crane Books, 359 pp.

Moore, M. 2002. Personal communication. Michael Moore lives in Bisbee, Arizona and is the principal of The Southwest School of Botanical Medicine. A conversation with Michael is like taking a sip from the well of knowledge—a surreal, mind-opening experience that generates waves of illumination punctuated by gruelling self-doubt (always a healthy combination).

Perry, Charles. 2001. Personal communication. Charles lives in Bath County, Kentucky, and is familiar with the Appalachian oral traditions, including medicinal plants and tobacco. He is a pioneering grower of a wide array of forest-dependent medicinal plants and does not get lost in the woods.

Phillips, B., R. Papowski, C. Franz, and P. Warren (1996). *Conservation Assessment and Strategy for Cimicifuga arizonica watson (Bugbane) on the Coconino and Kaibab National Forests.* Southwestern Rare and Endangered Plants: Proceedings of the Second Conference. United States Department of Agriculture, Forest Service, General Technical Report RM-GTR-283.

Steedman, E. 1928. *The Ethnobotany of the Thompson Indians.* Smithsonian Institution: Bureau of American Ethnology Annual Report No. 45, pp. 441-522.

USDA, NRCS. 2001. The distribution maps in this book were adapted with permission from the PLANTS Database, version 3.1 (http://plants.usda.gov). National Plant Data Center, Baton Rouge, LA 70874-4490 USA

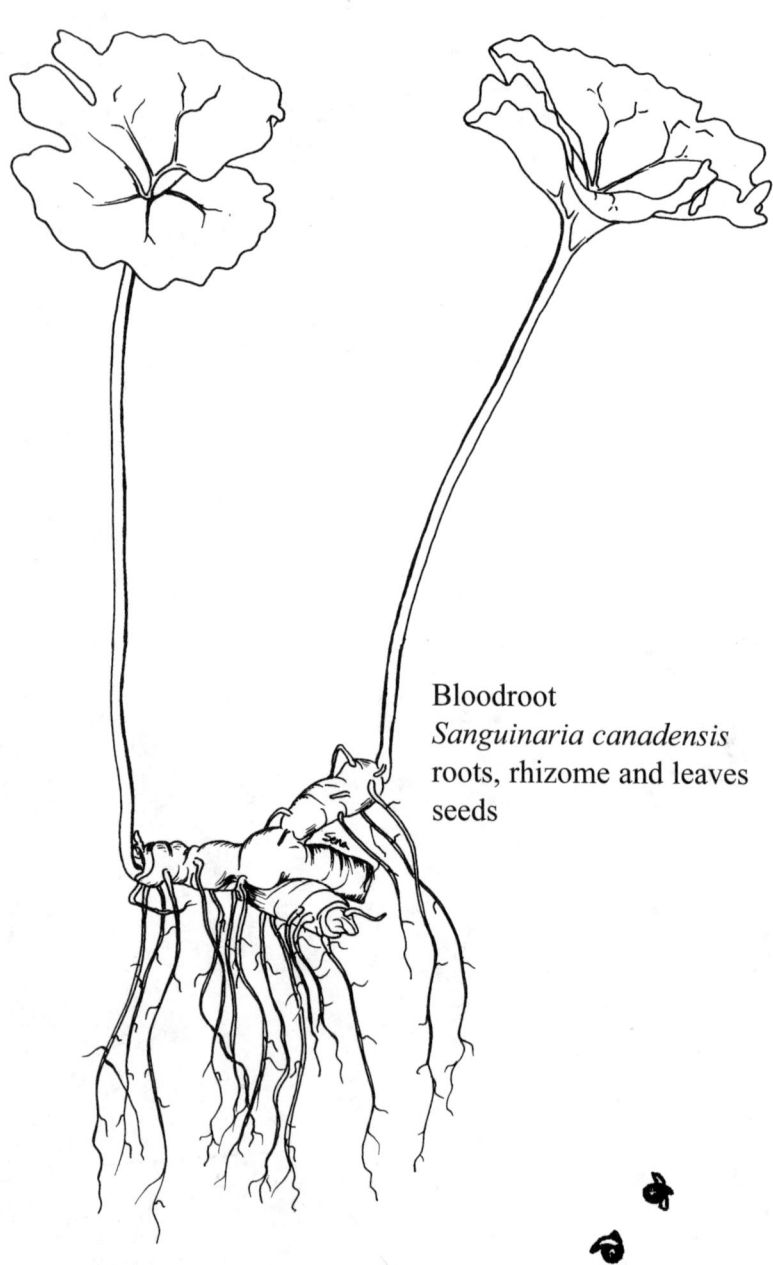

Bloodroot
Sanguinaria canadensis
roots, rhizome and leaves
seeds

Bloodroot
Sanguinaria canadensis L.
Family: *Papaveraceae*

Bloodroot is an herbaceous perennial forest dweller. The rhizome is dark brownish-red in color and filled with an orange-red juice that exudes from even the slightest injury. The broken rhizome looks like a severed finger, bleeding the alkaloid-rich juice that gives the plant its name, its medicinal activity and also provides the easiest method of identification. The rhizome occurs in jointed sections that branch freely, producing transparent, matted, amber-orange roots from the underside and scaled, tumescent buds from the growing tips. In the very early spring, each rosy bud gives rise to a single leaf and flowering stalk that emerge in coordination. The leaf is rolled around the flowering stalk, sheathing and protecting it as it pierces through the forest detritus, unfolding and expanding as the flower matures. The leaves are round-palmate, deeply lobed and grayish-green in color, with orange veins on the underside. The flower is shockingly white and waxy, yet devoid of nectar, sporting eight or more petals and golden anthers. This self-fertile flower lasts only a few days before giving way to the elongated, pointed, peapod-like, two-chambered seed capsule. The leaves and the seed capsule continue to enlarge as the season progresses. Eventually the swollen capsule splits apart, summarily scattering the seed near the base of the plant. The seed is a shining, mahogany orb attached to a worm-like, fatty protuberance known as a "raphe" (sometimes known as an eliasome). Forest ants consider the raphe a delicacy, and they carry the seed to their underground nests, eventually eating the germination-inhibiting raphe and abandoning the seed in a pile of backdirt or an unused passage. In this way the bloodroot is effectively disseminated in a kind of flea-circus symbiosis, otherwise known as "myrmecochery" or "ant-farming." The characteristic leaves continue to photosynthesize and feed nutrients to the expanding rhizome throughout the summer and into the autumn, usually disappearing entirely into an early dormancy prior to first frost.

29

Range. The native range of bloodroot is extensive, including all the eastern and midwestern states, from the Atlantic seaboard to the Rocky Mountains. The northern limits of its range take in southern Canada, from Nova Scotia to Manitoba.

Current Range of Bloodroot in the U.S.

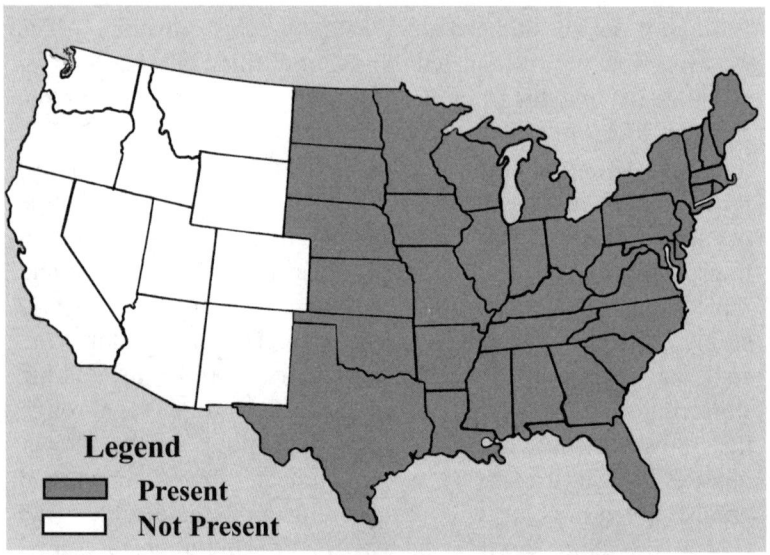

Legend
Present
Not Present

Hardiness and adaptability. Bloodroot is completely cold hardy and enters a strong winter dormancy, although severe cold is not a prerequisite to its growth. Also, the seed does not require cold stratification to germinate, so the plant reproduces successfully both in areas where the winters are very cold, and also where the winters are mild. Like many members of the poppy family, bloodroot grows most vigorously in the cool soils of spring. This is when it accomplishes the majority of its work, including production of the ephemeral flower, and when it invests great energy into the production of the nutritious seed. Probably the most significant requirements for successful domestication are partial to full shade and rich, forest-derived soils. Under its own volition, bloodroot never sailed the Atlantic or climbed the Rocky Mountains, but still it has been very successfully transplanted, becoming a favorite subject for shade gardens in Europe as well as the western United States.

Ecology. In nature, bloodroot prefers to grow in a mixed hardwood forest, occupying sites in the deep shade or areas of open woodland where dappled sunlight reaches the forest floor. Plants will occur lodged in moss on top of limestone outcrops, but they will also thrive in mulchy soils on hillsides or in bottom lands. The preferred soils are humus or clay, well-mulched with rotting leaves. The ideal acidity range is slightly acid, between pH 5.5 and 6.5. Although a certain amount of sand in the soil matrix is well-tolerated, pure sand soils are not. One of the reasons for this preference is that sandy soils are unlikely to contain the fungal symbionts that foster the growth of bloodroot and protect it from pathogens. Also, the breakdown of soil fungi provides gibberellic acid, a growth hormone critical to the germination and development of bloodroot seed (Deno, 1996).

Bloodroot prefers a climate that provides adequate moisture, and is subject to very early dormancy in a drought year. However the rhizomes will tend to rot in swampy ground, despite their heavy arsenal of alkaloidal sap, and they tend to crawl on or just below the ground surface in order to avoid overly damp conditions.

Bloodroot tends to grow in patches. Given ideal conditions a single plant left to spread by root and seed will make an impressive colony in a few years' time. Herbaceous plants often found in association with bloodroot in the eastern forest biome are dragon's tongue *(Arisaema dracontium),* Jack-in-the-pulpit *(Arisaema triphyllum),* wild ginger *(Asarum canadense)* and especially trillium *(Trillium* spp.).

Trees indicating good bloodroot growing habitat in the western states are alder *(Alnus* spp.), cottonwood *(Populus* spp.), maple *(Acer* spp.) and even the solitary oak *(Quercus* spp.). By this listing it should be clear that bloodroot is much more highly adaptable to varied forest ecologies in the West than are some of our more finicky forest-dependent medicinals (e.g. ginseng, goldenseal). Supplemental irrigation is almost always required during the dry western summers. Also, the fungal makeup of western soils is not the same as in the East, so it sometimes takes up to three years for transplants to sequester supportive fungi and to naturalize.

31

Life cycle. Bloodroot seed ripens early in the summer and falls directly to the ground. New seedlings are often found in the spring, in close association with the parent. Seeds may also be disseminated to a distance by birds or by ants, which are attracted to the fatty, grub-like raphe that is attached to each seed. Regardless of the method of dispersion, the seed must not completely dry out if it is to remain viable. Once they lodge in moist soil or well-rotted mulch, some of the seeds will swell, split and produce a radicle (embryonic root) by autumn, winter or early spring. The seed then produces a single true leaf as the soils warm in the midspring. Some of the seed will remain dormant until the second spring. The plant requires at least three years to produce an adult, flowering individual from seed.

Cultivation from seed. Bloodroot seed is best sown as soon as possible after it is ripe, in well-drained soil in forest nursery beds, in the shade garden or in shaded flats. Sow the seed ¼ inch (0.6 cm) deep in close furrows, or broadcast the seed, press it in and cover with a thin layer of soil. Finish with a layer of fine leaf mulch, which will help keep the soil from drying out through the summer and winter. This mulch will also harbor beneficial fungi, which in turn are likely to produce gibberellic acid (GA-4 and GA-7) as a byproduct of their life cycle. Bloodroot has been shown to be at least partially dependent on gibberellic acid to initiate germination (Deno, 1996).[1]

---

[1] The sea vegetable known as kelp (*Ascophyllum* or *Macrocystis* spp.) is a well-known biological source of potassium and trace elements. Kelp also contains relatively high concentrations of plant auxins and growth regulators such as indole-3-acetic acid (IAA) and gibberellic acid. Kelp tea, when used as a foliar feed or for watering plants, helps reduce transplant stress and encourages rooting. If used to soak seeds before planting, kelp tea may stimulate the germination response and increase germination rate. I use a large fistful of dried kelp per gallon of cold water, left to infuse overnight before use. Use kelp products sparingly and with respect—the overharvest of kelp from shallow seawater and intertidal zones is a significant threat to the sustainability of sea life as we know it (see Ryan Drum's excellent chapter on sea vegetables in *Planting the Future).* Better yet, beachcomb your own kelp when you visit the sea.

Mark the planting area with a permanent tag. Excessive moisture in the nursery bed or flat will do more harm than good, as the seeds are very liable to rot. I have achieved the best results with relatively little watering during the germination phase. At Horizon Herbs Seed Farm, seed sown on 6/19/01 began to emerge on 3/19/02, a germination period of 273 days. Germination is epigeal, but the seed leaves are tiny, cupped, vestigial and semi-subterranean, giving rise to 1 tiny, true leaf, which expands throughout the first season of growth. Average germination success is 30%, with higher rates possible. Zero germination is also possible, especially in soggy, oxygen-depleted soils. Seedlings are best grown out without disturbing them for 2 years, until they produce small rhizomes. Transplant to a finished spacing of about 6 inches (14.4 cm). Transplanting is best done in the fall or in the very early spring.

Cultivation from root sections. Large clumps of bloodroot rhizomes will boast many spreading branches that separate easily at the joints. These are natural transplants that may be broken apart by hand with an eye to producing the least possible amount of raw surface area. This is an important distinction, because transplants tend to rot back from the broken end before they root in and find balance in their new location. The more they are injured, the greater the potential for rot. The transplants are best planted barely below the soil surface, with the buds pointing up. Clumps of fibrous rootlets that hang down from the transplant should be spread out and dug in as deeply as possible in the underlying soil. Transplants boasting many rootlets have a better survival rate than bare rhizomes. Firm the soil around the transplant. If the "back" of the rhizome is just visible above the soil surface, protruding from the soil like a miniature surfacing whale, this is a good sign. Cover the transplant with mulch, and keep people and pets from walking on it. The plant will reemerge in the spring, and, given the right conditions, will rapidly establish itself.

Yield. In the spring of 2001 we dug a cultivated woodland patch of 3-year-old bloodroot grown from root sections, and weighed the roots in order to estimate average yields. Among 300 plants, the weight ranged between 8 and 40 grams, with an average individual root weight of 20 grams. The average number of stems per plant was 3. Average water content of the roots was 76%. Average number of fresh roots per pound was 23. Average dry roots per pound was 95. This means that every 10 pounds of fresh roots yields only 2.5 pounds of dried roots.

Harvest, processing and storage. Bloodroot may be dug in the fall or in the spring. The roots actually contain the highest concentration of the main alkaloid (sanguinarine) when harvested at the peak of flowering. To harvest roots during the spring instead of the autumn goes contrary to traditional herbal wisdom, but in this case the departure may be justified.

If destined for fresh extraction, the roots are best left dirty until just before processing. They are easily cleaned with a garden hose. If destined for drying, the roots are ideally washed in the morning, left whole and dried in the sun for a few hours until externally dry, then shade-dried. Very large roots may be first split along their length with a knife, thereby speeding the process considerably. I have dried bloodroot very successfully on screens near the woodstove, but they can also be dried in a very warm, shaded location with positive airflow, such as an attic. Take care not to allow the roots to take on moisture at night, or they can easily mold and be ruined. Therefore an herb dehydrator is very useful in drying bloodroot. Dry for 1 day at low temperature (70° F = 21° C) and high air flow, then turn up the temperature to 110° F (43° C) and dry the roots until they break without bending, making certain that the larger pieces are dehydrated all the way through.

Store dried bloodroot in sealed plastic bags or glass jars, out of the light. The roots will retain their potency for at least two years. Once the dried roots are ground up, they oxidize much more quickly, so the powder is best used as soon as possible.

Cautions. When handling fresh bloodroot, it is a good idea to minimize skin exposure to the fresh, acrid juices. A little sanguinarine on normal skin areas will not be likely to present a problem, but you do not want to get it in your eyes or delicate mucous membranes. If it is your habit to test medicinal herbs by taking a chew, even a cautious chew, take my advice and in this case stem the urge. Also, when grinding dried bloodroot, a filter mask should always be worn. The herb emits an acrid dust that can severely irritate the upper respiratory tract.

The main application for this herb is for external use against abnormal skin growths. The dried root is mixed into a salve base and applied on an ongoing basis until the problem is resolved. Alternately, the fresh root may be dug, sliced and rubbed on the affected area. In either case, ongoing treatment is likely to cause localized inflammation (Cech, 2000).

Bloodroot seed is round, slightly elongated at the hilum, dark reddish-brown when ripe, measuring ~4.5 x ~3.5 mm. The eliasome (or raphe) is translucent, undulating, worm-like, yellow, and ~5 mm in length. The seed coat is somewhat leathery. There are about 70 seeds in 1 gram of fresh seed.

It is easy to determine the viability of seeds by a cut test. Viable seeds sliced with a razor blade sport a solid, white or greenish-yellow endosperm, while nonviable seeds are filled with a putrescent mush.

Harvest the seed in the early summer when the capsule splits easily to the touch, and the seed is ripe and brown. Immature seed is white or green, and it is useless. Successfully picking this seed requires almost daily attention to the plants, as the harvest window is very narrow, a few days at best. You can pick the ripe pods and put them in a bucket, later separating the seeds from the pods by hand, with a screen or on an inclined plane. Keep the seed out of the direct sunlight.

Seed storage and viability. Bloodroot seed does not withstand dry storage. Once the ripe seed is removed from the mature pod, it must be planted immediately or stored with care to maintain viability. I have found that refrigeration of the newly harvested seed in moist medium is completely unsatisfactory. The raphe rots, and the seed follows suit. Moist storage at room temperature is a workable alternative, and seeds may be maintained for several weeks in this manner while beds are prepared, or while the seed is being shipped to another location. This method presupposes the willing participation of the primary sink-caregiver and is known as the "mesh bag technique." A finely woven mesh or cheesecloth bag is the tool of choice. Fresh seed is introduced into the bag, the top closed off with string or with a rubber band, and the bag hung from the faucet at the back of the sink. Most fresh seeds (e.g. goldenseal and trillium) require a daily rinsing or two, after which the bag is allowed to hang ingloriously and drip down the drain. However bloodroot really requires less rinsing than other fresh seeds, and I would suggest that it be rinsed thoroughly, and kneaded vigorously, only once every two days for maintenance. The rinsing rehydrates the seed while it leaches germination-inhibiting compounds out of the seed and the raphe. The physical kneading of the seed, performed under the constant flow of cold water from the faucet, serves to wear away the raphe and further accelerate the leaching of germination inhibitors. I find that seed can be stored for several weeks in this manner. One of the only drawbacks is that the regular hydration and stimulation in the presence of optimal oxygen flow may stimulate premature germination. Keep your eye on the seed, and if it is starting to sprout, plant it!

Conservation status. Even as far back as 1898, Felter and Lloyd stated that bloodroot was "rapidly becoming scarce in the New England states, where it formerly grew in great abundance" (Felter and Lloyd, 1898). As with other forest-dependent herbs, the fate of wild populations of bloodroot is linked to the fate of the forest that shades it.

A long history of wild collection to supply the nursery trade has brightened many a shade garden, but has also taken its toll in the wilds. The continued increase in the incidence of all kinds of cancer, and the resurgence of interest in bloodroot as an anticancer herb has also increased pressure on wild stands.

The part of bloodroot most traditionally employed is the root, used either fresh or dried. A few ethnographic accounts indicate that Native Americans sometimes used the entire plant internally as an infusion (Tantaquidgeon, 1928), or externally for treating wounds or for poulticing (Herrick, 1977). Actually, the medicinal activity of the aerial parts of the plant is very similar to that of the root, a difference more of concentration than of kind. Considering the acrid nature of bloodroot and its potent activity at low dosage, it makes sense to further investigate the substitution of leaf for root. By using the renewable parts of the plant we would be keeping the plant, and using it, too.

However, it is hard to teach old herbalists new tricks, because after all, our strength is largely due to the depth of our traditions. Our herbal elders will continue to teach about bloodroot, and the root will continue to be utilized far more often than the renewable portions. The answer to bloodroot sustainability is preservation through cultivation, and in the case of this garnet beauty of the deep forest and shade garden, the act of cultivation will be a pleasure, indeed.

Other species. Bloodroot is the only member of the genus *Sanguinaria,* but other members of the poppy family contain similar alkaloids and can really be used interchangeably with bloodroot. Greater celandine *(Chelidonium majus)* is native to Europe and Russia, and contains in its leaves and roots substantial quantities of sanguinarine and protopine alkaloids. The plant is considered immunotonic and has a long history of use in treatment of both internal and external cancers. Plume poppy *(Bocconia cordata)* is native to China and also contains sanguinarine and protopine alkaloids. Medicinally, the acrid juice is used externally, to resolve growths or to deaden the pain of insect stings (Cech, 2001). Both plants are highly productive.

References

Cech, R. 2001. *Horizon Herbs Catalog and Growing Guide, Spring/Summer 2002.* Williams (OR): Horizon Herbs Publications, 96 pp.

Cech, R. 2000. *Making Plant Medicine.* Williams (OR): Horizon Herbs Publications, 282 pp.

Deno, N. 1996. *Seed Germination Theory and Practice, First Supplement to the Second Edition.* State College (PA): Pennsylvania State University.

Drum, R. 2000. *Sea Vegetables* in: R. Gladstar (ed.) *Planting the Future: Saving our Medicinal Herbs.* Rochester (VT): Healing Arts Press, pp. 277-284.

Felter, H. and J. Lloyd. 1898 (Reprinted 1985). *King's American Dispensatory.* Portland (OR): Eclectic Medical Publishing, Vol. 1 & 2, 743 pp.

Herrick, J. 1977. *Iriquois Medical Botany.* Ann Arbor (MI): University Microfilms International.

Tantaquidgeon, G. 1928. *Mohegan Medicinal Practices: Weather-lore and Superstitions.* Smithsonian Institution Bureau of American Ethnology Annual Report No. 42, pp. 473-672.

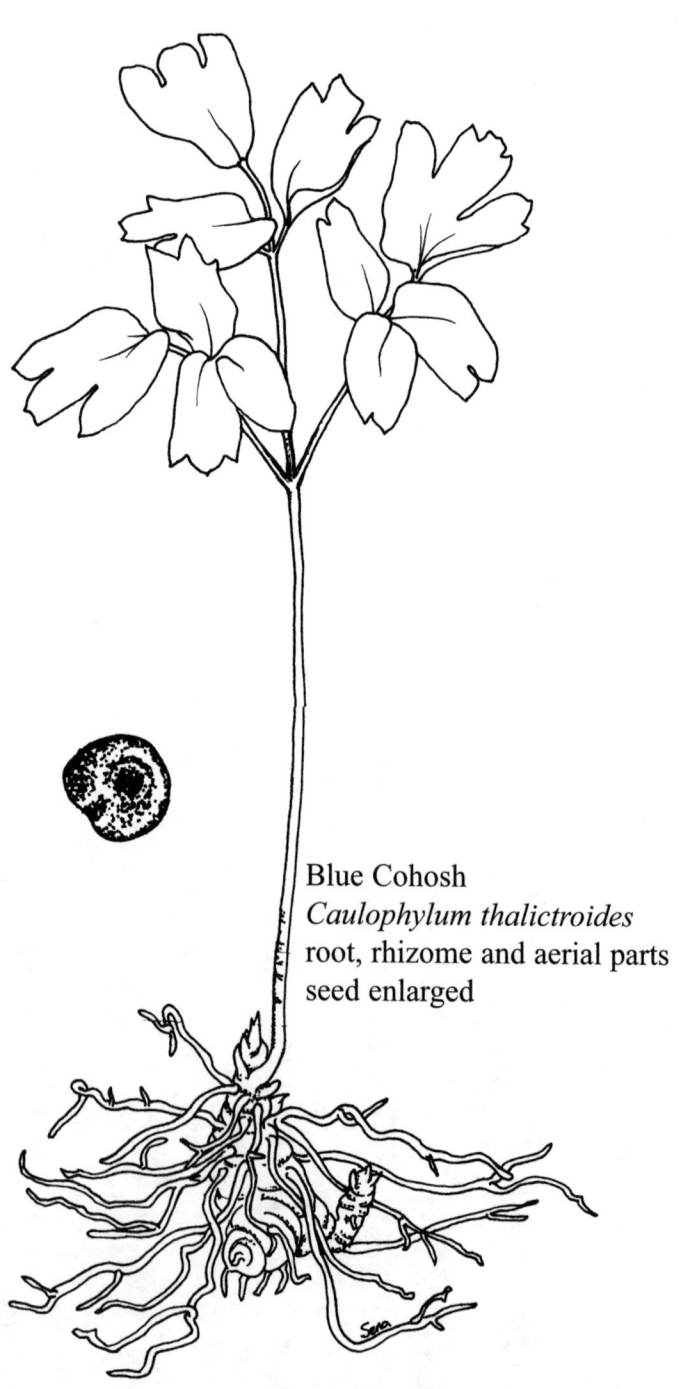

Blue Cohosh
Caulophylum thalictroides
root, rhizome and aerial parts
seed enlarged

Blue Cohosh

Caulophyllum thalictroides (L.) Michx.

Family: *Berberidaceae*

Blue Cohosh is a long-lived herbaceous perennial of the deep woodlands. The rhizome is light brown, roughly cylindrical and shaped like a crooked finger. At its largest, it is not much *bigger* than a finger, sometimes branched, punctuated by broad, craterous stem-scars on the upper surface, terminated by the primary dormant bud or buds that curve upward from the base. The nascent bud is shaped like the claw of a cat, complete with a fleshy cuticle. The rootlets are a crinkled, tough, golden-brown mass of fibers that radiate in all directions from the rhizome. On the upper surface of the rhizome, the rootlets are sparse, and on the lower surface they are very numerous. In the early spring each bud elongates into a smooth, forked stalk bearing purplish, three-lobed leaves and panicles of inconspicuous, star-shaped flowers colored brown, green and yellow. As the stalks spread up and outward to a height of no more than three feet, the leaves take on a soothing blue-green color. The flowers give way to pea-sized seeds, mahogany in color and cartilaginous, covered with a thin, royal blue skin. These fruits, rising in clusters above the plant foliage, are probably the most distinguishing characteristic of blue cohosh and once inspired the early settlers to give it the common name of "blueberry."

Range, hardiness and adaptability. Blue cohosh prefers the moist woodlands of the upper Appalachian Mountain Range, but may be found from New Brunswick south to South Carolina and across the hardwood forest biome, not extending very far west of the Mississippi Valley. The areas of greatest concentration are the Allegheny Mountains and the states of New England.

The plant is not hindered by cold winters, especially since in nature the dormant root is protected by the fallen leaves of the trees that define its habitat. Given a cold winter and a forested environment (or at least deep shade, water and leaf mulch) the plant may be readily naturalized or cultivated outside its native range, even in the mountains of the West.

41

Current Range of Blue Cohosh in the U.S.

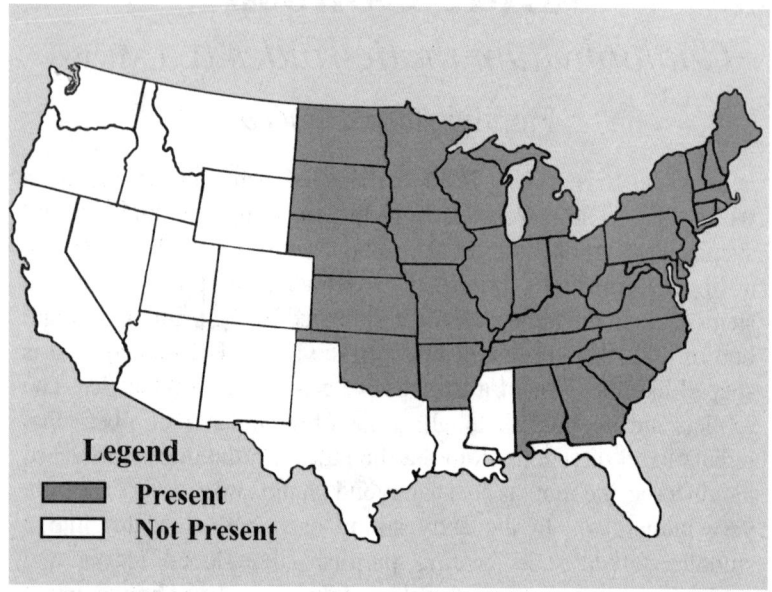

Legend
- Present
- Not Present

Environment. Blue cohosh prefers to grow in a moist, cool woodland setting, under the shade of a mixed hardwood forest. It is often found in patches in deep hollows or growing alongside a stream. The preferred soil type is slightly acid forest loam (pH 5-6). Clayey and sandy soils are tolerated, as long as there is sufficient organic content and a deep surface mulch.

The plant is sensitive to excess light, preferring to grow in areas of complete forest canopy. Occasional mottled light is excellent, but full sun exposure, even morning sun, can be detrimental. Therefore the plant does very nicely on northern facing slopes and in the shade of large forest features such as mature trees, rocky cliffs or watery clefts.

Blue cohosh tends to grow in self-supportive patches. The roots of associated plants in nature often grow so closely that they touch at the periphery. The ready availability of abundant water is an essential factor in supporting such close growth, and it is my experience that good blue cohosh habitat is usually moist and not necessarily well-drained. The rhizome of the plant is adapted to this situation, situated close to the surface, compact and rot-resistant, supported by the mass of tough and resilient rootlets.

BLUE COHOSH

Community. Blue cohosh prefers a mixed hardwood habitat, thriving in association with other water-loving and shade tolerant understory plants including goldenseal *(Hydrastis canadensis)*, Jack-in-the pulpit *(Arisaema triphyllum)*, ramps *(Allium tricoccum)*, Solomon's seal *(Polygonatum biflorum)*, spikenard *(Aralia racemosa)*, stoneroot *(Collinsonia canadensis)* and trillium.

In the western states, forests dominated by alder *(Alnus oregona)* and big leaf maple *(Acer macrophyllum)* define the ideal habitat. Common understory plants that indicate the right shade and moisture conditions for cultivation or naturalization of blue cohosh in the West would include Oregon grape *(Mahonia nervosa)*, petasites *(Petasites palmatus)* and California spikenard *(Aralia californica)*.

Life cycle. In nature, blue cohosh matures its seed in the middle to late summer, being disseminated by gravity or by foraging wildlife. The fleshy outer pericarp is readily rotted away by contact with the soil or by passing through the digestive tract of animals, in which case the indigestible seed is likely to be deposited at a distance from the parent plant. The seed remains lively as long as it stays moist, demonstrating resistance to fungal infection and bacterial rot. In the first or second spring after dispersal, the seed initiates the first phase of germination, pushing out a tough, blunt radicle (embryonic rootlet) from the dimpled opening, like a nose through a knothole. The radicle develops slowly during the spring and summer, becoming a branched rootlet, digesting the stored nutrients of the endosperm and setting a nascent bud (see illustration p. 45). The seed does all this without the advantage of photosynthesis. In the following spring, responding to warming soils and the abundant light of the spring forest (before the majority of trees leaf out and shade the forest floor), the bud quickly extends into a vigorous seedling. Germination is hypogeal, meaning that the seed remains underground, and the first leaves expressed are true leaves. The survival advantage of this two-phase germination is that the new seedling is able to respond rapidly from an established root system when conditions are right for optimal growth. The seedling can successfully compete for resources of water, light and nutrients against larger, established plants. Blue cohosh spreads in nature only by seed, and requires at least five years to reach maturity from seed.

43

Cultivation from seed. Newly harvested blue cohosh seed, once divested of its blue skin (the germination-inhibiting pericarp), must be kept moist until planting. Sow the seeds 1 to 2 inches (2.4 to 4.8 cm) apart and ½ inch (1.2 cm) deep, in prepared woodland nursery beds, in the shade garden or in shaded flats. It is important to keep the soil moist through the extended pregermination period (warm/cold/warm/cold), and this is best accomplished by mulching with well-rotted leaves. Mark the spot or the flat with an indelible tag, because it is easy to forget when and where the seeds were planted. Seed sown at Horizon Herbs Seed Farm on 10/22/97 emerged aerially on 4/12/99 (a 537-day germination period), demonstrating the typical time required for the completion of two-phase germination. Another planting started on 10/25/99 produced aerial parts for the first time on 4/1/02 (an 889-day germination period), demonstrating both double-dormancy and two-phase germination. Once the seedlings emerge, they may be grown at this original spacing for a full season or two, until they differentiate into a root-rhizome structure.

Cultivation from root cuttings. Blue cohosh is easy to propagate from root divisions. Divisions are best made from mature, seed-bearing individuals in the autumn, after the rhizome has set buds for the next year's growth. Dig the roots and shake them free of soil. Roots bound for storage or transport must never be washed, as the dirt protects them from rapid fungal deterioration. Each mature rhizome may be cut or broken into several transplants. Pieces sporting a nascent bud, no matter how small it may be, make excellent propagative material. Pieces of the rhizome without buds, if planted in propitious conditions, will sprout new buds from invisible eyes, producing plants sometimes in the first spring, and sometimes not until the second spring after dividing. Plants grown from cuttings usually take 3 years to produce a mature, seed-bearing individual.

Transplanting. Transplants grown from seed and root cuttings may be transplanted in similar ways. The rhizome is oriented horizontally, set shallowly into the mineral soil, with the rootlets secured underneath and the nascent bud or buds poking up toward the light. Space the transplants 1 to 2 feet (30 to 60 cm) apart and mulch.

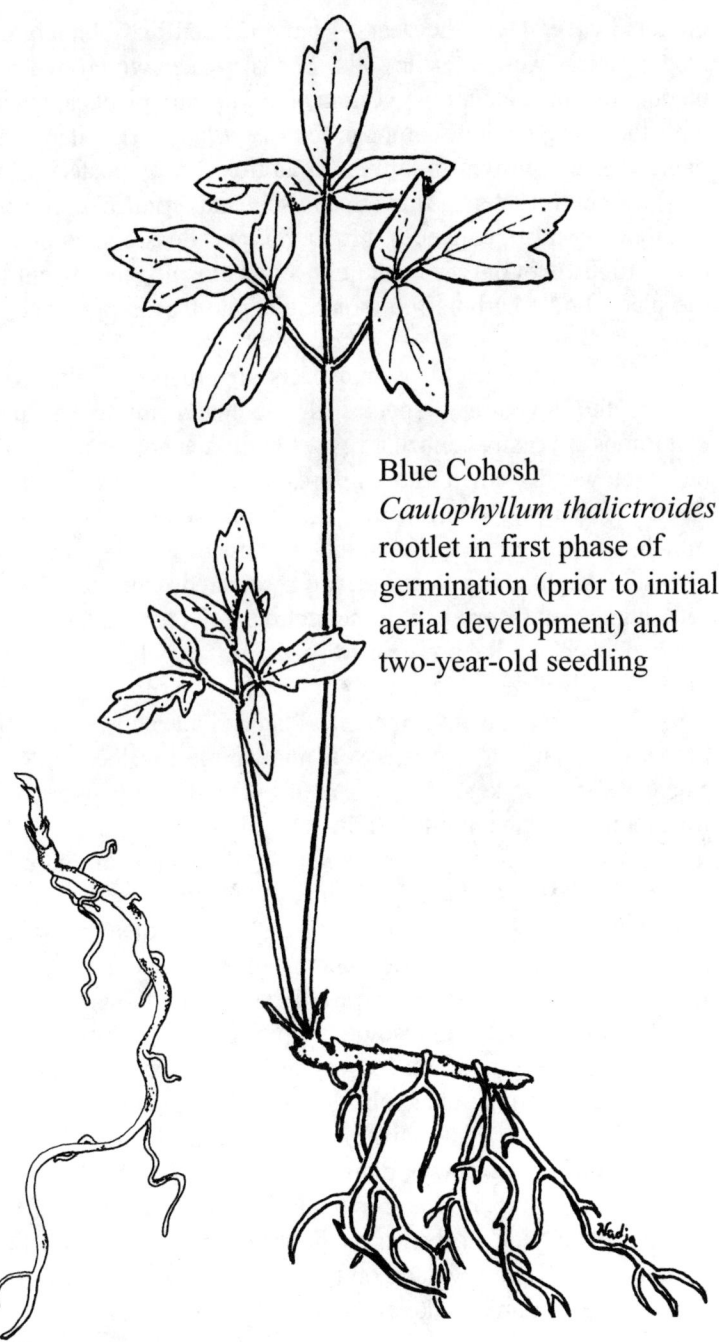

Blue Cohosh
Caulophyllum thalictroides
rootlet in first phase of
germination (prior to initial
aerial development) and
two-year-old seedling

General care. Over the years, I have learned that blue cohosh responds very well to fertile soils. Seeds covered with rotted cow manure demonstrate a high germination rate, and plants amended with the same mellow compost achieve a larger size than unamended plants grown in similar conditions. Composted plants produce multiple stems, flower profusely and produce more fruit. Composting also enhances production of dense, medicinally active roots. Not only is the compost nutritionally significant for the plant, but it harbors the moist substrate that is preferred by blue cohosh.

One of the most pleasant aspects of gardening in the shade is that the few weed species that actually thrive in these conditions are easily controlled. I wait until the hottest part of the day, then wander down into the forested area to cool off, pulling weeds or burying them with extra compost or forest-derived mulch, stopping often to check the progress of various patches of plants. I might stoop to read a tag associated with germinating seedlings in a nursery bed, or scratch tentatively in a bare nursery bed, checking the progress of seeds. After awhile, I sit down on a cushy bed of cleavers with my back to an old growth alder tree and observe the environment. Water trickles down from the higher mountains to the west. Minnows play in the shallows. The California spikenard reaches out its wide, compound leaves toward the sparse, mottled light that filters down through the treed canopy arching over the creek. In the woods on the other side of the creek, a squirrel gives away its position by the scritching of its toenails on the thick, resonant bark of a fir. Giant madrone trees, their trunks as smooth as leather, lean ponderously into the shadows. Just next to my hand, a slug crawls out of a patch of miner's lettuce, resolutely pouring itself over the turgid carpet of the forest, eating its way on to the next bite. But the slugs never touch the blue cohosh, and the deer don't, either.

Much time and work has gone into diversifying and enriching these woods with plants, but in comparison to the work involved with preparing and maintaining the fields and gardens on the upland side of the farm, the shade gardens require little maintenance. I put my hand on the smooth bark of my towering alder. Trees, I think, make awesome gardening partners.

Yield. The fresh or dried root and rhizome (the root) of blue cohosh is the part traditionally used, and there is very little historical evidence that other parts have ever been employed (Moerman, 1986). I once performed a chromatographic study of fresh vs. dry blue cohosh roots, testing the relative concentrations of active constituents (the alkaloids aporphine and magnoflorine, the saponin caulosaponin, triterpenes and steroids). The results of the study showed that some of the active chemistry of the root is lost during the drying process, so it makes sense to use the fresh root instead of the dry, since this saves plants in the long run (Cech, 2000). Combining blue cohosh with a demulcent herb (e.g. mullein) during therapy will mollify the acridity of the fresh plant.

The average fresh weight of a mature blue cohosh root is about 40 g. A pound of fresh roots contains an average of about 11 roots, and a pound of dried roots contains about 34 roots. The water content of fresh roots averages between 65% and 70%. Therefore, 10 pounds of fresh roots dries down to about 3.4 pounds of dried roots.

Harvest, processing and storage. Blue cohosh root is best harvested in the autumn, after the plant has fixed primary and secondary constituents in preparation for winter dormancy. Dig the roots, shake off the excess soil and keep them in a sack or in a bucket, protected from the light. If the roots are bound for transport in the fresh state, do not wash them. The native soil protects them from fungal disease, which can reduce washed roots that are stored too long in a sack or in a pile to a useless, white, spongy mass that looks and smells like tempeh.

Wash the roots with a pressure hose just before processing or dehydration. You may need to chop up some of the larger crowns in order to remove lodged mud or stones, but try to keep the roots entire in order to prevent undue oxidation.

Dry the roots in a warm place with positive airflow, turning often. I have laid out roots on open screens in the attic or behind the woodstove, but a forced-air dehydrator is preferable. Dry for 1 day with low temperature (70° F = 21° C) and high air flow, then turn up the temperature to high (110° F = 43° C) and dry the roots until they snap. The roots are best stored in plastic bags in lightproof sacks or drums, in a cool, dark and dry location. The dried roots retain their potency for up to two years.

Blue cohosh seed, once divested of its thin, blue-black skin (the pericarp), is swollen and globular, measuring ~9 mm in diameter (see illustration p. 40). It is colored chocolate brown, and sports a navel-like dimple which eventually gives rise to the radicle. Each seed weighs ~0.33 grams (3 seeds per gram). Contrary to other published accounts that report 2 seeds per fruit (Felter and Lloyd, 1898; Dinda and Craker, 1998), I have observed that the fruits are always 1-seeded.

Seed collecting, cleaning, storage and longevity. Blue cohosh seed ripens in the mid to late summer, turning from a hard green ball to a squishy-skinned fruit. Once ripe, the fruits detach readily from the thick stipe, and may be picked in much the same manner as one would pick blueberries or huckleberries. The seed is nicely preserved by the thin, moist layer of fruit that surrounds it, and is best left in the fruit during short-term storage or shipping. Refrigeration at this stage is not recommended, because it can cause extended dormancy.

It is important to remove the germination-inhibiting, fleshy skin from the seed prior to long storage or planting. This may be accomplished by individually popping the seeds out of their skin. (They tend to end up under the range, up against the cove or underfoot, in which case they are as dangerous as ball bearings.)

A more convenient and efficient method is to put the fruits in a mesh bag, soak briefly in water, then kneed the fruits by hand until the seeds separate from their skins. Then plop the whole mess out of the bag and into a bucket, pour in copious quantities of water and separate by flotation. This process is described in detail in the chapter on ginseng, but in short it involves separating the dense, viable seeds by repeatedly adding water and pouring away the fleshy, nonseed portion.

Regardless of how the seeds are cleaned, it is highly recommended to use the mesh bag technique, placing the bare seed in a mesh bag to hang at the back of the sink, rinsing twice daily for a period of at least 30 days before planting. This completely divests the seed of any clinging fruit material; it further leaches germination-inhibiting compounds out of the seed, and since the process is performed at room temperature, this practice nicely fulfills the initial warm stratification requirement.

After this extended rinsing, it is best to sow the seed immediately, but if necessary it may be stored for a time under refrigeration at 40° F (4.4° C). Storage in moist peat moss in a closed plastic bag is ideal. Seed stored in this manner will remain viable for up to 6 months. If stored longer than this, it may well begin producing rootlets. If this (first stage germination) occurs, the seed needs to be planted right away in a warm environment.

Conservation status. Wild-harvested blue cohosh root is sold both domestically and internationally. Demand is moderate, since this potent plant has a fairly narrow range of application and is therefore not prescribed as frequently as, for instance, black cohosh or ginseng. Another encouraging aspect is that blue cohosh grows in the mountains, and that it shyly sequesters itself in the deepest, least accessible parts of the forest. These locations are more likely to be chosen as nature preserves, and they are often not suited to development. However, the slow growth and complex germination of this plant (adaptive strategies that contribute to its longevity in nature) actually serve as stumbling blocks to efficient production of the medicine under cultivation. The nature of blue cohosh, consistently expressed through its choice of habitat, its chemistry, its medicinal application and its agronomy, is that of a complex plant spirit—best left alone unless called out in time of great need.

Other species. "Giant blue cohosh," otherwise known as "northern blue cohosh" is generally considered to be a variant of *Caulophyllum thalictroides,* but is listed in some publications as a separate species, i.e. *Caulophyllum giganteum* (Flora of North America, 1993). Giant blue cohosh has a sporadic distribution throughout the northeastern states, from Vermont across the shores of the Great Lakes and south as far as the states of North Carolina and Tennessee, where it is listed as a rare and endangered plant. *Caulophyllum giganteum* is larger and flowers earlier and more vigorously than *Caulophyllum thalictroides.* The plants sometimes occupy the same econiche, are difficult to distinguish (especially during dormancy) and for all practical purposes are treated as the same plant in herbal medicine.

References

Cech, R. 2000. *Blue Cohosh,* in Gladstar (ed.), *Planting the Future: Saving our Medicinal Herbs.* Rochester (VT): Healing Arts Press, p. 80.

_____. 1993. *Flora of North America.* New York (NY): Oxford University Press,Vol 3.

Dinda, K. and L. Craker. 1998. *Grower's Guide to Medicinal Plants.* HSMP Press, Amherst (MA).

Felter, H. and J. Lloyd. 1898 (Reprinted 1985). *King's American Dispensatory.* Portland (OR): Eclectic Medical Publishing, Vol. 1 & 2, 743 pp.

Moerman, D. 1986. *Medicinal Plants of Native America,* Ann Arbor (MI): University of Michigan Dept. of Anthropology, Vol.1, 534 pp.

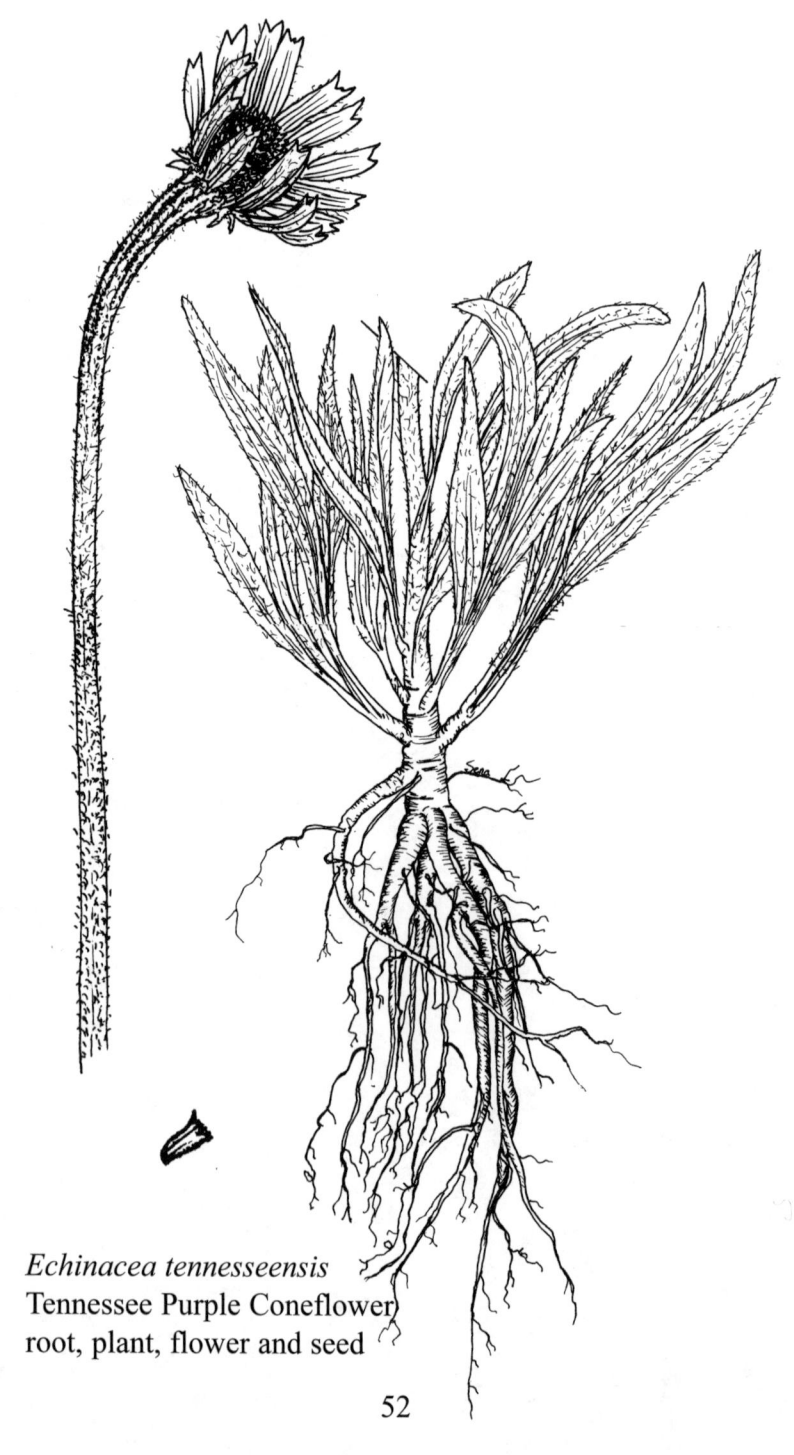

Echinacea tennesseensis
Tennessee Purple Coneflower
root, plant, flower and seed

Echinacea

Echinacea Moench

Family: *Asteraceae*

Echinacea is a widespread and diverse genus of plants consisting of nine unique species indigenous to open glades, woodlands, riparian lowlands, prairies and mountains in North America. The plant is an herbaceous perennial, anchored in the soil by either a spreading, fibrous root or a taproot, depending on the species. The roots are tough and earthy-smelling, with a crown that grows woody with age, giving rise to a full rosette of leaves. The leaf shapes may be narrowly lance-shaped and entire or broadly lance-shaped and toothed, depending on the species. Mature plants produce several flowering stalks, sometimes branched, with leaves occurring sparsely up the stem. They are crowned by the magnificent flower. Like all members of the *Asteraceae,* echinacea flowers are composed of multiple florets in a central disk, surrounded by infertile ligules (ray flowers) that rim the disk. The disk flower is blanketed by a bristling cone of spear-like paleae. The beautiful ray flowers vary in color from almost red to light purple, rarely white, and are even colored yellow in one rare, endemic species. The seeds are very numerous, wedged into the surface of the disk, protected by the bristling paleae. The seeds are tan or two-tone tan and brown, blunt at the base and concave at the top, the point of attachment for the corolla.

As one of the most striking of all North American wildflowers, the purple coneflower has been appreciated both in gardens and in nature for hundreds of years. Part of the lesson that flowers teach humans is to be aware of the moment, because their bright beauty is fleeting and impermanent. When the drying winds of early winter sweep off the mountainside and across the grasslands, laying down the first bleached blanket of snow, the purple coneflowers whither and dry. Perhaps the entire stalk blows over and lodges in the surface of a mounting snow-drift. Now the flower looks for all the world like a bit of ocean debris thrown up on a sandy beach, a likeness that long ago gave rise to its latin name *"echinos,"* meaning literally "sea urchin."

Native range. Viewed as a whole, the genus *Echinacea* is widely distributed across the United States and southern Canada, from the Rocky Mountains to the Atlantic. The center of diversity for echinacea arcs across Mississippi, Arkansas and Oklahoma. The overall distribution becomes much more meaningful when examined on the basis of the individual species, some of which occur over wide areas and others of which are endemic, meaning that their distribution is restricted to a particular area or region. For this concise review of the range of the nine species, the author is largely indebted to Steven Foster and his book "Echinacea, Nature's Immune Enhancer" which is a definitive work and highly recommended (Foster, 1991).

Echinacea angustifolia is the most northerly occurring of all the species, found in prairies and the rocky soils of mountainous areas in a wide band stretching from central Texas north to southern Saskatchewan and Manitoba.

Echinacea pallida has a more easterly range than *E. angustifolia,* although the two sometimes share the same habitat and are often misidentified and interchanged in commerce. The plant occurs in dry clay soils, in open oak woods and grasslands from northeast Texas all the way up to Minnesota.

Echinacea simulata is similar to *E. pallida,* but occurs in the Ozark Plateau: north central Arkansas, eastern and south-central Missouri, southwestern Illinois and west-central Kentucky.

Echinacea purpurea occurs only sporadically in the wild, growing in open woods and riparian lowlands from Louisiana, Texas and Oklahoma, north through Ohio and Michigan.

Echinacea laevigata is similar to *E. purpurea*, but is very rare. In fact, this is the rarest plant in the genus *Echinacea,* a federally listed endangered species limited to 23 known populations totalling only 6,000 to 10,000 individuals, occurring in Pennsylvania, Virginia, the Carolinas, Georgia and Alabama.

Echinacea atrorubens is a rare, endemic species that grows on prairies in a narrow band from Houston, Texas to Ardmore, Oklahoma and north to Topeka, Kansas.

Echinacea paradoxa is unique in that its ray flowers are yellow. This plant is also an endemic, growing in glades, open pine forests and prairies in the south central and western

Arkansas Ozarks and in a few locations in the state of Missouri.

Echinacea sanguinea is the most southerly ranging cone-flower, growing in open fields and pine woods in the West Gulf Coastal Plain, a region bounded by southwest Arkansas, southeastern Oklahoma, western Louisiana and eastern Texas.

Echinacea tennesseensis is an endemic species found in dry cedar glades in central Tennessee. The plant was listed in 1979 by the United States Fish and Wildlife Service as an endangered species (Federal Register, 1979).

Current Range of *Echinacea* Species in the U.S.

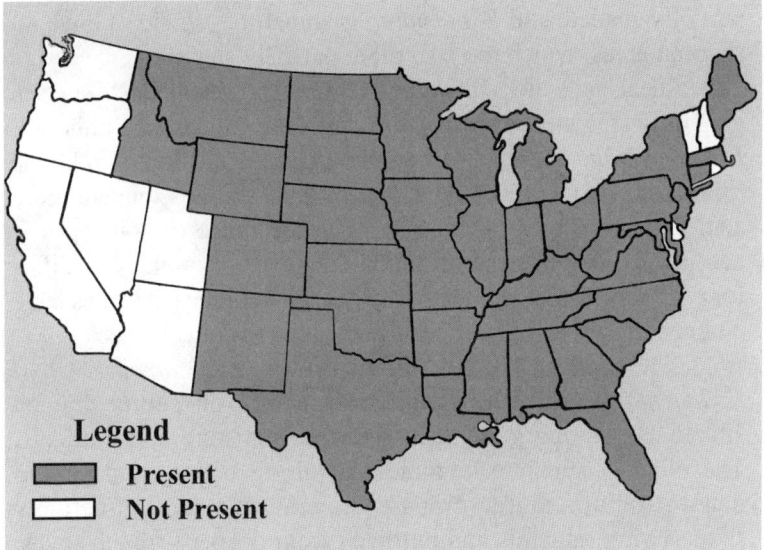

Legend
Present
Not Present

Hardiness and adaptability. Echinacea is relatively cold-hardy, evidenced by its far-ranging native distribution in temperate North America. The plant demonstrates a strong dormancy. The seed, on the whole, gives better germination if cold-stratified before planting. Literally every type of cone-flower is both beautiful and medicinally useful, so it makes sense for the gardener to choose the species that is best adapted for the local conditions. For instance, since *E. angustifolia* is the most northerly of all, thriving even at elevation in the Bighorn Mountains where the winters are very severe, this would likely be the species of choice for gardeners in Canada or Minnesota.

Conversely, the most southerly ranging of *Echinacea* species (e.g. *E. sanguinea, E. atrorubens)* would probably be most likely to grow well in Mississippi or Florida. Finally, *E. purpurea* has shown itself to be the best all-around candidate for cultivation, adaptable to a wide range of conditions, from the sweaty tropics of Hawaii to the frostbitten fields of Iowa.

Ecology. On the whole, echinacea prefers to grow in full or part sun, being first and foremost a plant of the prairie. Certain unusual species (e.g. *E. paradoxa* and *E. tennesseensis)* have adapted to living in woodland glades where they may be partially shaded, and *E. purpurea* is sometimes found in lowland riparian areas, which are also often partially shaded.

Ideal soils for cultivating any and all *Echinacea* species generally register a pH value between 6 and 7, although *E. angustifolia* and *E. pallida* prefer more alkaline conditions (pH 6.5 to 7.5). *E. paradoxa* and *E. tennesseensis* tolerate more acid conditions (pH 5.5 to 6.5). A wide range of soil types is acceptable, although the ideal soil composition is likely to differ for each species. Sandy loam, rocky clay and lime substrates have all been known to support healthy populations of echinacea.

The species with fibrous roots *(E. purpurea and E. laevigata)* are better adapted to growing in poorly drained situations, making good use of surface moisture and nutrients. The other species are taprooted, requiring better drainage and demonstrating more drought tolerance, also effectively sequestering minerals and nutrients from deeper soil substrates. However, echinacea is not a zerophytic plant, and when rainfall is not abundant, the plant suffers. Contrary to popular folklore, drought conditions do not cause the plant to "seed abundantly in a last-ditch effort to propagate in time of stress." Drought conditions may seriously reduce seed size, viability and production, while abundant moisture improves overall plant health and increases seed production.

Community. Echinacea is designed for life among the grasses. This is evidenced by the root form (especially the taproot), that utilizes a different soil horizon than do the grasses. The rosette springs from a cohesive crown, and the leaves push back the grasses and lay on top of them to photosynthesize, making room for the tall echinacea stalks. These stalks are in turn adapted to hold the flower and the seed out of direct competition with the grasses.

The plant also occurs in association with other forbs (broad-leaved plants) in loose communities that might include compass plant *(Silphium laciniatum)*, coneflowers *(Rudbeckia* spp.), milkweeds *(Asclepias* spp.), docks *(Rumex* spp.), wild carrot *(Daucus carota)* and perhaps the infamous echinacea adulterant known as wild quinine or prairie dock *(Parthenium integrifolium)*.

Purple coneflower itself occurs in self-seeded patches. The taprooted species tend to grow more closely in nature, because this root form allows for close spacing without too much intraspecies competition for resources. For instance, natural stands of *E. angustifolia* in the foothills of the Bighorn Mountains of Wyoming are visible during the flowering season as a purple-dotted patchwork, stretching from toe-tip to horizon. The species with fibrous roots *(E. purpurea* and *E. laevigata)* require a wider spacing and tend to occur as scattered individuals or in sparsely populated patches.

Life cycle. In nature, echinacea flowers in the summer and is pollinated by a diverse mix of flying insects, including native bees, wasps and butterflies. The primary flowers that cap the main stems are the largest and most productive. These flower first, followed by smaller flowers that occur on the secondary branches. Echinacea is an outcrosser, sharing pollen for miles around, the spread of pollen limited only by large land features and the practical range of the pollinators.

Once fertilization is complete, the ray flowers begin to fade and the cone itself swells and becomes nearly round as the seed matures. The pointed paleae protect the green seed, but when the seed ripens, it loosens in the conehead and begins to work its way out between the paleae. By autumn, some of the seed will begin to scatter in the wind. Small birds such as goldfinches, their beaks specially adapted to the work, dig in between the paleae and dislodge the seed, consuming much, but also scattering viable seed. The dormant seed falls to the wet ground or on top of the snow. The rains and snows of winter leach germination-inhibiting compounds from the seed, and the oscillating temperatures of winter and early spring help break the dormancy. As the soil warms in the spring, seeds having fallen on bare ground or buried shallowly in disturbed soil begin to germinate and grow. Germination is epigeal. Although the majority of seeds either perish or germinate within the first year, a small percentage will continue dormancy through to the second spring. In nature, echinacea spreads only by seed, and the plants require at least two years to reach maturity.

Cultivation from seed. Echinacea seed may be sown directly in the field or the garden in the fall or early spring. Although fertilization is not usually required before sowing the seed, it is a good idea to provide a dressing of ground limestone directly under the row.[1] A fine seedbed is required, since the seed is small and large clods reduce chances of germination and block penetration of the rootlet. Bed preparation and seed sowing is often easier in the autumn, when the soils are relatively dry. However, weed pressure is always a consideration, and the weeds have more time to develop when the fieldwork is done in the autumn as opposed to the spring. Regardless of how it is done, direct seeding is a challenge to even the most accomplished grower.

Seeds are best sown barely under the soil surface, spaced about 2 inches (4.8 cm) apart in rows 18 to 24 inches (43 to 58 cm) apart. The taprooted echinaceas are best thinned to a spacing of 6 inches (14 cm) apart, while the species with fibrous roots are best thinned to a spacing of 1 to 2 feet (30 to 60 cm) apart in the row. Once the seedlings develop their first set of true leaves, it is easier to cultivate around them, and field maintenance is even easier after the plants become self-mulching by the autumn of the first year. The first flowers will appear in the autumn of the first year, but commercially valuable flower and seed production does not occur until the second year. The plants are not harvested for the root until after year two or three.

---

[1] This alkalinizes the soil, approximating the limestone substrate that is the preferred wild habitat of several species. It is my experience that ground limestone, applied at the rate of 50 pounds per 100 linear feet to regular garden soil (pH 6.5), more or less depending on the relative acidity, is helpful in cultivating all species of *Echinacea.*

Much has been written about seed dormancy and stratification of the various *Echinacea* species, and the subject has become unnecessarily complex. Nature provides the appropriate conditions for breaking seed dormancy. A period of exposure to cold, moist, outdoor conditions followed by germination in the spring is the best way to assure success.[2]

In the case of direct seeding, these conditions are very simply met by sowing in the fall or in the early spring. In more controlled cultivation, the seeds are sown in flats or plug trays in an unheated greenhouse in the very early spring. Germination usually occurs within 30 days. My studies show that the ideal soil temperature for germination is a cool 55° to 60° F (13° to 18° C). Flats sown in February will produce plants ready to transplant into the field in May. If a greenhouse is not available, flats or plug trays may be set up on tables in a shady location outdoors, seeded in the early spring, protected by screens, and the seedlings transplanted to finished spacing after they attain the second set of true leaves. Most failures in controlled germination of echinacea may be traced to planting in soil that is too warm, which lowers the germination rate even when the seeds have been artificially stratified.

Echinacea purpurea and *E. laevigata* have a fibrous root system, and if their roots become bound in the pot or plug tray it is not a problem. They transplant readily and develop their roots in a natural shape. However, the other seven species of *Echinacea*

---

[2] Echinacea seed may be artificially stratified in moist medium in plastic bags in the refrigerator. The drawbacks of this technique are: 1) extra trouble, 2) lack of leaching by rain, 3) lack of oscillating temperatures, 4) lack of cadence with natural cycles. Similarly, experiments with echinacea seeds sown in sterile conditions in laboratories do not necessarily elucidate how the same seeds would perform in field conditions. *E. purpurea* germinates readily in a cool greenhouse *without* any stratification. Germination of the other species is improved by subjecting the seed to at least 30 days of freezing conditions. *E. paradoxa* and *E. tennesseensis* demonstrate the strongest dormancy, and 60 days of freezing temperatures may be necessary to obtain high germination rates. However, even *without* cold stratification, all species will show at least some germination within 30 days after planting in cool (55° to 60° F = 13° to 18° C) soils.

have taproots (although *E. atrorubens* has a short, stubby taproot), and the growth of these can be compromised if the root is not allowed to develop normally. This means that deep pots, flats or plug trays are required, and the transplant is best accomplished before the heavy taproot reaches the bottom of the container. If the root outgrows the container, the plant will stunt after transplant. If the plant is left in the container, it will never attain the size of a field-grown plant. Therefore, if production of herbs for medicine is desired, or if one is naturalizing the plant in the garden or landscape, it is highly recommended to transplant the taprooted echinaceas in the fledgling stage, or to direct seed them.

In mild winter areas such as the Pacific Northwest, California, and the South, a different cycle for establishing perennials with minimum labor and maximum returns is often employed. The seed is sown in the early summer into pots or plug trays. The seedlings are nurtured along until they produce the second set of true leaves, and are transplanted to the garden or to the field in the late summer to early autumn. This gives the plant plenty of time to root in before dormancy. Perennials established in this manner will produce large, flower-bearing individuals the next summer. The advantage of this system is that the gardener avoids an entire spring and summer of weeding, and this window of time can be used for growing (and subsequently tilling in) a revitalizing cover crop such as peas and oats or red clover. The disadvantage is that echinacea may be difficult to germinate in soils that are too warm. Therefore, this method is most applicable to the production of *E. purpurea,* because this species does not require cold stratification.

The shadehouse at Horizon Herbs Seed Farm is a framework covered with 66% shade cloth and fitted out with benches and prop-agation flats, watered by air-cooling misters. I have found this to be a very convenient place for plant propagation in the summer. The cool soils (~70° F = 21° C) and even watering actually give some germination on all species of *Echinacea* without stratification, and the delicate seedlings are shielded from the burning rays of the sun, reaching optimal size in time for the autumn transplant.

Cultivation from crown divisions. *Echinacea purpurea* and *E. laevigata* can be easily propagated from division of the mature, dormant plant. This is accomplished either in the fall or the early spring, by digging the root, shaking it free of soil and chopping it into several pieces. A good division sports several buds and a mat of hair-like feeder roots that will expand and nourish the new plant. In many cases, the central portion of the crown of older plants deteriorates, and many small offshoots are formed in a ring around the necrotic tissue. These offshoots also make very effective starts, developing into large individuals within two years of transplant.

The taprooted echinaceas, on the other hand, are difficult to propagate by crown division. I attribute this to the lack of hair-like feeder roots on or near the crown, resulting in insufficient water and nutrient assimilation to jump-start a new plant. However, it is a fact that pieces of echinacea taproot left deep in the ground after harvest often resprout and produce a new crown. These terminal ends of the taproot *do* have feeder roots attached. The presence or absence of hair-like feeder roots thus becomes a ruling factor governing whether or not a piece of taproot will produce a new plant by asexual means.

Adventitious reproduction. Echinacea is a pretty vigorous self-seeder, and one of the reasons that our established fields and gardens do not bristle with new plants is simply because the tiny seedlings are inadvertently removed during the spring cultivation and weeding. Careful observation in the field may reveal healthy seedlings that can be transplanted into prepared ground or pricked into pots. These may be grown out in the greenhouse for a few weeks, then transplanted into the field as a healthy start when conditions are right. It is good to remember that nature is, after all, our hardest working partner.

Fertilization. Purple coneflower responds favorably to occasional side-dressing with organic compost and composted manure. This improves overall health of the plant and increases drought tolerance. Yield of roots, aerial portions and seed is also increased by fertilization. Dilute foliar feeds, manure tea and seaweed tea also improve plant health and yield, and are particularly helpful to alleviate the stress of transplant. Leaving uncomposted manures in contact with the leaves will burn them.

Yield. The entire echinacea plant, including the root, stem, leaves, flowers and seed contains active constituents and may be used in the fresh or dry state for production of tinctures, capsules or teas. The root is generally considered to be the most potent and balanced portion of the plant for general use, and the stem is considered to be the least active plant part.

Echinacea purpurea is the most widely cultivated and utilized species. The mature, 2-year-old plant, harvested at peak of flowering in the summer of the second year of growth, yields on the average 2.25 pounds (1135 g) of aerial parts per plant. A second cutting in the same year is often possible, but this does sap the strength of the plant, and yields are substantially less than the yield from the first cutting. Stems constitute about 45% of the weight of the entire aerial plant. The water content of the leaves and flowers (stripped from the stem) averages about 75%. Therefore, 10 pounds of fresh leaves and flowers will dry down to 2.5 pounds of dried herb.

The roots of cultivated *Echinacea purpurea,* dug during plant dormancy, weigh on the average 0.5 pounds (227 g) fresh weight after 2 full years of growth. The water content of the fresh root ranges between 68% and 72%. Therefore, 10 pounds of fresh *E. purpurea* roots will dry down to about 3 pounds. Each pound of dried *E. purpurea* roots consists of between 6 and 7 entire roots.

The roots of cultivated *Echinacea angustifolia,* dug during plant dormancy, weigh on the average 0.25 pounds (114 g) fresh weight after 2 full years of growth. The water content of the fresh root averages 62.5%. Therefore, 10 pounds of fresh *E. angustifolia* roots will dry down to about 3.75 pounds. Each pound of dried *E. angustifolia* roots consists of about 16 entire roots. Our investigations show that these figures are generally applicable to all species of taprooted echinaceas.

The aerial parts of *Echinacea angustifolia* are nearly devoid of alkylamides (Cech, 2000) and are therefore considered less useful than the aerial parts of *E. purpurea.* More investigation into the utility of the aerial portions of all nine species is well-justified, since aerial parts (which are most often employed in tea blends) may be renewably harvested without killing the plant.

The green batch. The fresh roots of cultivated *E. angustifolia* are infamous among those that make liquid extracts, because they often produce what is known in the herb industry as a "green batch." The tincture takes on a bright neon green color during maceration, and the finished extract is malodorous, plagued by a mucky precipitate and an oily pellicle on the surface. Comparative constituent analysis of "green batches" and "normal batches" (colored brown) have failed to elucidate the problem. However, organoleptic analysis (simply tasting and smelling the extract) readily detects the green batch, which is usually rejected as unuseable. This is a blow to conservation-minded farmers and manufacturers, who would much prefer to use cultivated *E. angustifolia* over wild-harvested material. One answer is to use cultivated *E. purpurea* root for liquid extracts, and to use the cultivated *E. angustifolia* root for dehydration and encapsulation, which appears to be a completely valid and trouble-free application. *E. angustifolia* roots lend themselves to dehydration and grinding, because they are less fibrous than *E. purpurea,* making a fine powder with relative ease.

Harvest, processing and storage. Echinacea leaf and flower is best harvested at the peak of flowering, which usually occurs in midsummer. The stems are cut just above the first discolored leaves of the rosette, and the leaf and flower are stripped from the stem and used fresh or dehydrated. The flowers must be split at least once before drying, or they will rehydrate from internal moisture once put into storage. The leaf and split flowers are laid out on screens in a dark, airy and warm location and stirred daily until thoroughly dry. An herb dehydrator set at 110° F (43° C) is equally effective, and faster.

Echinacea root is harvested during the dormant period, preferably in the autumn after two or three years of growth. The species with fibrous roots are pried up with a shovel, and species with taproots are dug out with a sturdy spade. Mechanical harvest has also been developed, using a modified potato digger to lift the roots. Regardless of how the roots are dug up, they are then shaken free of dirt and piled in the shade. Roots may be washed with a specially designed root washer, or individually with a pressure hose. Large crowns will need to be hacked apart with a hatchet or machete in order to allow access to dirt and stones lodged at the base of the crown. Echinacea roots are pretty stable after washing, and may be cold-stored or shipped over a period of several days without molding. However it makes sense to process them as soon as possible after washing, which will minimize oxidation. Taprooted echinaceas are usually dried whole, while the fibrous-rooted species are best dried in pieces, as the crown is too big to dry efficiently in the whole form. The roots or root pieces are laid out on screens in a dark, dry location with positive airflow and turned often until dry. If using a forced-air dehydrator, it is best to dry the roots for 1 day at 70° F (21° C), then turn the temperature up to 110° F (43° C), drying the roots until they snap. Echinacea root is best stored in plastic bags in lightproof sacks or drums, in a cool, dry and dark location. The dried roots retain their potency for only one year in storage.

Echinacea seed consists of a soft, tan, tear-shaped ovule surrounded by a spongy pericarp. The color is tan or two-toned tan and brown, blunt at the hilum, longitudinally ribbed and convex at the top, which is the point of attachment for the corolla. The seed varies substantially in size and density, depending on the species and especially depending on the availability of water and nutrients during the growing season. For instance, a given accession of wild-harvested *Echinacea angustifolia* seed averaged 2 by 4 mm in size, with 270 seeds per gram. The same seed, once cultivated in organic conditions and fertilized, produced in 2 years' time plants that bore seeds averaging 3 by 5 mm in size and containing only 201 seeds per gram. The number of echinacea seeds per pound generally ranges between 96,000 and 145,000 for seed testing to 98% purity.

Seed cultivation. Echinacea is a wild one, and it is an outcrosser, so there are several relevant considerations before growing seed for replanting. The first is genetic diversity, that is, making certain that the harvest is from a sufficient number of plants to capture the range of variation that is the foundation of a stable race of plants. Failure to collect from a sufficient number of individuals can cause inbreeding depression, resulting in a lack of adaptability and vitality in subsequent crops. For this reason, it is recommended that seed be collected from several hundred individuals, and ideally from over a thousand.

Isolation is required in order to assure that only one species is present for cross-pollination and seed production. Preventing hybridization may be achieved by distancing the plants at least a mile away from other species of *Echinacea*. But isolation may also be achieved by using floating row covers (a commercially available, light weight fabric that isolates the crop from pollinators), or by relying on natural barriers in the landscape such as dense forests, a river or a mountain. Also, a cogent patch or field of echinacea is in itself a magnet to pollinators, and I have noticed that native bumblebees, for instance, will remain in the patch as long as pollen supplies last, remaining overnight on the plants in order to work there again the next day. So, planting a thousand individuals or more not only assures diversity, but also contributes to isolation.

The best seed is produced by plants that are two years old or older. Plants destined for seed production should not be harvested aerially that year, since the first flowers are also the largest and most vital flowers. Good fertility and sufficient water during the flowering phase will increase overall seed production, seed size and viability. However, once the ray ligules die back in the autumn and the seed begins to loosen in the conehead, it is best to let the field go dry. Wet conditions at this period, whether caused by injudicious irrigation or natural precipitation, will set up the conditions for mold. The highest quality seed is bright in color (not darkened by moist conditions in the field) and the best way to dry a seed is on the plant, not by artificial heat.

Seed collecting, cleaning, storage and longevity. When the flower stem directly below the conehead turns from green to brown it is a sure sign that the seed head is ready for harvest. Since the seed heads ripen differentially, there is an advantage in hand harvesting, where mature seed heads are picked and green seed heads are left on the plant. When harvesting by combine, it is necessary to wait until later in the season to harvest, when all the seed heads are mature and dry.

In order to clean the seed, the mature coneheads must first be broken up without injuring the seeds, either by running them through a combine or by using a hammer mill at low rpm with a 1-inch screen. This will produce a massive pile of chaff with seeds intermixed. This material can then be taken to a professional seed cleaner to process into pure seed, or the seed may be cleaned by hand.

Hand cleaning begins by running the dry chaff-seed mixture through a ¼ inch stationary screen. This will remove large stems and chaff. Then the remaining seed and chaff are shaken through a screen that is too small for the seed to pass. This will remove all dust and fine chaff, including the dense, dried corollas that look a little like seed but are slightly smaller and dark brown in color. The remaining product is composed of the seed and all the chaff that is approximately the same size as the seed. Since the bulk is substantially reduced, it will be easy to store the seed at this point in buckets or in drums.

The final cleaning is accomplished by winnowing. On a perfect day, when the wind wafts in great wide billows over the landscape in one consistent direction, you can do almost perfect wind separations. First lay down a clean bed sheet. Take this from the bed when the primary bedmaker in the home is not looking, or get one from Salvation Army. (Wash it before you put it back on the bed, or the dried bits of chaff will give you dreams out of the Dark Ages.) Pile the chaffy seed in a ¼ inch mesh hand screen, lift it head high and wait for the wind to be perfect. If it is helpful to you, you can imagine that you are surfing, waiting for the perfect wave—not as nice as surfing, perhaps, but no sharks. When the wind is right, shake the screen above the sheet. Light chaff will blow away, along with immature seed and empty seed coats. The heavy, viable seed will fall to the sheet in a pile, to be gathered up at the completion of the turn. Do this several times, until the seed meets your requirements for purity.

If the seed is not completely dry, it may be further dehydrated by piling on screens in a dark, airy place, where the heat does not exceed 90° F (32° C). Stir the seed on a daily basis. When it is completely dry, it may be stored in plastic bags in lightproof sacks or drums, in a dark, cool and dry place. Small quantities are best stored in sealed plastic bags or glass jars in the refrigerator. Stored in this manner, the seed will remain vigorous and viable for about five years.

Conservation status. Given the widespread popularity of echinacea as a medicine, the general preference for using the nonrenewable portion (the root) in medicine, and the continued use of wild-harvested echinacea in commercial preparations, there is good reason for concern about the sustainability of the remaining wild populations. Loss of habitat to encroaching farm, ranch and urban sprawl is a real problem. Harvest of wild echinacea for herbal use continues, although somewhat abated by the federal listing of *E. laevigata* and *E. tennesseensis* as endangered species, by recent legislation in Montana (Klein, 2001) regulating the harvest of wild *E. angustifolia,* and by an increasing awareness among consumers that a purchase of an organically grown echinacea product is also a vote for the conservation of the wild echinacea plant. Home herbalists that make their own medicine out of the garden, small-scale growers that offer echinacea products to the community and larger farmers who have adopted echinacea as a useful cash crop are all making a contribution.

The greatest strength of echinacea is in its genetic diversity, and the remaining wild stands of all nine species are living repositories of irreplaceable germ plasm. Harvest of pure and diverse seed from the native land races will help conserve these species through cultivation, also helping inject vigor back into cultivated strains. Further investigation into the active chemistry of the several species that have not been widely cultivated and studied will eventually contribute greatly to the continued role of echinacea in health care. I believe that the increasing public awareness of wild echinacea as a botanical treasure will result in the conservation of each species, both as a unique medicine that bolsters the human immune response, and as a wild beauty that augments the woody glades, the wide grasslands or the rocky mountainsides with its magnificent purple blossoms.

References

Cech, R. 2000. *Making Plant Medicine.* Williams (OR): Horizon Herbs Publications, 282 pp.

Federal Register. 1979. *Determination that Echinacea tennesseensis is an Endangered Species.* 44(110), pp. 32604-5

Foster, S. 1991. *Echinacea, Nature's Immune Enhancer.* Rochester (VT): Healing Arts Press, 150 pp.

Klein, R. 2001. Personal communication. Robyn lives in Montana and has been very active in making sure that the wild medicinal plant resources of that state remain stable and healthy. She served occasionally as a much-appreciated consultant and cheerleader during the writing of this book.

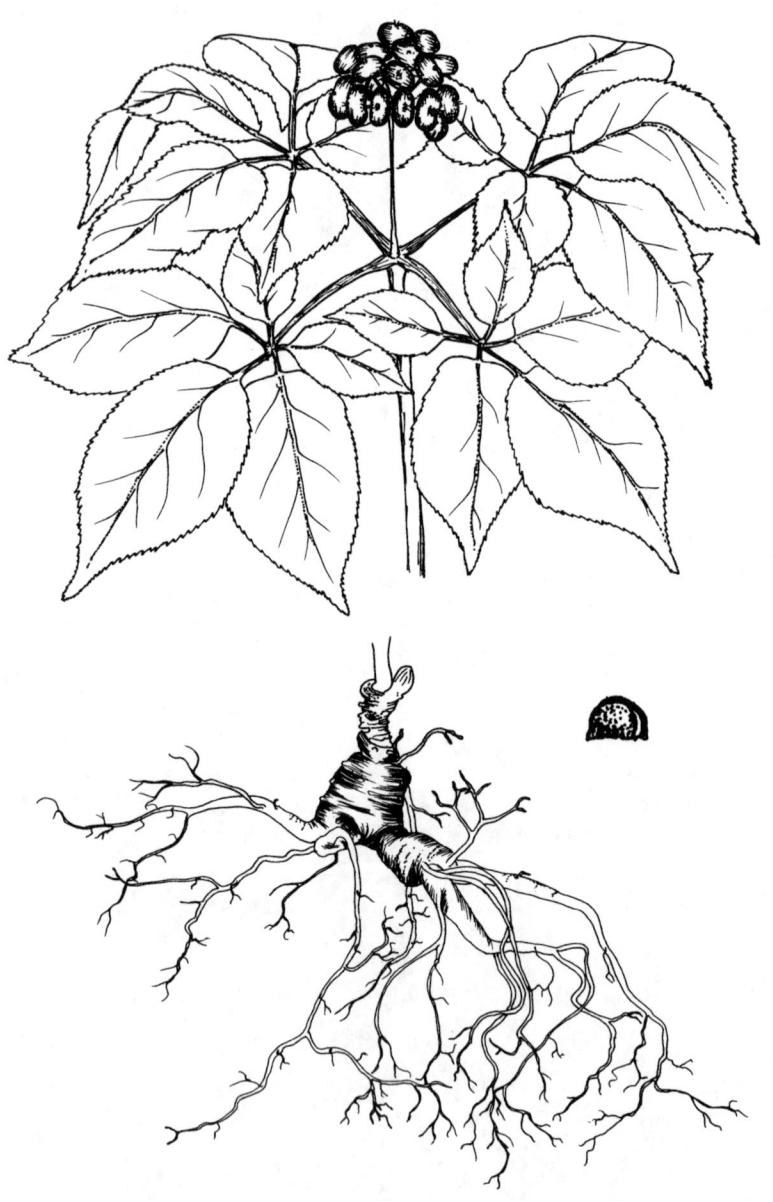

American Ginseng *(Panax quinquefolius)*
root and fruiting plant
seed slightly enlarged

Ginseng, American
Panax quinquefolius L.
Family: *Araliaceae*

Ginseng is a long-lived woodland herbaceous perennial. The barrel-shaped, off-white, fleshy body of the mature root is anchored in the soil by tapering, forked roots tipped with fibrous feeder roots. The overall appearance is humanoid, especially during dormancy when the soft, head-like nascent bud crowns the root. The main root gives rise to a small trunk (the rhizome), generally known as the "neck," growing longer with age and pocked with spiraling, ledge-like stem scars left from the growth of previous years. The round, smooth, green stem of the mature plant arises directly from the neck and is divided into several petioles that support palmate leaves numbering three to seven (usually five). The tip of the leaf is quite acute, flaring out to a broad lance shape, with a fine serration along the edges. I find that this characteristic tip of the leaf is the best way to differentiate *Panax* from other plants that resemble it, especially in the early season, prior to the formation of more indicative flowers and fruits. Among those that are familiar with the plant on a folk wisdom level, each set of compound leaves is known as a "prong." Counting the number of these prongs allows a good approximation of the age of the plant. A first-year seedling bears only three leaves, a second-year or older plant usually produces two prongs, a three-pronged plant is generally aged to three years or older, on up to very old plants that may boast as many as five prongs. The flower extends upward from the center of the plant, a rounded umbel colored greenish-white and giving way to the heavy cluster of berries. The berries are thin-skinned, shiny, plump, kidney-shaped and colored scarlet. They each contain one to three (usually two) seeds. An average mature root measures one inch or more in diameter and four to six inches in length. The plant usually flowers to about 20 inches, although a monumental individual measuring to 26 inches, with leaves as big as human hands, resides on the United Plant Savers sanctuary land in Meigs County, Ohio. Cultivated ginseng requires at least three full years of growth to produce a flower, but the plant may take longer to flower in a wild setting due to competition for resources. It is my experience that the plant may live longer than 90 years, evidenced by counting the stem-scars on older, wild-harvested individuals that I have seen in museums.

Investigators have shown that the concentration of active saponin constituents known as ginsenosides in cultivated ginseng roots increase rapidly during the first four years of growth (Court, 1996). In another study, a dramatic increase (~70%) in the concentration of ginsenosides was registered between year four and five, in conjunction with a marked increase in root weight (sometimes as much as 50% between the fourth and fifth year) (Soldati and Tanaka, 1984). Although these studies are not necessarily indicative of how ginseng performs under other conditions (e.g. wild or woods-grown), they do lend credence to the folk wisdom that older roots are more effective and more valuable than younger roots. So on the basis of reproductive cycle, a three-year plant may be considered "mature," while on the basis of medicinal activity, the plant may not be considered fully mature until at least year five.

Current Range of American Ginseng in the U.S.

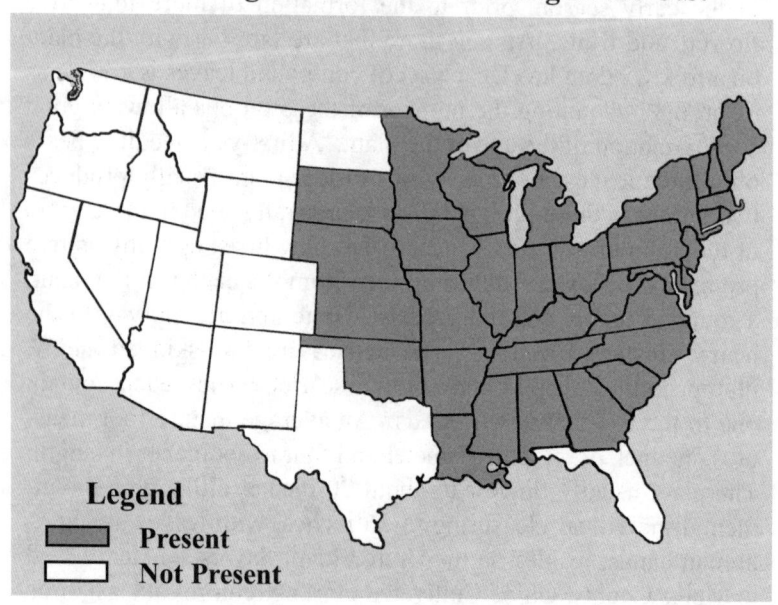

Legend
▬ Present
▭ Not Present

Range. The range of native American ginseng stretches from southern Quebec, Ontario and Manitoba south through the woodlands of the central United States, not extending far west of the Missouri River. Although the plant may be found throughout this range, only 16 states still harbor significant wild populations, with the highest concentration in the Cumberland Gap region of the southern Appalachian Mountains.

Hardiness. Cold winter temperatures are not only tolerated, but they are a necessary part of the life cycle of ginseng, strongly tied to dormancy and germination of the seed and the winter dormancy and reawakening of the plant. A minimum of 100 days of winter—soils at 50° F (10° C) or cooler, freezing if possible—is required to assure an adequate dormancy for the plant. This is why the distribution of wild ginseng dwindles toward the south. Cold temperatures, adequate drainage and wide spacing (planting so that the mature plants do not touch) also discourage the occurrence and spread of disease organisms (e.g. *Alternaria, Phytophthora, Rhizoctonia* and *Fusarium)*.

Adaptability. As long as the minimum requirements of appropriate temperature, soil and shade are met, some success in cultivating ginseng outside its native range is a reasonable expectation. For example, west of the Rockies the states of Oregon and Washington have proven fertile ground for both home-based gardening and large-scale farming of ginseng. Canada, with its cold winters and dry climate rates third in world production of ginseng. Agriculture and Agri-food Canada reports that over 5,000 acres of American ginseng were under shade cultivation in Canada in 1996, with production areas concentrated in southwestern Ontario and British Colombia. The majority of cultivated ginseng finds its way to Asian markets, but in a strange twist we have now begun to see Chinese-grown American ginseng entering the U.S. markets. Finally and perhaps most surprisingly, there is a solid and functional group of Australians that are growing ginseng "down-under" and finding local markets for their products, both fresh and dried.

Ecology. Ginseng prefers to grow under the shade of a mixed hardwood forest, usually on sloping ground with a northerly or easterly exposure. The degree of shade given to the plants is critical. Approximately 70% shade is often considered to be ideal, meaning that at any given time during the day the plants are receiving only 30% of the light that is shining on the uppermost leaves of the trees in the canopy above. This light will strike the plants as filtered light, reflected light and dappled sunlight, moving constantly as the earth revolves and as the trees and leaves sway and shift in the breeze. Ginseng can also be grown in complete shade, relying only on reflected light, and in certain circumstances it can tolerate more than 30% direct light, especially if that light is hitting the plants during the morning hours. Directional exposure, climate and elevation will influence the effect of light, while the microsite ecology, including companion plants, rocks and trees can readily assist plants to withstand greater amounts of sun than is normally considered ideal. To a certain extent, since the plant uses sunlight to manufacture its food, providing as much light as the plant can comfortably bear will speed growth and produce a larger root.

Soils. The best soils for ginseng culture are rich in humus, the wholesome product of decomposing leaves and wood. Humus contributes to the growth substrate for the plant, is the most significant source of needed nutrients and also provides a home for soil fungi that are symbiotic with ginseng (Whitebread, 1996).[1] The close proximity of large limestone features or smaller limestone rock to sweeten the soil is helpful. In the East, mixed hardwood forests predominated by oak, beech and

---

[1] Vesicular-arbuscular mycorrhizae (VAM) are branched, microscopic fungal symbionts that form within the living cells of the ginseng root. The interaction of VAM with the plant root hairs produces a high surface area interface allowing for efficient exchange of nutrients. The plant produces sugars that are utilized by the fungus, while the fungus breaks down nutrients, and by means of its extensive hyphal network enhances their absorption into the plant. Beneficial fungi also produce antibiotics that protect the plant from fungal pathogens, which is of particular advantage for the soft, susceptible roots of ginseng.

especially sugar maple (*Acer saccharum*) are particularly good for ginseng growing, although any mixed hardwood forest has potential, especially if wild ginseng already occurs in the area.

In the West, the best soils are those generated by a mixed maple and alder forest. I find that oak forests and coniferous forests in the West are poor sites for ginseng culture, but other growers have had success working under these trees. A clay or sandy loam with pH of 5.5 to 6.5 is ideal; heavy loam, sandy soils and clay soils can also be serviceable. The soil must be well-drained, either by dint of porosity of structure or because of a steep grade. Ginseng roots will rot in mucky ground.

Water. Ginseng requires at least 20 inches of annual rainfall for normal growth. If local conditions do not provide at least this much water, then supplemental irrigation will be necessary. Overhead sprinklers or misters are preferred to drip or flood irrigation, as they produce a more even distribution of the water and are less likely to cause puddling. In southern Oregon, we have found that misting during the summer effectively cools the plants, preventing summer burnout and improving overall health.

Community. Examples of plants that grow in close proximity to wild ginseng in the eastern states are black cohosh *(Cimicifuga racemosa)*, bloodroot *(Sanguinaria canadensis)*, goldenseal *(Hydrastis canadensis)*, Solomon's seal *(Polygonatum biflorum)*, spice bush *(Lindera benzoin)* and trillium *(Trillium* spp.). If these plants occur in the woods, it is likely that conditions are right for growing ginseng. Examples of plants that indicate good ginseng growing ground in the West are false Solomon's seal *(Smilacina racemosa)*, Oregon grape *(Mahonia nervosa)*, trillium *(Trillium* spp.) and wild ginger *(Asarum canadense)*. In cultivation, it is often preferable to mix the planting or at least alternate beds of ginseng with other shade-dependent herbs in order to approximate the natural forest community of plants. Monocrops deplete the soil, are subject to disease and generally require constant surveillance and chemical input. Mixed crops consisting of a diversity of species become mutually supportive, reducing the need for human intervention and promoting balanced soil ecology while increasing resistance to disease and pests.

Life cycle. In nature, ginseng ripens its berries in the summer months, usually in September or October. Birds or mammals eat the berries, or the fruits fall to the ground when fully ripe. The flesh surrounding the seed prohibits germination, as does the immature embryo in the new seed, which requires many months to mature. Successful dispersal involves removal of the fleshy portion and maintenance of seed moisture while the seed lodges below the natural forest litter, either in or on the mineral soil. The removal of the flesh from the seed is accomplished when the entire seed passes through the digestive tract of a bird or mammal or by rotting after the seed falls from the plant and is subsequently covered by autumn leaffall. The dense seeds tend to work their way down into the soil in cadence with the movements of small mammals, worms and the swelling and shrinking of the forest litter as it freezes and thaws. The seed must remain covered by reasonably moist soil through the following spring, summer and fall while it develops its embryo, after which germination occurs in the second spring, 18 to 20 months from the time it was dropped from the parent plant. In nature, it is common to find small seedlings growing in close association with the seed-bearing parent. Isolated individuals found at a distance from the parent are often the result of dispersal by animals, including purposeful reseeding by humans.

Advantages of woodland cultivation. Cultivation of ginseng in forest soils under the shade of the trees (producing woods-grown ginseng) offers several advantages. The alternative to growing in the woods is to cultivate in the open field, under shade cloth or lath. However, setting up shade structures is very expensive, and there is added labor and expense involved with bringing in the all-important, forest-derived mulch. It is much easier to make use of an intact forest ecology than to try to build a forest soil without trees. Ginseng blight *(Alternaria panax)* is less likely to infect wild or woods-grown ginseng, while it is a major problem in cultivated fields grown under shade cloth. Ginseng blight has led to the widespread use of fungicides in the ginseng industry, lessening the value of the crop due to potential chemical contamination and related health risks. Fungicides are very likely to have a negative impact on vesicular-arbuscular mycorrhizae that form a symbiotic relationship with ginseng. Soil, air and water quality are also degraded by fungicide use, while forest cultivation gives incentive to keep the woodlands intact, with a resulting improvement in the environment. Finally, the ginseng *connoisseur* can readily detect the difference between a cultivated and a woods-grown root, with the latter demanding a significantly higher market price. The differences are not only cosmetic, as wild or woods-grown roots tend to have a higher concentration of active constituents (Thompson, 1987).

Site preparation. To prepare a ginseng bed in the forest, choose an area that already has deep, well-drained soil and is on a slope. Trim the lower branches of trees to increase light and allow for free movement around the bed. Clear away all underbrush to expose the forest floor. Establish a clear trail next to the bed for access. Rake away the leaves, twigs and rotting wood from the surface of the soil, and save this natural mulch to the side, to be returned on top of the seeds or rootlets once the bed is planted. A good size for a ginseng bed is 5 feet wide and as long as you need to make it. You can establish several beds side-by-side with paths in between. Deeply fork the soil, cutting out surface roots with an axe and removing stones. If a large area is desired, then a rototiller can be of assistance. Always cultivate when the soil is relatively dry. This produces a fine, loose structure that is ideal for planting seeds or transplanting rootlets. Cultivating wet soil causes clods.

Seeding and germination. Ginseng seed is sown in the late summer or fall to a depth of about ½ inch (1.27 cm). Prepared beds may be direct-seeded (the seed raked in and tamped), or the seed may be cast onto the surface in the wild woodland and allowed to work its way in by gravity. Sowing in pots offers no advantage and is rarely done. Controlled organic cultivation of ginseng requires a much wider spacing than is normally employed in commercial fields. A finished spacing of 1 foot between the plants allows for sufficient air movement, thereby reducing the potential for fungal infection. A sowing rate of 15 pounds of seed per acre is a good rule of thumb for organic growers.

Ripe seeds may be simply squeezed from the fruit and planted immediately in the soil in prepared seedbeds or in likely spots in the forest. The leaf mulch is scraped back, thereby baring the mineral soil. The seed is planted individually or in rows and covered by soil. Then the mulch is replaced on the planting site. Germination occurs in 18 to 20 months.

Stratified seed is often employed. This seed has been washed free of the germination-inhibiting fruit and buried in damp sand for a full year prior to planting. Stratified seed is sown in the late summer or autumn and germination occurs the following spring. Germination is hypogeal. Ginseng does not express sporadic multicycle germination, but rather may be expected to germinate in coordination. Average planting success for properly harvested and stratified ginseng seed fall-planted in prepared beds ranges from 60% to 80%, but the tender seedlings are prone to physical damage from rodents, slugs and ill-placed footsteps. Substantial attrition is typical during the first 2 years of growth. Ginseng is self-thinning, so if the seedlings are left very close together, the larger and healthier seedlings will dominate, while less healthy seedlings will naturally die off. In nature, this process of self-thinning in dense stands occurs within the first three years of growth.

Mulching. If you choose to grow a crop under shade cloth or lath, then mulch will not be produced on site, so it will have to be brought in on a yearly basis. Application of extra mulch in woods-grown patches is also helpful. Mulch serves to hold moisture, build soil and buffer the plants against stress, especially drought and extreme cold. It is important to use well-rotted mulch composed of leaves of hardwood trees. The leaves are best passed through a chipper before piling, then allowed to break down for at least 6 months before use. This mulch is spread evenly to about 4 inches (10 cm) thick on newly planted beds, or is spread on older plantings after the plants die back in the autumn. Rotted sawdust (green sawdust that has been left to age in a pile for at least a year) may be used instead of leaf mulch, applied in a 2-inch (5 cm) layer. Rotted sawdust mulch often produces monumental plants. I have always recommended using rotted sawdust derived from hardwoods, but growers in the

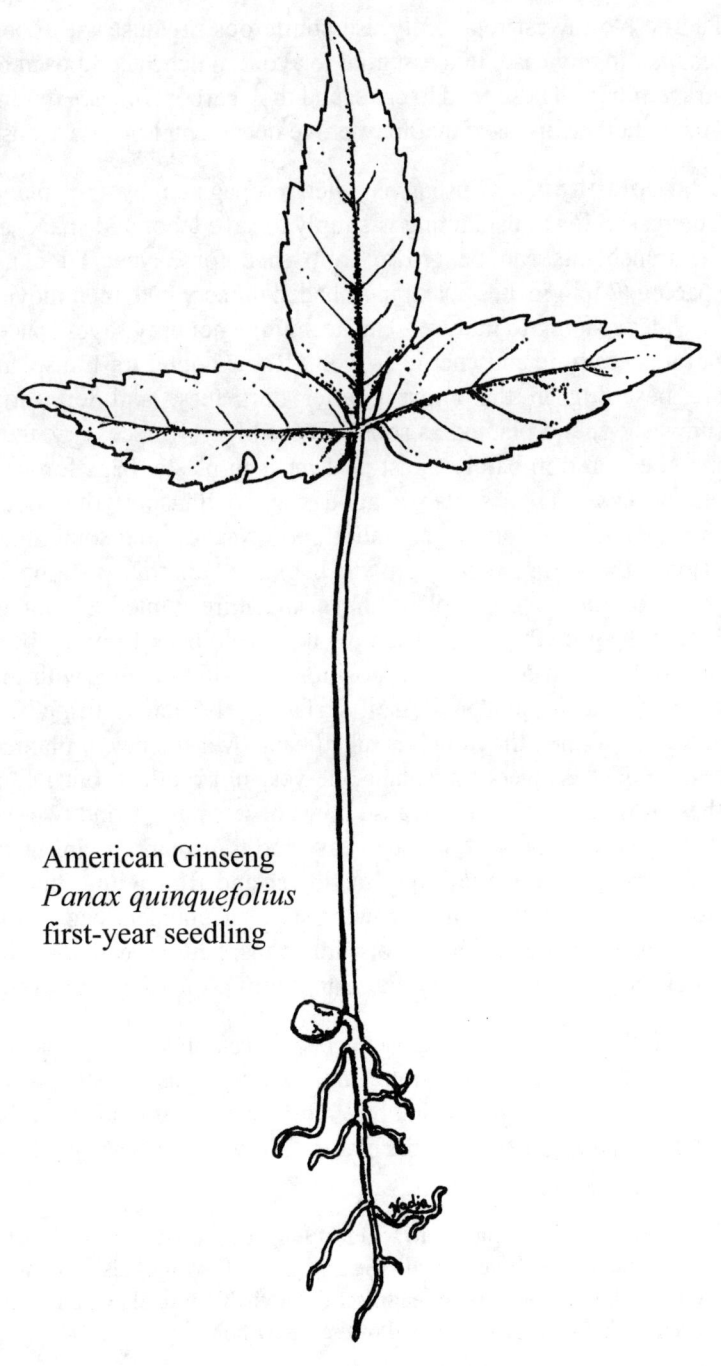

American Ginseng
Panax quinquefolius
first-year seedling

Pacific Northwest reportedly use coniferous sawdust with good results. In any case, it is essential to avoid mulches composed of straw or hay. These tend to cake, and they harbor *Alternaria* fungus and other diseases that may prove detrimental or disastrous.

Transplanting. Ginseng is often propagated by transplant. The reason for transplanting is simply to save labor and space, as the transplants can be grown from seed for 2 years at close spacing (2 to 4 inches apart) in a shaded nursery bed, then moved to wider spacing to mature. This technique not only saves space, but it saves time and energy as well. Roots bound for transplant are best dug in the autumn, after dormancy, and left dirty (unwashed) and planted as soon as possible.[2] If necessary, they may be stored in barely moist peat moss in plastic bags for several weeks. This is also a good way to transport the roots. Transplanting is done in the fall after dormancy, and sometimes also in the spring before growth begins. Fall transplanting is preferred, because the plants have an entire winter to root in before the growth phase. The mulch is raked back from the bed, the root nestled into its final position at a slight angle, with the nascent bud just under the soil surface. The soil is firmed all around, and then the mulch is raked back over the newly planted bed. Some growers transplant one-year-old rootlets, but I find these difficult to handle because they are so small. I find two- or three-year-old roots to be much easier to transplant, giving very satisfactory results and likely to flower and fruit within one or two years after transplant. Growing starts in a nursery bed on the farm is economical, but roots for transplanting can also be purchased by the root or by the pound from professional growers.

Challenges. Once the ginseng bed is established, it must be protected as much as possible from various pests. Mice like to chew off the emergent spring bud. Burrowing mammals love the fluffy soil and may uproot the plants. These animals are likely to

---

[2]Rootlets bound for transplant will last longer if you do not wash off the beneficial fungi that cling to their surface. They will also take to their new home much more readily if the invisible fungal symbiont is present to help inoculate the soil of their new home.

munch the roots, as well. Slugs can be a big problem in ginseng. Diatomaceous earth is a good preventive, but it must be reapplied after each rain. Avoiding use of straw and hay mulch helps limit slug habitat. Ginseng is very sensitive to being stepped on, so good paths are recommended—paths that route traffic around the beds, not through them. Care must be taken not to disturb the soil around the growing plants. Weeds are allowed to grow fairly large, then hand-pulled or flattened with additional mulch, avoiding disturbance to the root zone of the crop plants.

Fertilization. Ginseng is not usually fertilized, but a spare dressing of organic compost or well-aged manure is indicated if the native soils are not sufficiently fertile. This is best applied before planting, or in the spring prior to emergence, so the plants can make use of the nutrients during the growing season. High nitrogen fertilizers or fresh animal manure are definitely contraindicated, as these are not a part of the native soil makeup and will stress the plants. Many growers use ground limestone or wood ashes to sweeten the soil, especially if the pH is very low. Limestone or ashes are applied to the soil before planting, or applied to established beds in the fall after the plants have gone dormant.

Yield. The fresh or dried ginseng root is the part traditionally used. The average weight of a 5-year-old cultivated root is 40 to 60 grams, with 7 to 11 fresh roots per pound. The average water content is 70% to 74%. Dried ginseng roots weighing 1 pound would usually be composed of anywhere from 25 to 43 whole roots. Smaller roots are generally kept separate at harvest, transplanted and allowed to grow to a larger size before use. Larger roots weighing up to 180 grams apiece are not unusual. The largest root on record was planted by Don Hoogesteger of Ridgefield, Washington in 1990 and harvested in 1997. It weighed in at 2.35 pounds (1,067 grams) (Johnson, 2001).

Other plant parts. Although the root is the part of the ginseng plant most commonly employed, the Native Americans used other parts of the plant as well. For instance, the green portions of the plant were used as a poultice, applied to bleeding wounds by the Creek tribe (Taylor, 1940). An infusion of the aerial parts of the plant was taken by women of the Crow tribe to ease childbirth (Goldstein, 1975). On occasion I have eaten the fruit of ginseng, either out of curiosity or because I was keeping a few seeds, plucked on a hike through the woods, in the safest place I could find at the moment (the mouth). They taste much like ginseng root, and leave the typical acrid aftertaste in the back of the throat that is indicative of the saponin content. It may be significant to note that the aerial plant, including leaves, stem and berries do contain active principles, and that these parts can be renewably harvested without killing the plant. More research into the safety of aerial parts and their potential medicinal application is well-warranted.

Harvest and processing. Ginseng is best harvested at the age of five years or older, in the autumn, after the plant has matured its berries. During the growth cycle, the plant fixes primary nutrients (starches) and secondary constituents (saponins and polysaccharides) in the root. These are meant to protect and feed the plant through its dormant cycle. It is important to dig roots as soon as possible in the autumn, since ginsenoside levels decline after mid-September and by November may decrease by as much as 14% (Schooley and Reynolds, 1998). The roots are lifted with a spade or fork. Care must be taken to preserve the branching taproots and root hairs, as these are actually higher in ginsenoside content than the barrel-shaped body of the root, including the core. Ginseng is often appreciated (and priced!) on the basis of appearance, so this is another reason to keep the root whole and undamaged. Wash the roots briefly in clean water to remove any clinging dirt or debris. Extended washing leaches active water-soluble saponins from the root and must be avoided.

Drying. The roots are best dried on cloth or on screens in a dark place with positive airflow. Roots can be slow-dried in a warm room or attic, a process that may take up to six weeks. When using a dehydrator, avoid putting moist, fresh roots directly into the apparatus at the highest temperature. This will lock in moisture and make it very difficult or even impossible to dry the root completely. Instead, adjust the temperature to 75° to 80° F

(24° to 27° C), and, when after several days, the roots become noticeably shrunken and wrinkled, finish dehydrating at 90° to 100° F (32° to 38° C). The roots are best turned daily to encourage even drying, and the entire process can take up to two weeks. During the dehydration process, starches are converted to sugars, thereby improving the taste of the root, while the active constituents are fixed and protected within the root structure.

Storage. Dried ginseng is best stored in the whole form, in a moisture-proof container (plastic bag or glass jar) in a cool room, out of the light. Stored in this manner the roots maintain their potency for years. However, ginseng root powder quickly loses its potency due to oxidation. Therefore, once the roots are ground up, it is advisable to use them or make them into a tincture as soon as possible.

Ginseng seed is semicircular and flattened, colored tan. It reminds me a little bit of a very tiny whole wheat biscuit that did not rise very well, with one side flattened where it contacted another biscuit in the baking. There are approximately 12 to 15 seeds per gram, depending on seed size and moisture content. This results in a seed count per pound of approximately 5,400 to 6,800 seeds. The seeds measure anywhere from 6 to 9 mm in diameter and from 2 to 3 mm in thickness. The seed coat is leathery, splitting horizontally into equal halves, revealing a white endosperm. The seed does not withstand dry storage, but must be kept moist throughout processing, stratification and storage. Excess moisture, closed storage and warm temperatures increase the incidence of seed-borne diseases that may include bacterial decay or fungal organisms such as *Cylindrocarpon, Fusarium* and *Rhizoctonia* (Schooley, 2000).

Seed collecting and processing. The clusters of fresh berries are plucked from the ginseng plant when they are plump, scarlet and therefore fully developed. The berries are put in a bucket and mashed by kneading with the hands. Large quantities of berries may be more efficiently mashed on a table screen. After the berries are completely reduced, the mass is mixed with a little water and set aside at room temperature to ferment in a bucket for several days. The fermentation process helps break down the fruit surrounding the seed, a plausible substitute for the kind of "cleaning" a seed gets when it passes through the digestive tract of an animal. After fermentation, copious quantities of water are added to the bucket and the contents are swirled by hand. Infertile seed, diseased seed, pieces of stem and fruit debris float on the surface of the water or are suspended within the water, while the mature and viable seed sinks rapidly to the bottom of the bucket. The liquid is then decanted, pouring off all nonseed debris and leaving the good seed in the bottom of the bucket. This process is repeated several times until the wash water clarifies. Then the good seed is poured out on a screen and hand-sorted to remove any remaining foreign material. This entire process is known as "floating."

Seed stratification. The clean seed may be sown immediately or it may be artificially stratified. To stratify, the seed is first mixed with an equal volume of damp, coarse sand. The sand is best screened first in order to exclude larger pebbles. Small quantities of seed are usually stratified in a mesh bag, while larger quantities are better stratified in a wooden box with a screened-in bottom and top, made sufficiently tight to exclude rodents. The bag or the box is then buried in a moist, shady and cool location, often the eventual site for the ginseng planting. Once buried, the top of the bag or the lid of the box is left 2 inches (4.8 cm) below the soil surface. The site is then mulched and the location must be carefully marked, because it will not be necessary to disturb the seed again for a full 12 months.

Late the following summer, the seed is dug up, and the contents of the boxes are dumped out on a screen. Using a pressure hose, the sand is washed away, leaving the plump, stratified seeds on the screen. At this point it is a good practice to float them again, thereby selecting the finest, heaviest seed and pouring off any lighter seed that might be of low viability, rotted or diseased. The stratified seed, some of which may already be swelling and cracking open, is then drained and planted immediately, or it may be stored in a plastic bag in the refrigerator at 40° F (4.4° C) for several weeks. Storage at colder temperatures is best avoided, as it may drive the seed into extended dormancy.

Seed stored in this manner must be almost dry on the surface before bagging. Every few days the bag is removed from the refrigerator and the seed is stirred to aerate it. The seed may rot if it is too moist, indicated by heavy condensation on the inside of the bag. If this happens, dump the seed out and let it dry a bit before putting back in the refrigerator. If the seed becomes too dry, indicated by a total lack of condensation on the inside of the bag, then rehydrate it by squeezing out a wet paper towel in your fist and burying this within the stored seed. After long storage, obvious signs of deterioration will probably occur in the form of white or reddish mold cultures occurring on the seed coat of some of the seed. Infected seeds can be removed by hand sorting. The temperature, aeration and moisture tolerances for storage are narrow and critical, and the likelihood that disease will crop up increases with time in storage. The best advice is to get the stratified seed planted as soon as possible.

Conservation status. American ginseng is listed in CITES, and global trade in wild-harvested root is regulated. Under the direction of the United States Fish and Wildlife Service, individual states where wild ginseng is still found have developed programs to regulate harvest, and harvest is illegal in national parks and many other protected areas. The plant is designated by the Committee on the Status of Endangered Wildlife in Canada (COSEWIC)[3] as "threatened" in Canada, and no exportation of wild-harvested roots is allowed from Canada. However, government rules can only do so much to protect slow-growing and sensitive wild plants. Because there is an ongoing demand for wild or woods-grown roots, they are bound to disappear from areas where harvest is legal, while poaching increases from protected areas (Gagnon, 1999). In the face of this deterioration, it becomes increasingly important to protect and nurture remaining wild populations of ginseng. In replanting the wilds, it is important to use wild-derived and

---

[3]COSEWIC is a committee of representatives from federal, provincial, territorial and private agencies as well as independent experts that assigns national status to species at risk in Canada.

85

bioregionally cultivated seed from local land races in order to preserve any regional variations in the general gene pool. The genetic diversity of distinct wild populations will prove very useful in the future when we seek to breed vigor back into cultivated ginseng. In order to fulfill world demand, it is of paramount importance that we continue to cultivate ginseng, and we can rejoice that in the case of organic and woods-grown ginseng, we improve the local environment while contributing to the protection of an endangered plant. Ginseng is truly the most potent example of the value of conservation through cultivation, because without the concerted efforts of growers worldwide, the plant would be extinct.

Current Range of Dwarf American Ginseng in the U.S.

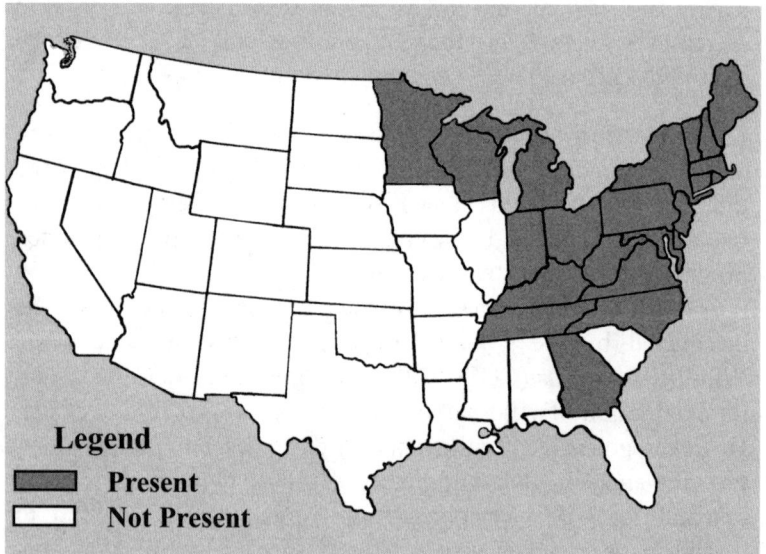

Other species. Dwarf ginseng *(Panax trifolius* L.) is the only other North American *Panax* species, native to a limited range in the eastern and northern United States. The plant is a perennial woodland ephemeral, emerging in the early spring then flowering, fruiting and senescing within the space of 2 months. Dwarf ginseng only grows from 2 to 8 inches tall, arising from a tiny, bulbous root (Foster and Duke, 1990). It is quite reclusive and little known. The Native Americans did use it medicinally, with applications ranging from indigestion to nervous debility

(Moerman, 1986), and some of these original uses are consistent with the way American ginseng *(Panax quinquefolius)* was used by Native Americans. More study and experimentation into the potential applicability of this plant in modern health care is certainly warranted, but given its diminutive size and ephemeral growth habits, it will probably prove to be a difficult plant to cultivate on a large scale.

References

Court, W., L. Reynolds and J. Hendel. 1996. *Influence of Root Age on the Concentration of Ginsenosides of American Ginseng (Panax quinquefolius).* Canadian Journal of Plant Science, 76, pp. 853-855.

Felter, H. and J. Lloyd. 1898 (Reprinted 1985). *King's American Dispensatory.* Portland (OR): Eclectic Medical Publishing, Vol. 1 & 2, 743 pp.

Foster S. and J. Duke. 1990. *A Field Guide to Medicinal Plants: Eastern and North America.* Boston (MA): Houghton Mifflin, 341 pp.

Gagnon, Daniel. 1999. *An Analysis of the Sustainability of American Ginseng Harvesting from the Wild: The Problem and Possible Solutions.* Final report to the Office of Scientific Authority of the US Fish and Wildlife Service.

Goldstein, Beth. 1975. *Ginseng: Its History, Dispersion and Folk Tradition.* American Journal of Chinese Medicine, 3(3), pp. 223-234.

Johnson, B. 2001. *Largest Ginseng Root Listed in Guinness World Record.* HerbalGram, No. 52, p. 15.

Moerman, D. 1986. *Medicinal Plants of Native America.* Ann Arbor (MI): University of Michigan Dept. of Anthropology, Vol. 1, 534 pp.

Persons, W. 1988. *American Ginseng: Green Gold,* revised ed., Asheville, NC: Bright Mountain Books, 203 pp.

Schooley, J. 2000. *Ginseng Seed Diseases.* Ontario Ministry of Agriculture, Food and Rural Affairs.

Schooley, J. and L. Reynolds. 1998. *Effects of Production Practices on the Quality of Ginseng Roots.* Ontario Ministry of Agriculture, Food and Rural Affairs

Soldati, F. and O. Tanaka. 1984. *Panax ginseng: Relation Between Age of Plant and Content of Ginsenosides.* Journal of Medicinal Plant Resources, Vol. 50 (4), pp. 351-352.

Taylor, L. 1940. *Plants Used as Curatives by Certain Southeastern Tribes.* Cambridge: Botanical Museum of Harvard University, p. 399.

Thompson, G. 1987. *Botanical Characteristics of Ginseng,* in L. Craker and J. Simon (eds.), *Herbs, Spices and Medicinal Plants: Recent Advances in Botany, Horticulture and Pharmacology.* Phoenix (AZ): Oryx Press,Vol. 2, pp. 111-136.

Whitbread F., T. McGonigle and R. Peterson. 1996. *Vesicular-Arbuscular Mycorrhizal Associations of American Ginseng (Panax quinquefolius L.) in Commercial Production.* Canadian Journal of Botany, 74, pp. 1104-1112.

Goldenseal
Hydrastis canadensis
roots and rhizome
plant with ripe berry
flower and seeds enlarged

Goldenseal

Hydrastis canadensis L.

Family: *Ranunculaceae*

Goldenseal is a long-lived herbaceous perennial of the deep woods. The horizontal rhizome creeps beneath the rich forest detritus, resembling a small, crooked finger. In very robust individuals, this rhizome becomes clump-like, with a dense crown and multiple buds. Fibrous rootlets extend out from the rhizome, sparse on the upper surface and more frequent toward the base. These fibers serve a dual function, absorbing water and nutrients from the surrounding soil, also occasionally giving rise at their extremity to small, knot-like buds that eventually develop into new plants. Both rhizome and roots (the root) are golden-yellow when fresh, and this color is intensified internally. In fact, this vivid color clearly identifies goldenseal, differentiating it from all look-alikes. Mature individuals produce at least two buds, slightly flattened, shaped like hands clasped in prayer. In the spring, each bud rapidly gives rise to an erect, rounded, slightly pubescent stem, the outer scales of the bud remaining to clasp the stem base. The stem is forked like a slingshot, each branch terminating in a characteristic, five- to nine-lobed, palmate leaf. The leaf is shaped similarly to that of the maple tree. One leaf is large, measuring up to eight inches in width. The other is noticeably smaller, occurring in direct association with the flower. Older individuals may actually produce a third leaf, above and parallel to the smaller leaf, partially clasping the flower. Occurring on a short stem at the base of the leaf, the ephemeral flower is concave, greenish-white and frilly, giving way to the bright red berry. Resembling a raspberry, this fruit is a composite of multiple two-seeded drupes, each crowned by a persistent style. The fruit is edible, if a bit bland, but is relished by wild turkeys. Given an abundance of rain, the leaves will persist until first frost, at which time they rapidly decompose back into the forest soil. However, the stem does not disappear without leaving its mark, a crater-like depression on the upper surface of the rhizome, resembling a waxen seal on an old-time letter—a golden seal.

Current Range of Goldenseal in the U.S.

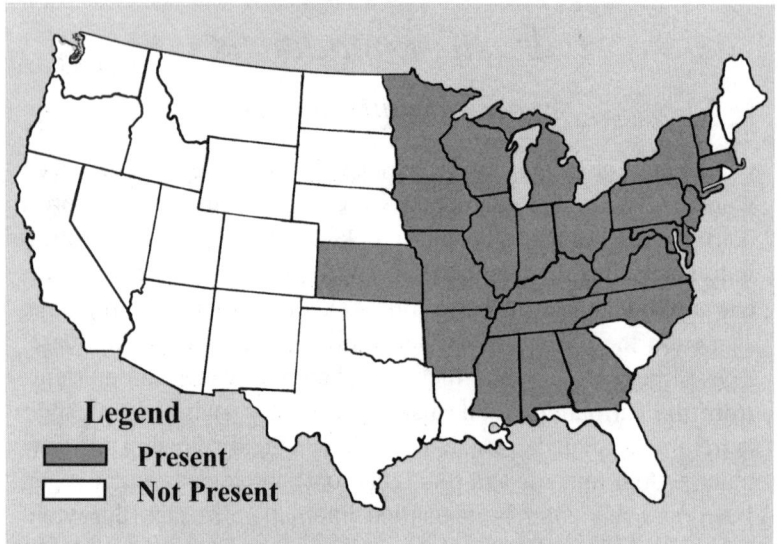

Legend
- ▓ Present
- ☐ Not Present

Range, hardiness and adaptability. Wild goldenseal has a wide distribution in the United States and southern Canada, stretching from the Appalachian mountain range through the forests of the eastern and central states, not extending far beyond the Missouri River valley. The original centers of distribution are the Ohio River valley and the Ozark plateau, and these two areas are still home to the most abundant wild stands.

The plant demonstrates a strong winter dormancy, and indeed a period of at least 3 months of cold soil temperatures (less than 40° F = 4.4° C), preferably freezing, is required for normal development. Cold temperatures are also a necessary part of the germination cycle of the seed, and are a significant deterrent to fungal disease. This cold dependency is partially responsible for limiting the distribution of the plant. The gulf coast is too hot. The great plains of New Mexico, Colorado and Wyoming are also uninviting to the spread of a demure, forest-dependent plant, and the Rockies have proven unsurmountable.

Nonetheless, given a cold winter, rich soil and protection from the sun, goldenseal can be successfully cultivated outside its native range. In fact, the coastal rain forests of the western states of Oregon and Washington have proven particularly well-adapted to goldenseal culture. For instance, in the early 1900s the Skagit Valley Goldenseal Farm in Mount Vernon, Washington produced substantial quantities of goldenseal for market (Gillis and Langenhan, 1931), and the herb is currently cultivated under shade cloth and under natural forest canopy in several locations ranging from southern Oregon to British Columbia. Goldenseal has even crossed the Atlantic, making an appearance, albeit somewhat rarely, in European shade gardens.

Ecology. In nature, goldenseal grows in communal patches, usually on gently sloping land, often on a northern or northeastern exposure, under the shade of the mixed hardwood forest. Climax deciduous forests are the preferred habitat, since they provide a high canopy that shields these delicate understory plants from the sun. The shade of mature trees also reduces competitive brushy growth, and their deeply excavating roots leave the surface soils unencumbered. The plant is generally considered to require about 70% shade, best received in the form of dappled sunlight. Full morning sun may be tolerated, but the plants definitely need protection from perpendicular sun. So long as the leaves do not burn out from excessive exposure, the more sun they receive, the more the plants are nourished through photosynthesis.

The soil most preferred by goldenseal is a rich, forest-derived humus with a slightly acid pH (5.5 to 6.5). The presence of copious quantities of leaf mold and a thick mulch of decomposing hardwood leaves is essential. A balanced supply of nutrients is required for vigorous growth, and in nature this is supplied by the breakdown of carbonaceous leaves and other forest debris. Leaffall from nitrogen fixing trees such as locust or alder is an ideal source of assimilable nutrients.

Although the plant is water-loving, good drainage is a prerequisite to healthy growth. Goldenseal does not occur in marshy ground. Regular summer rainfall is required and high humidity is relished. The plants will suffer and droop during dry periods, but as long as the tissues do not desiccate completely, a timely summer rain is likely to cause an almost miraculous revitalization. Nonetheless, extreme summer drought will send the plants into an early dormancy. As long as they have time to set buds for the next year's growth, such setbacks are not normally fatal.

93

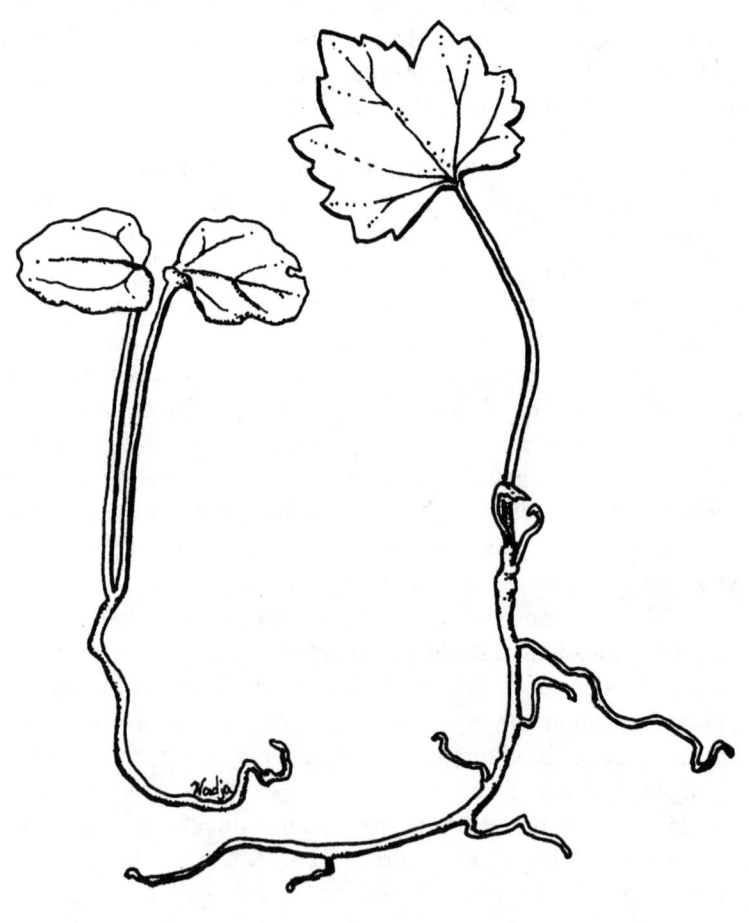

Goldenseal
Hydrastis canadensis
newly germinated seedling
two-year-old seedling with first true leaf

In the native environment, goldenseal grows in patches under the shade of mixed hardwoods such as beech, hickory, locust, maple, white oak and tulip poplar. Herbaceous plants associated with goldenseal include the entire grouping of forest-dependent, at-risk plants including American ginseng *(Panax quinquefolius)*, black cohosh *(Cimicifuga racemosa)*, blue cohosh *(Caulophyllum thalictroides)*, bloodroot *(Sanguinaria canadensis)*, trillium *(Trillium* spp.) and wild yam (mainly *Dioscorea quaternata)*. Twin leaf *(Jeffersonia diphylla)*, a forest plant that grows in communal patches and resembles goldenseal in size and root form, also occupies the same microniche. I consider this to be a pointer plant for goldenseal. This similarity has not gone unnoticed, giving rise to a long history of purposeful adulteration of goldenseal root with twin leaf root (Felter and Lloyd, 1898).

In the West, ideal soils for woodland cultivation of goldenseal are found under mixed alder *(Alnus oregona)* and big leaf maple *(Acer macrophyllum)* forests. Understory plants that are indicators of good ground for goldenseal cultivation in the West include sword fern *(Polystichum munitum)*, Oregon grape *(Mahonia nervosa)* and trillium *(Trillium* spp.). In cultivation, it is preferable to alternate beds of goldenseal with other shade-dependent herbs in order to approximate the natural forest community of plants. Alternation of crops promotes balanced soil ecology, where the plants sequester certain fungal symbionts in order to assist in nutrient assimilation and to protect against pathogenic organisms. This interrelationship becomes evident when alternate beds of several exotic species (e.g. goldenseal and ginseng) outperform the same plants grown as a monocrop.

Life cycle. The goldenseal berry matures in the early summer, ripening from an emerald green to a deep red color. As the berry softens, it is likely to detach from the plant and fall to the forest floor, where it eventually rots, leaving behind its load of up to 30 shiny black seeds. Alternatively, the fruit may be eaten by birds or mammals and the berry passed through the digestive tract, the seeds subsequently deposited (in association with a little nitrogenous fertilizer) at a distance from the parent plant. In either case, if the seed remains reasonably moist throughout the process, it will retain viability and with luck will lodge in the soil.

After overwintering, the seed will germinate in the spring, or may rest for another full year and germinate in the second spring following dissemination.[1] Multicycle germination of this sort is of survival advantage to a delicate plant that may be challenged by adverse environmental conditions or human activity. However, I have noticed that in the wild, seeding in is not the primary means of reproduction. Rather, seed dissemination is significant in establishing individuals at a distance from the concentrated population, while the patch itself is increased largely by means of root runners.

Germination is epigeal, producing a long, delicate, yellow taproot, a tiny bud and two spoon-like cotyledons (see illustration next page). The first year after germination is a particularly vulnerable period for a goldenseal seedling, and rates of attrition are quite high. The infant seedling is vulnerable to dehydration and footstep, may be irretrievably covered by autumn leaves, and indeed is likely to perish if the soil is even minimally disturbed by burrowing animals or excessive frost activity.

---

[1] Recent observations in the forest propagation beds at Horizon Herbs Seed Farm have elucidated further complexities in the germination habits of goldenseal seed (Cech, 2001). By recording the planting locations and dates, then carefully observing the status of germinating seeds (both in the ground and above ground) we have shown that goldenseal under some circumstances, may demonstrate two-phase germination. This means that a certain number of the seeds that germinate in the first spring after planting may not develop aerial parts until a year later. During the first growing season, a root and bud are formed, nourished solely by the energy reserves of the seed and by directly absorbing soil nutrients, perfectly healthy without the benefit of photosynthesis. In the following spring, fully 20 months after the seed first came into contact with the soil, the seedling emerges energetically. Germination is hypogeal, without photosynthesizing cotyledons. There is rapid emergence of aerial portions from an already-established root system in the very early spring when the woodland floor is sunny, and before other plants begin to compete for resources. Similar adaptive strategies have been reported for blue cohosh and trillium (Deno, 1996).

In the summer of the first year or in the second year, the seedling produces a single true leaf, a branching root system and a more pronounced nascent bud. From this stage on, the plant is much better equipped to survive in the wild, and by the third year is able to effectively compete with surrounding forbs. In nature, the plant takes from five to seven years from seed to reproductive maturity.

Germination and development of goldenseal.

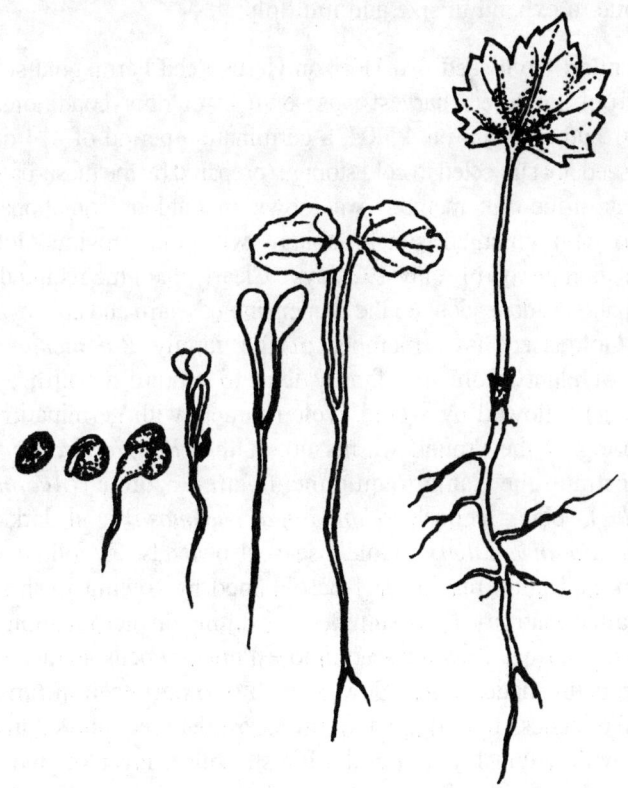

The goldenseal patch evolves over time. At first, a few scattered individuals will send out fibrous roots just under the soil surface, producing nodules that develop into buds, eventually forming new plants at a distance of up to 36 inches (86 cm) from the parent. The new plants are clones of the parent, but they do individuate, forming a distinct rhizome-root structure and fruiting, usually within 3 years. These plants in turn begin sending out fibrous roots to a distance, and in this manner a dense patch is formed. As long as environmental conditions are conducive, a climax patch will occupy the same location for decades. However, as the patch ages, the overall rate of growth of plants within the patch will begin to decrease. Their root weight will lessen, the incidence of flowering individuals will decrease and fungal deterioration may begin to affect the larger rhizomes. Still, given the right conditions, the plants on the periphery will continue to expand in size and multiply.

Cultivation from seed. At Horizon Herbs Seed Farm, cold-stored seed from the recent harvest was sown in outdoor conditions on 2/15/01 and emerged on 4/5/02, a germination period of 414 days. Fresh seed not subjected to cold storage (prepared by the mesh-bag-at-the-back-of-the-sink method) was sown in outdoor conditions on 9/25/01 and emerged synchronously with the previous lot, a germination period of only 192 days. Clearly, the time required for germination is dependent on the sequencing of warm and cold cycles.

Goldenseal is a member of the family *Ranunculaceae.* Seeds of plants from this family tend to require a warm cycle (summer) followed by a cold cycle (winter) with germination in the spring as the ground warms up. Other *Ranunculaceae* that demonstrate the same requirements are: aconite *(Aconitum napellus)*, black cohosh *(Cimicifuga racemosa)* and larkspur *(Consolida orientalis).* Goldenseal also tends to follow this pattern, and good results may be obtained by sowing fresh seed soon after maturity (late summer), resulting in germination the following spring. Sow the seed in forest nursery beds, in the shade garden or in shaded flats. Sow ¼ inch (0.6 cm) deep in furrows spaced 6 inches (14 cm) apart, or broadcast the seed, press it in and cover with a thin layer of soil. Finish with a layer of fine leaf mulch, which will help keep the soil from drying out through the autumn and winter. A germination rate of 75% is typical.

Emerging seedlings are very delicate and must be kept carefully watered, weeded and protected from slugs. Grow the seedlings at close spacing until they form a definite root-rhizome structure. This usually requires 2 years' time. Transplant to a finished spacing of between 6 inches (14 cm) and 1 foot (28 cm) apart. Transplanting is best done in the fall or in the very early spring before the plants break dormancy.

Cultivation from rhizome cuttings. The mature goldenseal rhizome has the potential to be divided into several viable transplants. Even unbudded pieces of the rhizome are covered with tiny, dormant eyes (adventive buds) that will produce new buds when planted under the right conditions. The rhizome is typically broken or cut apart into sections of approximately ½ inch (1.2 cm) length, complete with any attached rootlets. The section containing the dormant bud produces the most vigorous plants, and may even give rise to flowers and fruits in the first season.

The transplants are best spaced between 6 inches (14 cm) and 1 foot (28 cm) apart, planted just below the soil surface, with the buds pointing up. The fibrous rootlets that hang down from the transplant may be spread out and dug in as deeply as possible in the underlying soil. Alternatively, long rootlets can be trimmed back to 2 inches (5 cm), thereby stimulating root growth and simplifying planting. Firm the soil around the transplant, and cover with mulch. Mark the area well and keep wild animals, people and pets from walking on it. The plants will reemerge in the spring, and given the right conditions will become rapidly established. Goldenseal grown from cuttings usually attains harvestable size in three years' time.

Cultivation from root runners. As long ago as the early 1900s, goldenseal investigators discovered that wild plants produce reproductive buds on the fibrous rootlet at a distance from the parent, and that these roots with attached bud could be replanted to produce mature plants (Harding, 1972). It was further observed that naked root fibers form nodules (and eventually reproductive buds) even when removed from the parent plant, as long as they are planted in mellow soil, weeded and kept moist. The fibrous roots leftover from "trimming" rhizome cuttings can be spread out like a sparse helping of spaghetti on a few inches of soil in a flat or in a nursery bed, covered with an inch of rich soil or compost, and new plants will eventually emerge. If the fibers are layered in this manner in the autumn, then new plants will emerge in the first spring. If they are layered in the spring, new plants will emerge on an ongoing basis within a month or two. Warm temperatures definitely stimulate this kind of reproduction, and thus a shaded greenhouse is the preferred environment. Also, I have found that watering the flats with willow tea^2 substantially speeds the process, producing a profusion of new, vigorous plants. Plants propagated in this manner usually attain harvestable size and reproductive maturity within four years.

Goldenseal in the greenhouse. The most consistent commonality among all good goldenseal growing habitats is high summer humidity. Coupled with the requisite amount of shade, the well-watered solar greenhouse that is allowed to go cold in the winter is therefore a very effective place to grow this plant. I find that the area underneath the slatted wooden benches in my simple plastic tubehouse is sufficiently shady for goldenseal, and the plant benefits from the nutrient-rich water that drips down when the flats above are watered. I made raised beds in this area one autumn and planted root cuttings. They flowered in the first year, and after three years of growth one representative plant was dug. The rhizome measured 4 by 6 inches (10 by 14 cm), weighed 513 g (more than a pound) fresh weight and bristled with 49 nascent buds! This kind of productivity is exactly what is needed to justify the increased use of world resources involved in manufacturing a habitat (i.e. the greenhouse) as opposed to using the natural habitat (i.e. the tree-shaded garden or woodland).

General care. Because goldenseal grows in patches, it makes sense to prepare a wide bed (minimum 4 feet = 120 cm), pulling all competitive species and removing surface tree roots, making room for the transplants to take over the entire bed area. If soil humic content is low, the bed should be amended with organic compost and decomposed leaves prior to planting. The level of fertilization is best adjusted according to existing conditions. If the plants are

---

^{2} Willow *(Salix* spp.), is the classic weeping (or not weeping) tree that graces yards in the city and in suburbia, and is a dominant species along many waterways throughout the United States. The tea is made by soaking the growing tips of the branches (about as long as your forearm) in a bucket of warm water for a period of several days. The "tea" thus formed is imbued with tannic acid and loaded with growth hormones—a natural and harmless organic replacement for powdered "rooting hormones."

set in loamy soil in a deep forest situation where drought may occur, then fertilization is contraindicated and may cause more harm than good. If the plants are set in regular garden soil in an artificially shaded environment and are regularly watered, then the addition of compost is very appropriate and will substantially increase yields. In keeping with the natural pattern of leaf mulching in the fall, compost and mulch is best applied prior to planting in the fall, or to existing plants in the fall after dormancy. Only natural fertilizers (e.g. stove ashes, limestone, organic compost, rotted manure, decomposed forest debris, rotted bark mulch and/or rotted sawdust) should be used. Uncomposted straw and hay mulches are contraindicated because they harbor fungal diseases.

Goldenseal is a shy forest dweller, and it likes to be left alone. So the job of caring for the plants is largely one of maintaining a conducive environment and allowing the plants to develop undisturbed. Weeds are best hand-pulled or smothered under mulch or organic compost. Weeds are usually a problem when growing in garden soils under shade cloth, and they are rarely a problem in growing under the natural forest canopy.

Although the plant requires only moderate drainage, very poor drainage sets up conditions for slugs, which can be quite bothersome as they chew their way across the patch like the glutenous gluttons they are. Poor drainage also supports various pathogens and diseases including root knot nematodes, *Alternaria, Rhizoctonia* and *Fusarium* wilt (Davis, 1999). I have also observed spider mite infection in cultivated goldenseal in the western states. Diseases do not much affect forest plantings, where balance is maintained by the trees themselves, but plants grown in amended soils under shade cloth are more susceptible. Still, the plant is not disease-prone and is generally vigorous.

Goldenseal really needs regular watering to thrive. If rains are not forthcoming, a weekly irrigation is indicated. Sufficient water in the late summer is particularly important, since lack of water at this time will cause premature dormancy and reduced yields.

Yield. The fresh or dried goldenseal root and rhizome (the root) contains the highest levels of active alkaloids in comparison to other plant parts, and the root is the part traditionally used.

Further, the rhizome itself contains significantly higher quantities of active alkaloids than do the fibrous rootlets (Gillis and Langenhann, 1931). The aerial parts (consisting of leaf and stem) also contain significant quantities of isoquinoline alkaloids (Cunningham et al 2002).[3] Goldenseal leaf may be renewably harvested in the autumn after the plant has matured its berries, but harvesting the goldenseal root kills the plant. Goldenseal leaf is used in herbal tea and as an ingredient in salve. It has a marked antimicrobial effect, and may also be expected to tonify the mucous membranes, although it is not as bitter as the root.

The weight of goldenseal leaf and stem is fairly consistent on a per-plant basis, regardless of whether the plants are from wild or cultivated sources. Weights range between 2 and 5 grams or more fresh weight per plant, depending on the age, the vitality of the plant and the number of leaves.

There is a large degree of variation in fresh (undried) root weights of individual mature goldenseal plants (between 2 g and 500 g or more) depending on the availability of shade, water and nutrients. Wild-harvested goldenseal roots are generally very small (between 2 g and 7 g or more), mainly due to competition from other plants, but probably also due to harvest pressure, where larger individuals are first removed, leaving smaller roots to be harvested as the plant becomes increasingly rare in the natural habitat. Woods-grown roots, cultivated under the forest canopy but without use of fertilizer and without irrigation, are larger (between 5 g and 10 g or more), mainly due to the increased space afforded by clearing the space for the patch and by pulling competitive weeds. Plants grown under shade cloth with fertilization and irrigation attain much larger size (between 25 g and 300 g or more), since all contributing factors are optimized.

The average water content of fresh goldenseal root is 68%

---

[3] "Quantitation based on chromatographic peak area indicated the same alkaloids can be found in the aerial portions of goldenseal as in the roots. Although the roots are higher in alkaloid content than the aerial portions (approximately 5% vs. 1%, W:W), it appears that aerial portions do represent a valuable source of alkaloids."

to 73%. This means that 10 pounds of fresh roots will dry down to about 3 pounds of dried root. The average water content of goldenseal leaf and stem ranges between 71% and 76%. This means that 10 pounds of fresh leaf and stem will dry down to about 2.3 pounds of dried herb.

There is an ongoing concern that although root *yield* is substantially increased through cultivation, that which is gained is offset by a deterioration of *concentration, quality or effect*. However, I have examined this issue for years, especially in relationship to goldenseal (due to the conservation relevancy) and have determined that any concerns about the utility of organically cultivated root are unfounded. Large cultivated plants are generally vigorous and healthy, a good choice for parental stock in production of root cuttings and seed. The root and rhizome are intensely golden in color, indicating a high concentration of berberine; and they are bitter! Furthermore, my chromatographic comparisons of goldenseal root, although they showed a marked degree of variation between cultivated roots from various farms, gave no indication of a comparative diminution of active constituents as a result of cultivation (Amarquaye and Cech, 1996). Further experimentation undertaken by Nadja Cech and her research team at the University of North Carolina in Greensboro yielded similar results, using the technique known as electrospray mass spectrometry (ESI-MS) (Cunningham et al 2002).[4] These findings are also supported by an early and comprehensive study that was published in the Journal of the American Pharmaceutical Association (Gillis and Langenhann, 1931) of the total alkaloid content of rhizomes cultivated at the Skagit Valley Farm. The results showed an average alkaloid content of 2.82% in roots and rhizomes of cultivated plants that averaged 6 years of age. This

---

[4] "Both the quantity and identity of alkaloids present in goldenseal plants varies from individual to individual. However, the levels of active constituents do not seem to be consistently higher in wild-harvested goldenseal than they are in cultivated plants . . . On the basis of these data, concerns that the larger roots yielded by cultivated plants may be lower in active constituents seems unfounded."

falls well within the generally accepted range of 2.5% to 6.5% total alkaloid content in wild plants, as expressed by various investigators (Wagner et al, 1984; Galle et al, 1994; Gocan et al, 1996).

Harvest, processing and storage. Goldenseal root is best dug during plant dormancy in the autumn, winter or early spring. During the months of September through May, the concentration of total alkaloids is at its highest (Gillis and Langenhann, 1931). It makes sense to harvest the plant after midsummer (after the maturation of the fruit and seed) in order to encourage proliferation. The root has a higher water content in the spring, and a lower water content in the autumn. Therefore, in order to optimize medicinality, conservation and ease of dehydration, it makes sense to plan on harvesting the roots in their autumn dormancy.

The roots are best dug with a fork, in order to preserve the long fibers. Shake the roots free of dirt, and keep them together in a clean sack or a bucket. It is best to harvest when the soil is fairly dry, in order to reduce the amount of dirt that clings to the rhizome and roots. Keep them covered from the sun so they don't dry out. If the roots are to be stored in the fresh state for any period of time, do not wash them. The covering of dirt will help keep them from getting moldy in storage or in shipping. Just prior to tincturing or dehydration, thoroughly wash the roots with a pressure hose. Do not rinse them repeatedly, as one of the main alkaloids (berberine) is water soluble. Alternatively, you can wash the roots in a clean stream or by agitating them in a bucket of water. Commercial goldenseal root is infamous for containing a lot of dirt and sand. Cleaning is labor intensive, and dirt and sand are valuable commodities when sold at goldenseal prices. Also, roots that look passably clean in the fresh state may look unacceptably dirty once they dry. This is because the root shrinks in dehydration, and the dirt therefore gains predominance, crusting on the shrunken surface of the rhizome and catching in the tangle of brittle root fibers. Considering the standard use of dried goldenseal as an antimicrobial (used internally, externally, and as an ocular wash), the presence of large quantities of dirt are clearly contraindicated. Therefore, those who pay attention to thorough cleaning of cultivated roots will be justified in asking premium prices. Once all the root pieces are clean, they are best processed immediately in the fresh state or promptly dehydrated.

Very large plants may have to be split apart with a knife, snips or machete in order to facilitate washing and subsequent dehydration, but generally goldenseal is dried in the whole form. This helps prevent undue oxidation and loss of medicinal activity.[5] Dry the roots in a warm place with positive airflow, turning often. The roots are hygroscopic, and if drying in an open area or under a shed roof they must be protected from dew. An herb dehydrator is very helpful in drying goldenseal. Dry for 1 day with low temperature ($70°$ F = $21°$ C) and high air flow, then turn up the temperature to medium ($95°$ F = $35°$ C) and dry them until they snap with a clean break, making certain that the larger pieces are dehydrated all the way through. Once they are thoroughly dry, the roots are best stored in plastic bags in light-proof sacks or drums, in a cool, dark and dry location. Stored in this manner, they retain useful potency for about three years. The appearance of a green core in goldenseal roots is caused by long storage or dehydration at very high temperatures and indicates a deterioration of quality.

Goldenseal leaf and stem is best harvested in the late summer, after the plant matures its fruit. Early harvest is ill-advised since the leaf continues to photosynthesize and nourish the plant throughout the summer. I once did a comparative analysis of cultivated goldenseal leaves, and discovered that the alkaloid content deteriorated markedly after the first frost (Amarquaye and Cech, 1996). So the leaves are best picked while they are still green and turgid, before the first frost and before they begin to turn yellow. Dehydration of goldenseal leaf is very easy. It dries within 24 hours in an herb dehydrator at moderate temperature ($95°$ F = $35°$ C). Alternatively, the leaves may be laid out on screens in any dark, dry, warm and airy location and will dry in a few days' time. They may be stored in a cool place, in plastic or glass, and should be protected from the light. Stored in this manner, the herb will retain useful potency for up to two years.

---

5 Although berberine is stable under a wide variety of conditions, hydrastine (an active alkaloid particular to goldenseal alone) is susceptible to oxidative degradation (Upton ed., 2001).

Goldenseal seed is smooth, black, shiny, globular (tear-shaped) and barely ridged at the hilum. The seed measures approximately 3 mm in diameter. In 1 gram of moist seed there are about 50 seeds. The endosperm is bright golden-green with a tiny embryo at the base. The seed does not withstand dry storage, and suffers noticeably if allowed to dry out for a few days' time. This can be determined by examining the endosperm, which turns a translucent gray in color. However, as long as this dehydration does not continue for very long, the seed can be brought back to life by rehydration, after which the endosperm will return to a healthy golden-green color. Nonviable seed in cold storage will mold, and if stored in the presence of much water or planted in a place with poor drainage, the seed will rot, maintaining for a while the black testa, but filled with putrescent goo.

Seed collecting, cleaning, storage and longevity. The ripe goldenseal berry contains on the average 26 seeds. Interestingly, the seeds mature at a faster rate than the berry, and it is not unusual to find fully developed, black seeds in a green fruit. Still, to attain optimal vigor and viability, it makes sense to allow the seeds to mature completely by harvesting the fruits when fully ripe. Once they are ripe, however, they should be picked immediately or they will be eaten by wildlife. The berries are hand-picked and stored in any convenient vessel in preparation for the next step.

If the berries are still very hard, then it makes sense to mix them with a little water in a bucket and allow them to ferment at room temperature for a few days until they are soft enough to mash. Otherwise, the ripe berries may simply be kneaded between the hands until the fruit is mashed. The fruit-seed mash is then spread out on a screen (too small for the seeds to go through) and sprayed with a pressure hose. This divests the seeds of much of the fruit. The process of mashing and spraying is repeated until the seed is relatively clean. At this point the seed can be "floated" by introducing it into a bucket with plenty of cold water and swirling. Remaining fruit debris and empty testa will float, while the dense, viable seed sinks to the bottom. Then the debris is decanted along with the water, taking care to preserve the viable seed by pouring at the last moment into a strainer or a cloth. The seed may then be planted immediately.

If the seed is destined for travel or for storage, then it must be cleaned more thoroughly. The seed is spread out on a cloth, and any nonseed remnants are hand-picked from the sample in order to obtain 100% purity. This is important, since any necrotic debris will spread disease into the moist seed while it is in storage, a tiny example of the "bad apple in the barrel" scenario. The seed is then stored in a mesh bag (hung at the back of the sink) at room temperature and rinsed twice daily with cold water. This rinsing should continue for at least 3 weeks before the seeds are placed under refrigeration. This method not only satisfies the warm stratification requirement, but also serves to clean the seed very thoroughly while it leaches germination-inhibiting compounds from the seed coat, performing the same function as autumn rains and snowmelt. Interesting how you can find all this at the back of your sink . . .

Premature cooling of the seed will cause extended dormancy. Seeds removed from the fruit and stored immediately in cold, moist conditions (refrigeration at 40° F = 18° C) will remain dormant, germinating sporadically or not germinating at all until the second spring. This is confirmed by my own experiments, and is a nuance that could prove useful to anyone interested in long-term storage of goldenseal seed under refrigeration.

Small samples of goldenseal berries may be processed in a much simpler way. The ripe berries can be introduced immediately into a mesh bag and squeezed, kneaded and rinsed repeatedly over a period of a few days. This will separate the seeds from the fruit, and clean them up pretty well. However, the primary sink person in the house may object to copious quantities of bright red fruity debris going down the drain, in which case other methods may be devised. Then the contents of the bag are emptied into a vessel and the seeds are floated. At this point the seeds may be planted, or if destined for storage they may be introduced into a clean bag and rinsed twice daily at room temperature for at least three weeks.

Clean seed that has been subjected to the warm stratification period can be stored for several months by keeping it in moist peat moss under refrigeration (40° F = 18° C). The peat moss is nice because it approximates natural conditions, separating the seeds from each other and allowing for oxygen flow. Otherwise, it is possible to store the seed in the mesh bag, inside a plastic bag. If using this method, it makes sense to take the mesh bag out from time to time, in order to rinse the seeds and give them some oxygen. If the seed begins to split and sprout, this is a sign that the pre-treatment regimen was completely successful, and it is also an indication that the seed must be planted immediately. Like ginseng, goldenseal seed that sprouts and begins to *grow* in cold storage develops abnormally once it is planted in a soil medium.

Conservation status. Goldenseal *(Hydrastis canadensis)* is the quintessential indigenous North American medicinal herb, the only member of its genus in this hemisphere. Despite its diminutive size and shy habits, the rare beauty and unquestionable medicinality of this plant have enthralled herbalists for over a century. In 1898 Felter and Lloyd wrote that the plant "figures conspicuously among the leading Eclectic drugs, and few have been in greater esteem." They go on to make the first mention of habitat degradation and diminution of supply by stating "the plant disappears as soon as the ground is disturbed by the settler" (Felter and Lloyd, 1898).

Much water has gone down the Ohio River since 1898. By the 1930s, the advent of sulfa-type antibacterial drugs largely supplanted the use of goldenseal in medicine, and partially as a result of this disinterest native stands of goldenseal held their own in many areas. However, the recent resurgence of interest in botanical medi-cine has caused increased pressure on wild populations. In 1997, goldenseal was given a CITES listing, which regulates international trade in the raw herb. However, this listing does little to control international trade in manufactured goldenseal products, and it does not affect domestic trade in goldenseal, which is used largely by American herbalists in American healthcare.

The current distribution of wild goldenseal populations includes 26 states as well as southern Ontario and Quebec. The plant is listed by state governments in six states as endangered, and otherwise variously listed as threatened, rare, vulnerable, or of special concern in the remaining states and in Canada.

Wild harvest of goldenseal root continues at an alarming rate. In 1997 Joseph Brinkman estimated that between 200,000 and 300,000 dry pounds of goldenseal were harvested on a yearly basis (Cech, 1997), and these harvest figures have since been confirmed by other investigators (McGuffin, 1999; Upton ed., 2001). Since a dry, wild-harvested goldenseal root averages about 2 grams in weight, this means that it takes about 227 plants to produce a dry pound. Therefore, during the 1990s, wild harvesters dug between 45.4 million to 68.1 million goldenseal plants out of the forest on a yearly basis!

In the year 1999, Michael McGuffin of the American Herbal Products Association sponsored a survey of the herbal industry in an attempt to evaluate commercial scale cultivation of goldenseal. The survey gave good reason for optimism in that it predicted a yearly availability of 200,000 pounds of dried goldenseal from cultivated sources by the year 2003, a quantity that would supply as much as 78% of the total projected requirement for goldenseal root. However, given the fledgling state of large-scale goldenseal growing, the majority of plants would be propagated not from seed or nursery-grown stock, but from division of roots that were harvested from the wild. Despite this caveat, the trend seems to be positive in the direction of supplanting wild-harvested goldenseal with cultivated goldenseal, and we can expect that as an eventuality the planting stock will be acquired from nurseries, not from the wild. Perhaps goldenseal will then follow in the rootsteps of American ginseng, a success story in domestication of wild medicine and a good example of conservation through cultivation.

References

Amarquaye, A. and R. Cech 1996. *The Presence of Significant Quantities of Berberine and Hydrastine in the Leaf, Stem and Root of Organically Cultivated Goldenseal (Hydrastis canadensis).* Unpublished study performed at the Herb Pharm analytical laboratory under the direction of Ed Smith.

Cech, R. 1997. *An Ecological Imperative, Growing a Future for Native Plant Medicinals.* United Plant Savers Newsletter, Vol. 1(2).

Cech, R. 1999. *Balancing Conservation with Utilization: Restoring Populations of Commercially Valuable Medicinal Herbs in Forests and Agroforests.* Herbalgram, No. 45, pp. 58-60.

Cech, R. 2001. *New Observations on the Germination Habits of Goldenseal.* Journal of Medicinal Plant Conservation, Spring, p. 18.

Cunningham, C., R. Gilmer, H. Hash and N. Cech. 2002. *ESI-MS for the Identification and Quantitation of Bioactive Alkaloids in the Aerial Portions of the Endangered Medicinal Plant Goldenseal (Hydrastis canadensis).* Presented at the 50th ASMS Conference on Mass Spectrometry and Allied Topics.

Davis, J. 1999. *Forest Production of Goldenseal.* AF Note—16, USDA Natural Resources Conservation Service.

Deno, N. 1996. *Seed Germination Theory and Practice, First Supplement to the Second Edition.* State College (PA): Pennsylvania State University.

Felter, H. and J. Lloyd. 1898 (Reprinted 1985). *King's American Dispensatory.* Portland (OR): Eclectic Medical Publishing, Vol. 1 & 2, 743 pp.

Gillis, E and H. Langenhan. 1931. *A Phytochemical Study of Hydrastis Canadensis (Goldenseal).* Journal of the American Pharmaceutical Association, 20(3): pp. 210-224.

Harding, A. 1972. *Ginseng and Other Medicinal Plants,* Revised Edition. Columbus (OH): Harding, 385 pp.

Galle, Bladt and Wagner. 1994. *Deutsche Apotheker Zeitung.* 134, pp. 35-44.

Gocan, Cimpan and Muresan. 1996. *Journal of Pharmacy and Biomedical Analysis.* 14, pp. 1221-1227.

McGuffin,1999. *Having Our Goldenseal and Growing It, Too.* United Plant Savers Newsletter, Vol. 2, No. 1.

Upton, R. (ed.). 2001. *American Herbal Pharmacopoeia and Therapeutic Compendium: Goldenseal Root (Hydrastis canadensis) Standards of Analysis, Quality Control and Therapeutics.*

Wagner, Bladt and Zgainski. 1984. *Plant Drug Analysis.* New York (NY): Springer-Verlag, pp. 80-83.

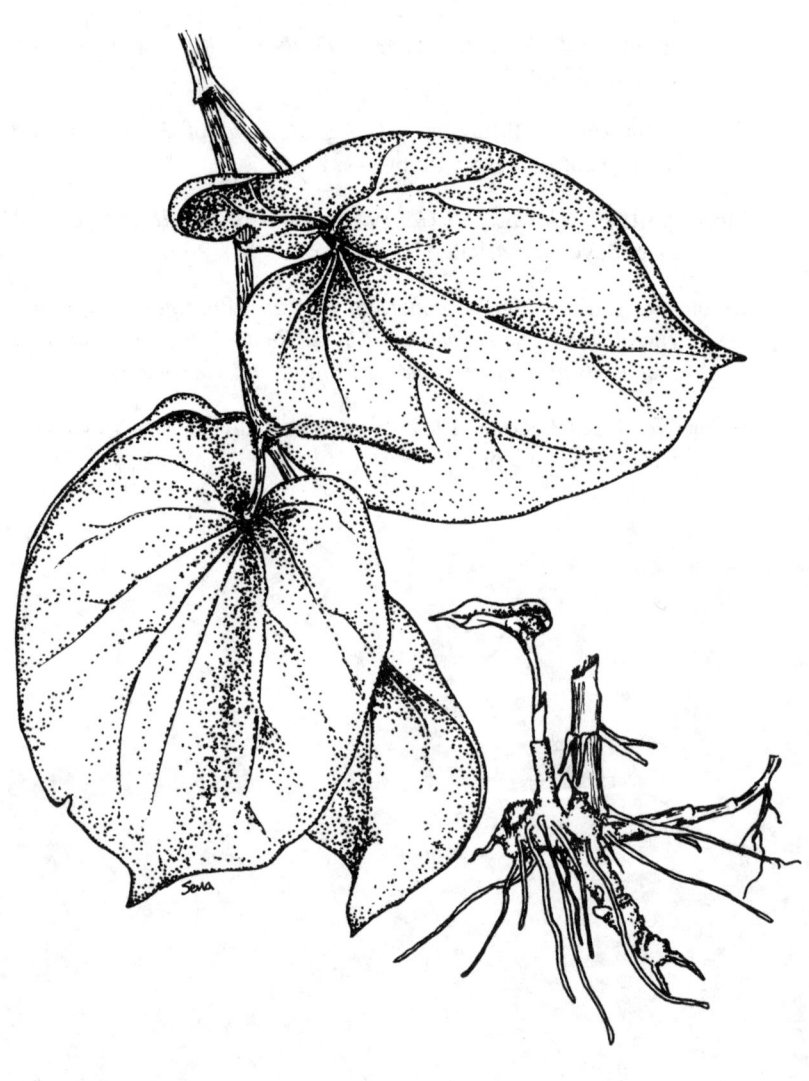

Kava Kava
Piper methysticum
mature leaves and sterile flower
stump, roots, new sprout and
jointed stem with adventitious rootlets

Kava Kava
Piper methysticum Forster
Family: *Piperaceae*

Kava kava is a long-lived shrub of the tropical rain forest, a sterile cultigen of the original wild progenitor (*Piper wichmannii*). The mature kava root is monumental, consisting of a massive, amorphous, tough stump and a spreading mat of woody, lateral roots that anchor the plant. These roots may extend out to a distance of 10 feet (~3 meters). The crown of the stump gives rise to multiple, jointed, bamboo-like stems. The swollen stem nodes that occur close to the ground are often encircled by adventitious rootlets. The stem varies in color from green to black, meandering upward to a maximum height of about 15 feet (~4.5 meters) or more, branching freely, presenting clumps of leaves to the mottled sunlight of the forest understory. The smooth, dark green, pointed, heart-shaped leaves occur alternately on the branches, often in close association with the flowering spikes. The flowers may be male or female, but they are sterile and do not produce seed. They remind me of catkins.

Range. Domestication of kava probably started around 3,000 years before the present time on the Pacific islands of Vanuatu, spreading as a part of the Polynesian culture westward to New Guinea and eastward into Fiji, Tonga and Samoa and finally northward to the islands of Hawaii. Stem cuttings from preferred varieties accompanied the islanders during migrations, resulting in a wide distribution of the plant throughout the three ethnogeographical regions of the Pacific: Polynesia, Melanesia and Micronesia. The wild species *Piper wichmannii* is native to New Guinea, the Solomon Islands and Vanuatu (Lebot, 1989).

Kava is most readily cultivated as an understory plant in the tropical rain forest. As long as the requirements of temperature, humidity, wind protection, shade, fertility and good drainage are fulfilled, the plant will adapt to cultivation in any tropical or subtropical area. Specimen plants may also be kept as a curiosity in heated greenhouses in the temperate zone.

113

The Islands of Oceania, the Traditional Home of Kava

Environment. Kava grows as an understory to the higher canopy[1] of the tropical rain forest, and if planted thickly enough will create a patch to the exclusion of other shrubby species. The plant prefers partial shade, and has adapted the dark green coloration of its leaves to make optimal usage of available sunlight. The understory of a tropical rain forest only receives 5% to 20% of the sunlight available to the canopy. Up to the age of two years, kava plants absolutely require shade. Older plants may withstand full sun (being partially self-shading) but the outer leaves tend to get sunburned and turn yellow.

---

[1] The tropical rain forest is generally considered to be composed of four layers, each associated with a related community of insects and vertebrates. The "emergent layer" is defined by the tallest trees, which often reach a height of 200 feet (60 meters) and are buttressed at the base to withstand high winds. The "canopy" is the primary layer, generally rising to a height of 150 feet (45 meters), consisting mainly of spreading, smooth-leaved trees that shed water quickly. The "understory" is made up of shrubby species and dwarf palms that are adapted to making optimal usage of limited light resources. The "forest floor" is covered with a thin litter of rapidly decomposing vegetation, teeming with bacteria, fungi and microfauna. All species compete for available nutrients.

114

Kava thrives in areas of high rainfall, but prefers soils that drain quickly. Good drainage is characteristic of island soils that are derived from porous volcanic cinder or coral. Kava requires plenty of water to thrive, and is very sensitive to the effects of drying winds. The plant is relatively inefficient in bringing water up to its leaves, and may go vegetatively dormant during dry spells, only to arise again with vigor when water is again consistently available. Drying winds will adversely affect the health of kava plantations, causing yellow spots on the leaves and inviting mite infestation; protection from the trade winds[2] contributes significantly to overall plant health.

Kava prefers soils that are rich in organic content. As a result of intense biological activity, organic matter in rain forest soils is quickly consumed, so kava grows best in soil pockets that are generated by the decomposition of detritus from carbon-producing understory species such as palms and tree ferns.

In Hawaii, a typical emergent species that might be found in association with kava[3] is koa *(Acacia koa),* an aromatic, nitrogen-fixing tree that is highly prized for its wood. Ohia *(Metrosideros collina)* is a typical canopy plant that may be found shading kava in the rain forest. This tree is a pioneer species in lava flow areas and is a soil builder. Kava itself prohibits the rooting of other plants within its drip line.

---

[2] In Hawaii, these would be the northeasterly trade winds. South of the equator, they would be southerly trade winds.

[3] Since the plants were originally introduced, this is not necessarily a "natural association." According to Tane "Since all plantings were originally done by people, it is likely that remoteness was one of the parameters for planting, to protect the plant from poaching." Naturalized kava in the Waipio Valley is found in remote sections growing along stream banks. In Kona it grows in the koa forests. The area where it historically grew best (fastest) was in the lowlands of Kalapana, which had cinder soils, low winds, plentiful rain and sun. This area is now covered by fresh lava.

Kava in the traditional garden. Kava plants that are cared for by humans will grow faster and give improved yields over plants left unattended in the rain forest. This is especially true if kava is planted in organic compost or fed with a side-dressing of organic compost or composted manure.

In traditional gardens, the plant is often cultivated along with food crops so that it may be watched over and found right at hand when needed. Typical companion plants in the garden would be bananas *(Musa* spp.) and cassava *(Manihot esculenta).* Kava might also be planted on the outskirts of the taro *(Colocasia antiquorum)* patch.

Kava also has a preference for growing in marginal areas, including boundary zones between forests and clearings. The plant also sometimes thrives in back dirt or trashy areas consisting of jumbled rock and organic debris.

Life cycle. Since kava is a cultigen (a plant that is the result of selective breeding by humans), there is really no such thing as a "wild" plant. However isolated patches of kava that were originally planted by oceanic voyagers have naturalized in the rain forest, long forgotten by humans. These plants represent a valuable genetic heritage to the Polynesian culture,[4] and it is because of the need for preserving them that kava now appears on the at-risk list. Undisturbed in the forest, plants will spread by means of creeping roots. The original stump may rot away, leaving a circle of plants that slowly gravitate out from the center. Stalks that fall over may also resprout at the nodes, creating new plants at a short distance

---

[4] The original wild progenitor *(Piper wichmannii)* contains a prevalence of dihydrokavain and dihydromethysticin, kavalactones that can cause adverse reactions, including nausea. High-quality cultivated kava contains low levels of these undesirable kavalactones and higher levels of psychoactive constituents (e.g. kavain, methysticum and yangonin). This shift of chemistry is the result of thousands of years of human selection, where plants demonstrating positive qualities were chosen, cultivated, transported, replanted and protected. For a more complete discussion of the physiological effects of various kava cultivars, the reader is referred to Tane Datta's excellent chapter on kava in *Planting the Future* (Datta, 2000).

from the mother. In this way, kava becomes self-replicating and may live for centuries in the forest without human intervention, awaiting rediscovery and further cultivation.

Propagation. Kava does not make seed; the plant is propagated asexually by division or by making stem cuttings. Division of the stump involves cutting back the mature stems, digging up the stump with attached roots, dividing the stump into two or more pieces and replanting the pieces at a distance of approximately 10 feet (~3 meters) apart. When dividing the stump, any young shoots with immature leaves may be left intact; these will then become primary stems of the new plant.

A typical stem cutting contains 2 to 4 nodes. Cuts may be made with snips or a machete. The cuttings are layered end-to-end and a few inches apart in shallow trenches in the shade garden or in trays in the greenhouse. The preferred soil is high in organic content and drains quickly. A mixture of 1 part organic compost and 1 part coarse sand or cinder is serviceable. Warm temperatures, high humidity and good drainage stimulate formation of the sprouts and rootlets at the nodes. Adequate air movement discourages disease.

**Rooted and sprouted three-node cutting,
age three months, ready for transplant.**

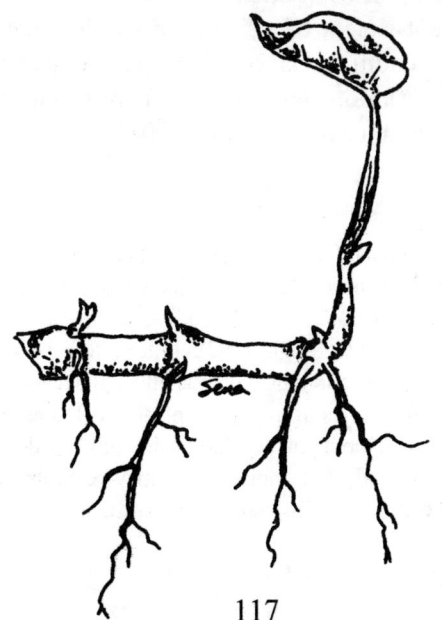

117

Transplant and cultivation. After developing for about 3 months (after initial signs of sprouting), the rooted cuttings may then be transplanted to pots for further maturation before replanting, or may be transplanted directly to the shade garden or rain forest. Plants are set about 10 feet (~3 meters) apart in rich, well-drained soil. Keep the plants moist and weeded until they bush out, at which point they become self-mulching. The plants need to be protected from the trade winds, which can cause damage through dehydration. Supplemental water may be necessary to carry the plants through periods of drought, and a side-dressing of organic compost or rotted manure will increase plant health, size and yield. Optimal shade conditions range between 70% and 90%.

Yield. The entire kava plant (including roots, stump, stem and leaf) contains varying quantities of the active kavalactones, and all parts of the plant have been used. The strongest and most preferred portion is the root and stump (kava root),[5] which contains the highest proportion of active constituents. The root may be used fresh or dried. Roots that contain a high percentage of kavalactones will appear yellow on the interior. The water content of kava root varies depending on the woodiness and the age, generally ranging between 60% to 80%. Therefore, 10 pounds of fresh kava root will dry down to between 2 and 4 pounds of dried roots.

Average root weight of a fresh, 2-year-old plant cultivated under excellent conditions is 20 to 25 pounds (~9 to 11 kg). By the age of 5 years or older, the root may attain 150 pounds (~68 kg) fresh weight or more (Datta, 2001).

---

[5] Average dried roots contain 43% starch, 20% fiber, 12% water, 3.2% sugar, 3.6% protein, 3.2% minerals and 15% kavalactones. Kavalactone content may vary between 3% to 20% depending on the age of the plant and the cultivar (Lebot et al, 1992; Singh, 1992). Fifteen different kavalactones have been isolated, each contributing a unique effect; the relative percentage of each kavalactone also varies from plant to plant. Therefore, there is a huge range of variation in both potency and quality of kava, depending on the cultivar. The overall effect of drinking kava may be attributed to synergy between the various psychoactive constituents.

Harvest, processing and storage. Minimum plant age for harvest is 2 years, and given that the root increases rapidly between years 2 to 5, it makes sense to wait longer than 2 years to dig the root. Besides, digging kava is hard work, and you might like to put it off for awhile. When you *do* decide to dig, bring a mattock and a 6-foot metal digging bar (if you have one). This will help dislodge the stump, which can be quite well-seated, especially in heavy soils. Make sure you get all the larger lateral roots, as well (the mattock helps). Lateral roots suitable for medicine-making are at least the diameter of your finger. Shake the roots free of dirt, cut apart as necessary to dislodge stones, cut off and discard all rotted portions and wash the root thoroughly, using a stiff brush and elbow grease.

Fresh roots may be processed immediately or cut up into chunks and dried. Native preparation often includes an initial sun-drying process. The roots are left in full sun for a period of several days (often laid out on corrugated steel or bamboo racks) and protected from rain, until they become partially dry. This process discourages formation of mold, which can be a real problem in the humid tropics. Roots are then dried to completion in an open shed or hut, where they are laid out on screens or hung in bundles from the rafters. The high-grade lateral roots may be partially dried in the sun, then formed into a large bundle while still pliable, finally hung to dry. Good quality dried kava root smells earthy, is colored bright golden-brown and is free of dust and mold. When stored in air and lightproof packaging, dried kava retains its goodness for at least three years.

Ceremony. The kava ceremony is the ideal context for experiencing the effects of the plant. The kava-maker begins by pounding or grinding the dried[6] root pieces to a powder, which is then introduced into a cloth bag. This bag is wetted with pure water and kneaded by hand over a large, carved bowl. Water is continually poured over the bag as it is squeezed and worked. This results in a suspension of the active plant resins in the water, producing eventually a starchy, thick, slightly nauseating, cold-processed brew.

---

[6] In Hawaii, the fresh root is also used in ceremony.

119

The household and guests, including the kava-maker, gather around in a circle. The eldest and most respected are the first to drink, receiving the polished coconut cup from the cupbearer and swigging at once the entire contents. The cup passes on to other participants, accompanied by prayers, laughing, the unison clapping of hands and exhortations *(bula-bula!)*. After a cup or two, drinkers experience enhanced sensory and mental awareness and a sense of psychic connection. Oral communication and understanding is improved, emotions are soothed and an aura of reciprocal understanding and compassion spreads. Imbibing increased quantities of kava causes a slowness of motor function, lack of coordination between mental impulse ("now it is time to walk") and actuation ("but my knees do not want me to walk") and finally drowsiness. These effects are consistent with the medicinal use of kava, which is generally prescribed as an antidepressant and a relaxant to the skeletal muscles.

Recent investigations into the safety of using kava have raised concerns about potential liver toxicity. In my opinion, occasional use of drinks prepared from whole kava root in a ceremonial or therapeutic context is unlikely to cause liver damage. However, before embarking on a program of using kava frequently (especially in its extracted and concentrated pharmaceutical form), it makes sense to consult a qualified healthcare professional.

Conservation status. Kava has recently experienced a huge resurgence of popularity. Given the pantropic ease of cultivation, and despite potential regulation and toxicity warnings, the plant will be fine. The cup will continue to pass and doctors will prescribe kava to treat depression and back pain. Chemists will continue to pull apart the kavalactone, while growers search for the ultimate cultivar. To the furtherance of all this, naturalized stands of heirloom kava need to be protected, enhanced and replicated.

In response to escalating prices and burgeoning demand for raw materials, the diversity of certain island ecologies have actually been harmed by large-scale cultivation of kava.[7] However, in Hawaii, pioneering farmers are following the principles of permaculture, converting farmlands once dedicated to sugar and pineapple monocrops into sustainable systems planted in nitrogen-fixing shade trees and kava. This is a preferred scenario that deserves replication.

Other species. Plants in the pepper family (the *Piperaceae)* are herbally significant worldwide. This family consists of nine genera and over 1,000 species, including our kava kava *(Piper methysticum)* and the universally popular black pepper *(P. nigrum)* which is native to India. The long pepper *(P. longum),* otherwise known as *pippali,* is an herb of the Ayurvedic tradition that is used as a digestive and upper respiratory tonic. In China, Southeast Asia and Oceania, the betel nut *(P. betle)* is chewed for its digestive and stimulant properties. Cubeb berries *(P. cubeba)* are similarly employed. In Mexico and South America, several related species including *P. angustifolium, P. auritum* and *P. sanctum* are used medicinally for their urinary antiseptic, antispasmodic and digestive effects. They are a pungent spice.

---

[7] For instance, the island of Pohnpei in Micronesia has recently received grants implemented by The Nature Conservancy (TNC) "to control destructive kava cultivation in upland forests through developing environmentally compatible enterprises . . . to promote effective, long-term, community-based conservation of Pohnpei's globally significant biodiversity."

121

References

Datta, T. 2001: Personal communication. Tane is an organic farmer who lives with his beautiful family on the Kona Coast of the big island of Hawaii. He grows rain forest-shaded kava at his farm "Adaptations." Tane served as a patient informant and reviewer for this chapter.

Datta, T. 2000. *Kava* in: R. Gladstar (ed.) *Planting the Future: Saving our Medicinal Herbs.* Rochester (VT): Healing Arts Press, pp. 130-138.

Lebot ,V. and J. Lévesque. 1989. *The Origin and Distribution of Kava (Piper methysticum Forst. g. and Piper wichmanni C. DC., Piperaceae): A Phytochemical Approach.* Allertonia, 5, pp. 223-280.

Lebot, V, M. Merlin and L. Linstrom. 1992. *Kava: The Pacific Drug.* New Haven (CT): Yale University Press,10.

Singh, Y. 1992. *Kava: An Overview.* Journal of Ethnopharmacology, 37(1), pp. 13-45.

Lady's Slipper Orchid
Cypripedium pubescens
root, rhizome and flowering plant

Lady's Slipper Orchid
Cypripedium L.
Family: *Orchidaceae*

Cypripedium is a widespread and diverse genus of terrestrial orchids consisting of twelve unique species indigenous to North America. The ecologies that harbor these plants are as varied as the orchids themselves, including rich deciduous woodlands, coniferous woodlands, mountain forests, cold streams, rocky outcrops, flood plains and bogs. Regardless of where they are found, and despite a few pockets of local abundance, lady's slipper orchids are rare in the wild. The various species are represented by scattered populations consisting of few individuals, separated by vast areas of land stretching from the Atlantic to the Pacific and from the deep South all the way to the Yukon territories.

The lady's slipper root consists of a horizontally flattened rhizome, punctuated on the upper surface by multiple concise, craterous stem scars. An interwoven mat of coarse, wiry, kinky rootlets splay out and down, an adaptation that serves well in anchoring the plant in marshy, rocky or otherwise unstable soils. The rhizome gives rise to one or more pointed buds that develop in the early spring into the leaves and stem. The leaves are bright green, graceful, broadly lance-shaped and longitudinally veined. The single shared characteristic of all lady's slipper orchids is the flower, consisting of a pouch-like "slipper" (known technically as the labellum), framed by showy petals and sepals that contrast handsomely. The labellum itself is an amazing adaptation, a pendulous, inflated and sensuous offering that invites the bumblebee to enter and perform the rites of pollination. Unfortunately the plant is nectarless, so pollination is often accomplished only by naive bees that soon learn to go elsewhere in search of sustenance, and some lady's slippers must make do with self-pollination. For these reasons seed production often suffers. Germination of the tiny seed and development of the seedling requires an almost miraculous symbiosis between the developing germ plasm and mycorrhizal fungi, a rare dance in nature and a difficult performance to reenact in cultivation.

Once known as "American valerian,"[1] the roots of lady's slipper have a relaxing effect on the human nervous system, used historically in treating headache, insomnia, irritability, depression and menstrual irregularities. The signal attribute of lady's slipper root is that it promotes a feeling of tranquility by calming nervous irritability. Resulting sleep is without twitches, worries and bad dreams. Surely there are common herbs (e.g. valerian, passionflower and skullcap) that give similar results, but to say that the activity of these herbs is identical to that of lady's slipper would be incorrect.

The yellow lady's slippers are actually represented by three distinct species: greater yellow lady's slipper *(Cypripedium pubescens),* lesser yellow lady's slipper *(C. parviflorum)* and Kentucky lady's slipper *(C. kentuckiense).* At one time, these were all considered official in medicine (Felter and Lloyd, 1898). The greater and lesser yellow lady's slippers are often seen in the literature grouped as variants of a single species *(C. calceolus),* but are treated here as separate species.

The root of moccasin flower *(Cypripedium acaule)* and white lady's slipper *(C. candidum)* were also harvested in devastating numbers for home use and for export. These were considered medicinally interchangeable with the official species (Felter and Lloyd, 1898). Native uses of moccasin flower as an "analgesic and sedative" have also been recorded (Hamel, 1975). Similarly, there is evidence that other species (e.g. *C. calceolus)* were also used in native medicine (Herrick, 1977).

According to *King's Dispensatory,* "There are several varieties of it, all of which possess similar virtues, and the roots of which are undoubtedly collected, sold and indiscriminately used with the official article" (Felter and Lloyd, 1898).

The deterioration of native stands of lady's slipper may be attributed to: loss of habitat (especially the draining of fens and the logging of old growth forests), harvest of plants to supply home

---

[1] A singularly unfortunate epithet; this name highlights the sedative and nervine aspects of the root while it masks a rare herb in the guise of an easily cultivated and common garden medicinal.

gardens and the horticultural trade and wide-scale harvest to supply the medicinal herb industry. A.R. Harding, in his classic manual on cultivation and wildcrafting of native American medicinal plants called *Ginseng and Other Medicinal Plants,* recorded that prices paid to collectors (in the early 1900s) were 32 to 35 cents per pound for the dried roots (Harding, 1972).

Starting lady's slipper plants from seed is likely to require facilities and materials not available to the common gardener (and the author hastens to add that he is a gardener of just this variety). Laboratory produced seedlings are increasingly available through several technically advanced nurseries. However, even when seedlings are purchased, the cultivation of lady's slipper requires very specific environmental conditions. The best results will be obtained by replicating the natural habitat and by choosing the species that is native to your area. The next portion of this chapter is a concise overview of the twelve North American species, including their range and ecology. This is given so that the reader may determine which species is appropriate to grow, and what conditions are likely to result in success.

Greater Yellow Lady's Slipper Orchid
(Cypripedium pubescens)
Syn. *Cypripedium calceolus var pubescens*

Range. The plant occurs mainly in the eastern and midwestern United States, but populations have been recorded in a few western states, in the western boreal forest of Canada and in the northern circumpolar reaches of Canada.

Description. *C. pubescens* is robust and hairy; flowers 1 to 2 per stem; leaves 3 to 6 per stem; multistemmed to a height of about 30 inches (~80 cm). The pouch is bright yellow, spotted inside with purple. The sepals are often twisted, colored brown and streaked with green.

Habitat. The plant prefers rich deciduous woods and thickets; limestone outcroppings; and wet meadows and bogs.

Notes. This is the main species that has been used in medicine. It is difficult to start by seed, but is fairly easily propagated by division. The plant is tolerant of a wide range of soil types.

127

Current U.S. Range of Greater Yellow Lady's Slipper

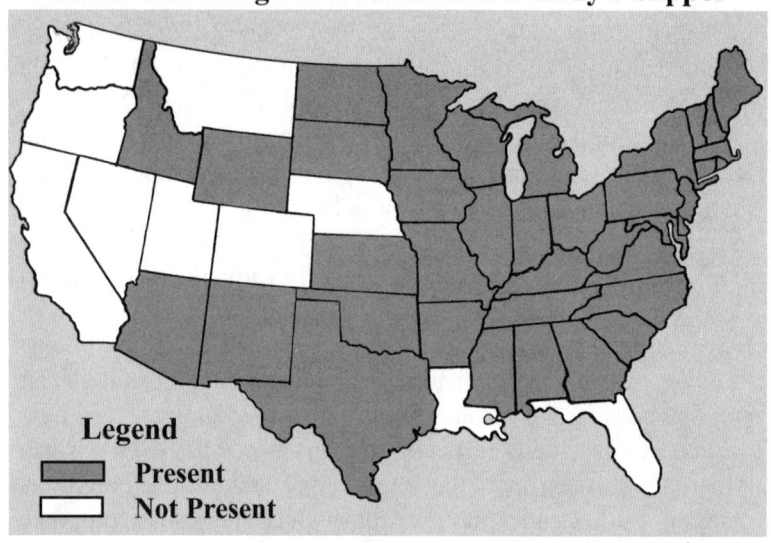

Current U.S. Range of Lesser Yellow Lady's Slipper

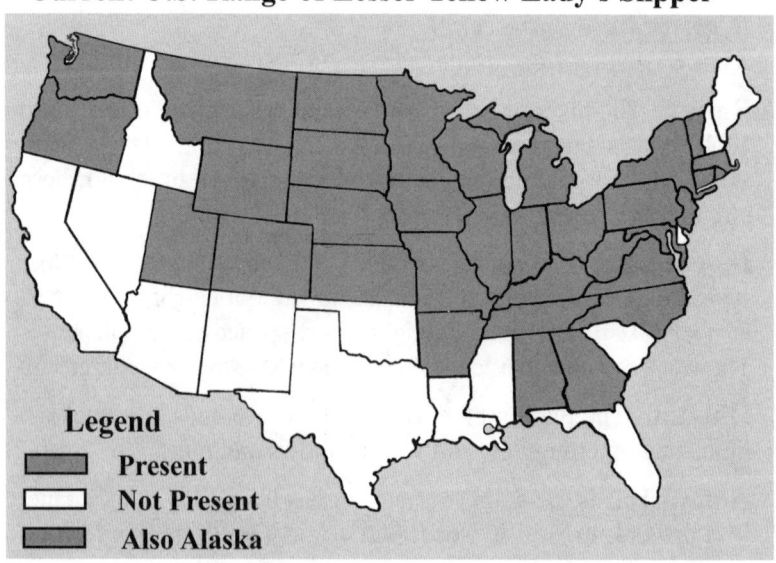

Lesser Yellow Lady's Slipper Orchid
(Cypripedium parviflorum)
Syn. *Cypripedium calceolus var parviflorum*

Range. The plant occurs mainly in the northern and western United States and Canada, including Alaska.

Description. *C. parviflorum* is smaller and less hairy than *C. pubescens,* with smaller flowers; flowers 1 to 2 per stem; leaves 3 to 6 per stem; multistemmed to a height of about 14 inches (~35 cm). The pouch is bright yellow, spotted inside with purple. The sepals are highly twisted, colored dark reddish-brown.

Habitat. The plant lives in shaded fens, bogs and moist meadows, in acid, well-drained soils. In the Ozarks, the plant occurs in oak-hickory or pine-oak slopes along streams.

Notes. This species, along with *C. pubescens,* is considered official. *C. parviflorum* is more common in the West, but it is often difficult to differentiate from *C. pubescens,* and indeed the two are known to intergrade freely in shared habitat.

Kentucky Lady's Slipper Orchid
(Cypripedium kentuckiense)

Range. The plant ranges across the southern states, from Virginia to Kentucky and Tennessee, as far south as Alabama, then across to Texas.

Description. This is the largest of our native lady's slipper orchids, with flowers measuring (including sepals) up to 5 inches (13 cm) across; flowers and leaves several per stem; multistemmed to a height of about 40 inches (~100 cm). The pouch is bright yellow with maroon stripes.

Habitat. *C. kentuckiense* prefers moderately moist flood plain forests and the slopes of ravines. The plant is sometimes found next to springs and seeps, generally in acid soils.

Notes. Wildcrafting herbs and roots has been an integral part of the lives of many who live in the southern Appalachian range and contiguous territories. Given the close resemblance of this plant to the official species, it has been heavily impacted by harvest activities. However, remaining populations are strong and stable.

Moccasin Flower (Pink Lady's Slipper Orchid)
(Cypripedium acuale)

Range. The plant occurs across the eastern United States and southern Canada.

Description. The plant consists of 2 basal leaves, giving rise to a leafless stem that carries a solitary flower, rising to a height of 16 inches (40 cm). The pouch is colored magenta to whitish-pink, with darker pink venation. The pouch may be differentiated from all other species of lady's slipper by the fact that it is split up the front (instead of demonstrating the usual round opening).

Habitat. *C. acuale* prefers medium-moist (mesic) to dry, acidic soils in pine, hemlock or other coniferous forests.

Notes. Although this plant is not yellow-flowered, it has a history of medicinal use, both by the Native Americans and by the eclectic physicians (Moerman, 1986; Felter and Lloyd, 1898).

White Lady's Slipper Orchid
(Cypripedium candidum)

Range. The plant occurs mainly in the New England states and across southern Canada; also found in the Rocky Mountain states and in Alabama.

Description. *C. candidum* is small but robust; flowers 1 to 2 per stem; leaves 2 to 5 per stem; multistemmed to a height of about 18 inches (~40 cm). The pouch is a shiny, waxy white and is internally streaked with purple. The sepals are twisted, colored greenish-yellow and also streaked with purple. The flowers are exceptionally fragrant.

Habitat. The plant prefers clay-loam soils and alkaline conditions in wet prairies, prairie swales or calcareous fens; low, wooded slopes bordering streams.

Notes. In *Flora of Missouri,* Steyermark states that the plant was "very rare" in Missouri in 1963 (Steyermark, 1963). White flowered species have been the "Moby Dick" of plant collectors. In the early 1900s one collector (in Waubun, Minnesota) blithely picked and pressed 43 plants as voucher samples (Saupe, 2002). One plant would have sufficed.

Showy Lady's Slipper Orchid
(Cypripedium reginae)

Range. The plant occurs across the eastern and midwestern United States.

Description. This plant is robust; flowers 1 to 3 per stem; leaves 3 to 5 per stem; multistemmed to a height of about 35 inches (~90 cm). The pouch is colored white, suffused with deep rose to magenta, often with white veins; rarely entirely white, pink or rose.

Habitat. *C. reginae* grows in alkaline or limestone soils or on rocky outcrops, preferring deep, humusy soil where the crown remains aerated, but the roots are kept constantly moist. The plant may be found in peat bogs, but with roots growing through the peat into underlying alkaline substrates. If growing in swamps, the plant is found on hummocks that lift the crown above the water; also inhabits rich, moist woods or open wetlands.

Notes. This species is less dependent on a strong winter dormancy than most lady's slipper orchids, but it is more dependent on having a consistently moist root zone. In cultivation, it is best grown in a medium containing a high percentage of woody debris, and must be mulched heavily.

Mountain Lady's Slipper Orchid
(Cypripedium montanum)

Range. The plant occurs from California north through Alberta and British Columbia to Alaska. It is very sparsely distributed over a large range of territory.

Description. *C. montanum* is robust; flowers 2 per stem; leaves 4 to 6 per stem; multistemmed to a height of about 24 inches (~60 cm). The pouch is colored white, veined with purple, with highly twisted, dark red-brown sepals. It is faintly perfumed.

Habitat. This species grows in moist to dry, deciduous or coniferous forests on subalpine slopes. This orchid may be found on rocky, shrubby slopes in association with Indian paintbrush.

Notes. *C. montanum* is distinguished from *C. candidum* by the much longer sepals.

California Lady's Slipper Orchid
(Cypripedium californicum)

Range. The plant is native to a limited range in southern Oregon and northern California. Although the orchid has been described as a "Siskiyou Mountain endemic," scattered populations occur outside the Siskiyous. *C. californicum* occurs in local abundance in the Illinois River valley in the Kalmiopsis Wilderness, just over the mountain from the author's home.

Description. This is an atypical lady's slipper orchid, with upright stems that are leafy to the top. The flowers are borne at intervals along the stem; flowers 3 to 12 per stem, rising to a height of 24 inches (60 cm).

Habitat. The plant grows in moist woods and damp areas, especially at the edges of streams or on tiny islands within streams. I consider it to be a semiaquatic species, very similar to stream orchid *(Epipactis* spp.). *C. californicum* occurs in association with California pitcher plants *(Darlingtonia californica),* and is especially fond of growing in cold rivulets that run through serpentine slopes down to bigger water.

Clustered Lady's Slipper Orchid
(Cypripedium fasciculatum)

Range. The plant occurs in the Pacific Northwest and Rocky Mountain states, especially the Cascade Mountain Range, continuing up into Saskatchewan, Alberta and British Columbia.

Description. This is another atypical lady's slipper orchid. It is very inobtrusive, with 2 leaves per stem; 1 to 6 flowers per stem; flowers occurring in an open cluster, to a height of 8 inches (20 cm).

Habitat. *C. fasciculatum* grows in moist to dry, acid soils in coniferous forests, at elevations up to 10,000 feet; it is often found in Douglas fir-ninebark associations. In the forest, the plant may be found hiding at the base of ferns or next to rotted logs, rooting into deep humus and sheltered by these larger features.

Notes. This plant is rare; it is highly impacted by logging activities, due to its association with market-sized timber. Environmental impact statements should take this into account.

Ram's Head Lady's Slipper Orchid
(Cypripedium arietinum)

Range. The plant occurs in the northeastern and Great Lakes regions of the U.S.; Nova Scotia to eastern Saskatchewan.

Description. *C. arietinum* is small, with 3 to 5 leaves per stem; flowers solitary, attaining a height of 12 inches (30 cm). The pouch is colored crimson, with a conical projection below. The sepals are horn-like, pointing forward as if ready to charge.

Habitat. The plant grows in cool soils in coniferous forests; soils derived from old sand dunes; in cedar bogs or woodlands, often in association with limestone or dolomitic outcrops. The plant even grows in moist, partially shaded road ditches.

Sparrowegg Lady's Slipper Orchid
(Cypripedium passerinum)

Range. This is a subarctic species distributed transcontinentally in Canada, also occurring in Montana and Alaska.

Description. The plant is small but robust; 3 to 5 leaves per stem; 1 to 3 flowers per stem; multistemmed to a height of 12 inches (30 cm). The pouch is colored white to rose, with small purple spots. The flower is very fragrant. The plant is a self-pollinator.

Habitat. *C. passerinum* will grow in both acidic and alkaline soils of moist, coniferous forests; gravely or sandy shores of rivers and lakes.

Spotted Lady's Slipper Orchid
(Cypripedium guttatum)

Range. In the northern reaches of Canada, the plant is circumpolar.

Description. *C. guttatum* has only 2 leaves, which give rise to a leafless, single-flowered stem, rising to 12 inches (30 cm). The pouch is colored white and blotched or checked with magenta; it is unusual among the lady's slippers, in that it is shaped like a cauldron, with the lip turned out, an adaptation devised to temporarily trap pollinators.

Habitat. The plant occurs in association with birch and poplar, on the lower reaches of forested mountain slopes.

Life cycle. Most species of *Cypripedium* are highly dependent on cross-pollination between individuals in order to assure production of viable seed. The highly colored and sometimes sweetly aromatic, pouch-like labellum is designed to attract the midsize to large, native bees that are most likely to pollinate it. The flowers are long-lived in order to maximize the potential for this much-anticipated visit. The bee circles the flower, considering for a moment before alighting. "Isn't this one of those flowers that smells so good, but doesn't make nectar?" Although the bee has a very long *genetic* memory, its *short-term* memory is flighty. "Better go in to make sure," it says. The bee alights, enters the labellum and finds itself trapped for a moment. It buzzes around inside (the whole plant vibrates), looking for a nectar source. Disappointed, the bee then discerns an exit, a narrow passageway at the back of the flower, where a little sunlight peeps through. In the process of crawling out, pollen from the dusty anthers of a previously visited orchid are transferred to the sticky, receptive stigma of this flower. As the bee exits, its back is dusted with new pollen from the parting anthers of this flower. The bee bumbles away, planning a visit to a nearby meadow where there is mullein at the edge, and red clover in the middle. On the way it encounters a beautiful flower, dangling invitingly from a familiar, hairy stalk. The bee considers for a moment, "Isn't this one of those flowers that smells so good, but doesn't make nectar. . ?"

After pollination, the flower wilts and the ovary swells. Over a period of weeks, the seed capsule ripens and matures. A large seed capsule produces as many as 20,000 seeds. The elongated, papery capsule eventually splits, opening its valves and dispersing the seed to the slightest breeze. The seeds are about the size of a dust mote. They contain no endosperm (nutrient reserves), but a certain percentage of them do contain germination-inhibiting compounds. Therefore, seeds may remain dormant and viable in the soil for several years until they perish or (very rarely) meet with the necessary conditions for germination and development.

Germination begins as the embryo is invaded by a mycorrhizal fungus (*Rhizoctonia)*. Germination continues as the embryo expands and the seed coat splits, eventually forming what is known as a "protocorm." The protocorm is non-photosynthetic, developing in union with the fungal symbiont. The fungus lives on the protocorm as an intracellular coil or "peleton," serving the plant by breaking down nutrients and enhancing their absorption by means of its fine-rooted, hyphal network. It is a typical marriage, in that the partners are not always harmonious. The fungus would really like to eat the protocorm, and the protocorm responds by producing antifungal compounds.[2] During the symbiotic phase, when the fungus is supplying the protocorm with carbohydrates and the production of antifungal compounds is at a minimum, then the plant grows. But sometimes the fungus eats the plant, and they are both then subsumed by the soil.

Barring this event, the protocorm develops until it produces a small dormant eye bud and root system. It is now a seedling. After overwintering, the seedling produces a green leaf and begins to photosynthesize. At this point, reliance on the fungal symbiont is lessened, and after several years of development the rocky marriage ends unhappily in divorce. The plant produces a healthy rhizome and a mass of feeder roots, and no longer needs the mycorrhizal fungus. The fungus retreats, only to revisit if unfavorable growing conditions weaken the plant. Lady's slippers require a moist root system, but the crown of the plant must reside in loose, aerated soil. If conditions become anaerobic, then the fungus may return. It returns not as a former lover, but as a disgruntled "ex," and it bears in hand a nasty court summons, at the top of which is written in hyphal scrawl "crown rot."

---

[2] This is not to be confused with the phases of my marriage where I ask too much of my wife, when she feels consumed by her lists of things to do, and responds by making popcorn, her "happy food." So in no way should the term "protocorm" be confused with "popcorn," although the existence of each may be the result of the whole marital relationship, where harmony is preserved only by a level of giving that appears disproportionate to each partner.

The life cycle of the lady's slipper is tenuous and complex; it is not surprising that seedlings are a rare find in the wild. In nature, the underground development phase may last anywhere from 3 to 7 years, and it may require an additional 5 to 10 years for the photosynthesizing plant to reach maturity. Therefore, it can take anywhere from 8 to 17 years for a plant to grow from seed to flower. Barring human disturbance or natural disasters, populations of lady's slippers remain stable in the wild. This is not because the plant reproduces easily, but because once it is established, it may live for over a century (Klein, 1999).

Cultivation from seed. Given optimal conditions of temperature and moisture, it is possible that lady's slipper could be successfully direct seeded, especially in areas where the plant is already growing. Pick the ripe seed capsule and worry it slightly until the seed begins to float away, making sure that it lands on a likely bed (according to the habitat requirements already listed for each species). For example, *Cypripedium fasciculatum* seed could be scattered in a coniferous forest at the base of a rotting log. *Cypripedium pubescens* might do well planted on acid soil and covered with leaf mold in the shade garden. However, most serious propagators of lady's slipper rely on laboratory techniques to enhance germination rates and provide a carefully controlled environment for the development of the protocorm.

In laboratory culture, sterilized seeds are sown on agar plates containing a nutrient solution. The agar may contain ground oats, or may be a specific recipe designed for propagation of terrestrial orchids (Anderson, 1990). The agar plates are further inoculated with the fungal symbiont, which is obtained from the roots of immature lady's slipper plants. This is known as a "symbiotic medium." Sometimes mature seeds are used. Because mature seeds contain high quantities of germination-inhibiting compounds, this practice often results in a poor germination rate. For this reason, many propagators use seed from green capsules. This seed sometimes gives better results, due to the lack of inhibiting factors, but may in turn give low germination rates due to the immaturity of the seed itself. The happy medium seems to be to use capsules that are about 60 days old (since pollination).

The cultures are kept in the dark at room temperature (approximately 70° F = 21° C) for the early stages of germination. Then when the protocorms develop, they are reflasked and placed on agar medium in bottles at a spacing of about ½ inch (1.3 cm) apart. The flasks are again left in the dark, and the protocorms enlarge and continue to develop. Once the leaf bud is formed, the plants are deflasked and planted in a loose potting soil. This transplant should occur in the autumn. It is possible to plant the seedlings directly to their final location at this point, but most propagators put them in communal pots. After a period of overwintering (minimum 4 months of cold temperatures) the buds will produce the first leaf, and the plants will grow and develop slowly from this point on.

Transplanting to the fens, woodlands or shade garden usually takes place when the seedling is 1 to 3 years old. Higher rates of success may be expected when working with larger, more established individuals. Planting beds are best prepared in advance so that the plants may grow for many years with a minimum of disturbance. The soil and moisture requirements of the specific species must be taken into account. In general the best results are obtained by choosing a spot with morning sun that is otherwise shaded. The moist soil may be amended with composted leaves, peat moss and sharp sand. The plant is settled into the bed, the roots are spread apart and firmed in and the bud is situated with the point up. Well-drained, airy mulch is then introduced around the crown. Most lady's slippers thrive under these conditions.

Upkeep from this point on is relatively simple. If the area becomes dry, it must be watered, and watering from below is preferred over watering from above. Natural water sources are ideal (rain, pond, stream or river water), and chlorinated water is not good. In the autumn, the area is best mulched manually, unless mulch occurs as part of the natural cycle of leaffall. Acid-loving species are best mulched with decomposed pine needles or with peat moss. Alkaline-loving species will benefit from a side-dressing of ground limestone or dolomite, applied in the autumn and covered with a layer of decomposed hardwood leaves. The plants do not require or appreciate additional fertilization.

Cultivation from root division. Any lady's slipper orchid plant that has multiple stems may be divided. Dig the plant in the autumn, after the aerial parts have gone down. Shake it free of dirt and examine it closely. Divisions are by far most successful if they contain at least one dormant bud. Snip the rhizome transversely, leaving 1 or more buds on each cutting. A single mature plant may make up to 6 transplants. Replant immediately, following planting and care instructions already given. Plants are best spaced at least 1 foot (30 cm) apart.

Yield. The dried root and rhizome (the root) of lady's slipper orchid is the part traditionally used. The reason for drying the root is because the main active constituents are not water-soluble, and therefore drying the root improves extraction. However, most modern herbalists will *not* use it. The plant is too slow-growing, too rare and too pretty to sacrifice. Valerian and passionflower are substituted. There is some ethnographic evidence that Native Americans used a decoction of the whole plant for treating intestinal maladies and pain, or used the aerial portions as a poultice (Moerman, 1986). Since the roots of this precious plant are so very slow-growing, it might make sense to investigate the safety and possible applicability of the fresh or dried, aerial parts as a substitute for the root.

For the purposes of this study, I sacrificed one of my oldest greater yellow lady's slippers *(Cypripedium pubescens)* that was growing in a small patch in the alder-maple woods here at Horizon Herbs Seed Farm. In agreement with normal harvest practices, I dug it in the autumn. Sena was then able to sketch in the root section of the plant (see illustration at beginning of this chapter). She had already illustrated the aerial parts in the spring, lying on her stomach in the cool woods while the yellow flower dangled a few inches from her nose. The plant was at least 15 years old, and to tell you the truth, it really hurt to dig it up.

The fresh root weighed 96 grams and measured 7 inches (18 cm) from rootlet tip to rootlet tip. The root had set 4 nascent buds, which would have been flowering stalks the next spring. I counted 30 stem scars, the evidence of stems and flowers gone by. The root dried down to a weight of 38 grams, indicating a water content of about 60%. Therefore, 1 pound of fresh roots would consist of 5 plants, and 1 pound of dried roots would consist of 12 plants. On the basis of this test, 1 pound of fresh roots would dry down to less than 0.5 pound of dried roots.

Conservation status. As a terrestrial orchid, lady's slipper is listed in CITES Appendix II, which means that international trade in the raw herbal material, fresh rootstock and plants harvested from the wild is strictly forbidden. In the case of lady's slipper, this is an effective designation, because the international trading of live, wild-harvested plants as horticultural curiosities is a more relevant concern than is the vestigial practice of harvesting for herbal use. However there is *no* level of harvest that can be claimed to be sustainable, and many states and national governments have recognized this in their conservation listings. For instance, greater yellow lady's slipper is listed as "imperiled" in Oklahoma, of "special concern" in Georgia and is "critically imperiled" in Wyoming. Lesser yellow lady's slipper is considered "endangered" in Illinois, Indiana, Kentucky and Massachusetts, "rare" in Colorado and has been extirpated in my own state of Oregon. The list goes on and on (Marshall, 1993).

Generally academics and naturalists view the idea of reintroduction of plant species into the wild with a great deal of suspicion. They ask, "Will it be the right 'landrace'[3] for the chosen locality, and what will the consequences be for other native plants?" However, in the case of lady's slipper, there is certainly a softening of this attitude, and various groups encourage reintroduction to the wilds—and why not? The plant belongs there, and lady's slipper itself, with its bright yet demure flowers and sweet demeanor seems to elicit this assistance. Therefore, I encourage all who have the opportunity to protect and augment the native stands to do so, and I pray for all who care for land that they may have the opportunity to replant this beauty.

---

[3] A "landrace" is a local strain of a plant that has evolved independently. The genetic specificity caused by environmental seclusion often gives rise to useful characteristics such as northern hardiness, shade tolerance or even variation in the chemistry or concentration of secondary constituents. Plants on *this* side of the mountain may not be quite the same as plants on the *other* side of the mountain.

References

Anderson, A. 1990. *North American Terrestrial Orchid Propagation and Production.* Conference proceedings. Chadds Ford (PA): Brandywine Conservancy.

Hamel, P. and M. Chiltoskey. 1975. *Cherokee Plants.* Sylva (NC): Herald Publishing.

Harding, A. 1972. *Ginseng and Other Medicinal Plants,* revised ed., Columbus (OH): Harding, 385 pp.

Herrick, J. 1977. *Iriquois Medical Botany.* Ann Arbor (MI): University Microfilms International.

Klein, R. 1999. *How Old are Our Medicines?* United Plant Savers Newsletter, Vol. 2 (1), pp. 5-10.

Marshall, N. 1993. *The Gardener's Guide to Plant Conservation.* Baltimore (MD): World Wildlife Fund, 186 pp.

Moerman, D. 1986. *Medicinal Plants of Native America.* Ann Arbor (MI): University of Michigan Department of Anthropology, Vol. 1, 534 pp.

Saupe, S. 2002. *Morality in the Herbarium.* Collegeville (MN): College of St. Benedict/St. John's University.

Steyermark, J. 1963. *Flora of Missouri.* Ames (IA): Iowa State University Press, 1724 pp.

General references

Johnson, Kershaw, MacKinnon and Pojar. 1995. *Plants of the Western Boreal Forest and Aspen Parkland.* Canada: Lone Pine Publishing and the Canadian Forest Service, 392 pp.

Foster, S. and J. Duke. 1990. *Peterson Field Guide to Eastern/Central Medicinal Plants.* New York (NY): Houghton Mifflin, 355 pp.

Peck, M. 1941. *A Manual of the Higher Plants of Oregon.* Portland (OR): Metropolitan Press, 866 pp.

Lomatium
Lomatium dissectum
seeded umbel and mature leaf
seeds

Lomatium

Lomatium dissectum (Nutt.) Mat. & Con.

Family: *Apiaceae*

Lomatium is a widespread and diverse genus containing 80 species of native American dryland herbaceous perennials. Some of these were once significant food plants for native peoples, and there is one *(Lomatium dissectum)* that is still used in herbal medicine. This plant (otherwise known as desert parsley, fernleaf biscuitroot, cough root and Indian balsam) is hereinafter referred to as "lomatium." Medicinal lomatium may be differentiated from the many allied species by its large size and by close examination of the flowers and seeds, but the easiest way to know it is by the characteristic root. This thickened, branching taproot looks like a giant, brown-skinned beet suffering from elephantiasis. The flesh is firm, but yielding—humanoid and cream-colored. The terminal taproots are fibrous, but easily damaged. When cut or bruised, the root yields a yellowish latex in greasy tears. The odor is clinging, celery-like and intense. The root is capped by a flat crown that is studded with ingrown rocks and woody detritus, covered with amorphous gnarled, fleshy nubs. Some of these are artifacts of previous stems, and some give rise to the living stems. The stems are many and tightly grouped; they are hollow and finely grooved. The flattened, compound leaves occur most frequently at the base of the plant; they are deeply divided and ferny. Each stem produces a single, large umbel. There is substantial regional and microsite variation in the leaves and flowers of *Lomatium dissectum,* and the plant has been loosely grouped into two varietal forms: *var. multifidum* that is yellow-flowered, and *var. dissectum* that has flowers tipped in purple or chocolate-brown. The flowers give way to large, oval, flattened seeds held aloft on a radiating cluster of stems. The seeds occur in pairs, with many pairs per stem. They are green and turgid when young, then split apart and become papery at maturity. Each seed is rimmed by a narrow wing and sports three raised ridges on the dorsal surface. These are a characteristic identifying feature, which comes in very useful given the early dormancy of the plant.

Range, hardiness and adaptability.   Lomatium ranges across the drylands of the western states and up into Alberta and British Columbia, not occurring far east of the Rocky Mountains. The area of highest concentration is the dryland expanse located in the rain shadow of the Cascade and Sierra Nevada Mountain Ranges—the Columbia Plateau and the Great Basin.

The plant grows best in the winter, spring and early summer and goes vegetatively dormant (while ripening its seeds) during the hot and dry summers. Winter cold is well-tolerated, but prolific rainfall or snow cover in the winter is likely to damage the root. The plant thrives during the winter and early spring on minimal moisture. Average rainfall in the Great Basin is 16 inches (41 cm). Attempts to cultivate the plant outside its native range have not been particularly successful, but then, attempts to cultivate the plant *inside* its native range have also met with frequent failure. The plant requires a full sun exposure, mild winter or springtime weather patterns and a very dry summer. It is possible that areas of New Mexico and Texas meet these criteria, but it is unlikely that lomatium would naturalize or prosper in gardens east of the Missouri River.

Current Range of *Lomatium dissectum* in the U.S.

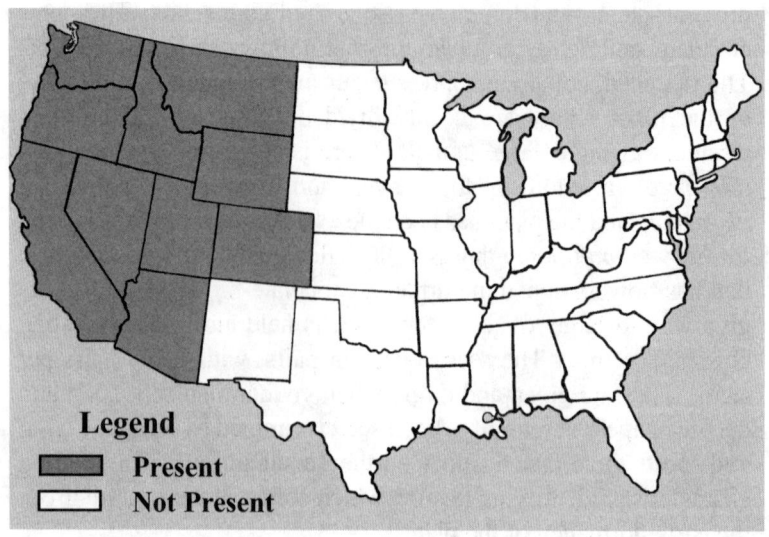

Legend
- Present
- Not Present

Ecology and plant community. Lomatium grows in dry and rocky habitats, where there is little organic matter in the soil. It has a high tolerance for alkalinity. It is often found on a south slope in the full sun, or as an understory plant to dryland trees such as oak, madrone, manzanita or pine. The plant has a preference for extremely well-drained soils, including trashy, disturbed soils and talus slopes. It is a pioneer plant to landslides.

Lomatium is patch-forming, and may be seen to dominate local areas of land as the main plant species. It occurs this way in ideal habitat, and maintains its dominance of the microsite by means of its extraordinary longevity. Moore mentions that arrowleaf balsam root *(Balsamorrhiza sagittata)* is an indicator plant for lomatium habitat, and goes on to state that "Finding your first *Lomatium dissectum* can be maddening, since large stands, growing in the right circumstances, may be 100 miles apart" (Moore, 1993).

In less ideal habitat, *L. dissectum* may occur singly or in very sparse colonies. In Oregon, I have seen the plant grow on rocky ridges overlooking streams and rivers, often in direct association with poison oak *(Rhus diversiloba),* which is a classic indicator of depleted soil and strong light. I have also found lomatium growing in partial shade in richer, bottom land soils. However, the plant produces its active medicine in response to the severity of the growing conditions, and plants found in mellow areas may be less potent.

Life cycle. Lomatium seed drops from the dehiscent umbel during the late summer and early winter, sometimes lodging in the cracks between rocks and coming into contact with a little soil or sand. The seed overwinters in this position and germinates during wet weather in the winter or very early spring, while the soils are still very cold. Germination is epigeal, with two elongated seed leaves followed immediately by several true leaves, deeply divided and very similar to the form of the leaves of the adult plant. The seedling produces a long taproot during the first year of growth. The taproot of a 3-month seedling measures up to 6 inches (15 cm), an adaptation designed to solidly establish the water collection and water-nutrient storage capacity of the seedling before the advent of summer drought.

In nature, the seedlings often root in along the underside of large slabs of rock, where shade alleviates the heat, and where some water resources will be available throughout the summer in the form of condensed dew. Seedlings that fail to sufficiently establish their roots perish during the first summer.

The seedling turns vegetatively dormant by midsummer, in cadence with the cycling of older plants. The plant then reemerges in the midwinter in mild areas, and in the early spring in very cold areas. The main period of vegetative growth is in the early spring to early summer. In this manner, lomatium slowly establishes itself in an unfriendly environment, taking advantage of the fact that in such a place there is little or no competition from other plants. From year to year the seedling continues to store water and energy reserves in its fleshy root, which expands and resolutely pushes aside heavy sand and rocks. A thick oleo-gum-resin is produced and stored in the taproot as the plant matures, providing protection from browsers and from the dessicating heat. After two or more years of growth, the plant produces a single umbelliferous flower. As it grows and develops, lomatium may expand hugely, producing in good years multiple stems and several thousand seeds, which in turn scatter into the environment. The cycle repeats.

Perennial plants that demonstrate strong, consistent seasonal dormancy patterns often tell the story of their years by producing countable growth rings. By cross-sectioning large roots, I have discovered that plants live as long as a century, and this estimate is confirmed by Alan Adessey (Adessey, 2002). I have never seen an instance of rot or disease on a lomatium root, but very old individuals become completely woody, and in this manner eventually return to the earth (or rock, as it were).

The green seeds of lomatium are the preferred target of the seed parasitic Greya moth *(Greya subalpa)*. The little gray-winged female moth cuts and oviposits into the green fruits, and the larvae drill into and feed on the developing seeds. This moth does much damage to wild stands of the plant, and in many areas is responsible for the extremely low germination rate of naturally disseminated seed.

146

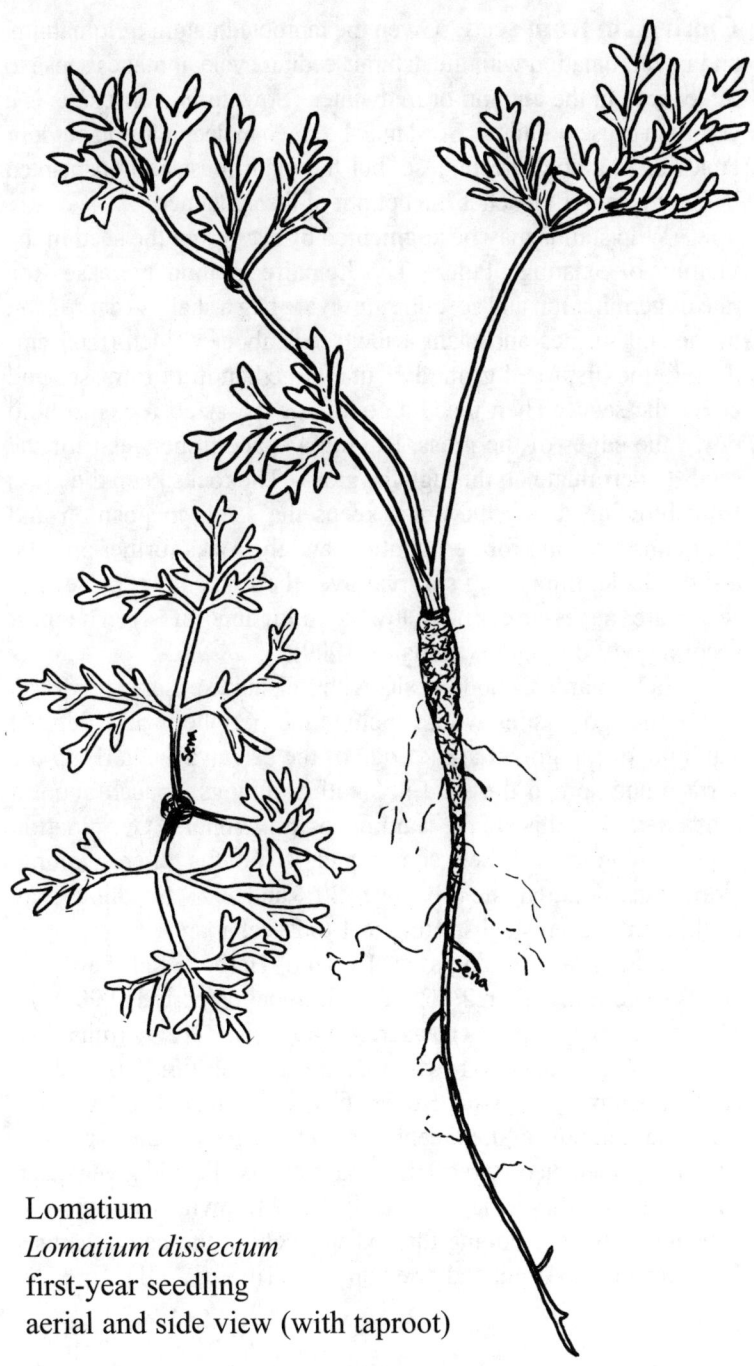

Lomatium
Lomatium dissectum
first-year seedling
aerial and side view (with taproot)

Cultivation from seed. Given the taprooted nature of lomatium, and in coordination with the natural seeding cycle, it makes sense to direct seed in the autumn or midwinter. Sowing in warm soils is a common cause of failure. Seed may be sown in deep flats on outdoor tables or in a cold greenhouse, but the plant must be transplanted before the taproot reaches the bottom of the container.

Wild stands may be augmented by scattering the seed in the vicinity of existing plants. The Lemaire method increases the rate of germination and seedling survival. Dig a shallow depression in the soil surface and plant a few seeds about ¼ inch (0.63 cm) deep in the disturbed ground. Cut a large handful of grasses and cover the seed. Then place a couple of fist-sized rocks to hold down the edges of the grass, leaving a space in between for the seeds to germinate up through the grass. The rocks keep the grass from blowing away, the grass keeps the seeds in position and maintains moisture for germination, and the rocks further provide a little shade, improving survival over the first summer. Several seeds are necessary, given low germination rates. The best seedling will dominate (Lemaire, 1999).

In the garden, choose a site with full sun exposure and dryish soil. Other good sites would include the periphery of a defunct sandpile, or the gravel at the edge of the driveway. Work up the surface and spread the seed in small groupings, spaced about a foot apart. Do this in the autumn or midwinter. Germination occurs in cold soil between 2 and 4 months after planting. Normal germination rate is between 20% and 90%. Seedlings may be thinned to a finished spacing of 1 to 2 feet apart.

Seed sown outdoors at Horizon Herbs Seed Farm on 10/10/99 germinated on 2/8/2000, a germination period of 90 days. The soil temperature was measured at 45° F (7° C) at germination.

I have tried to grow lomatium several times by taking cuttings from the crown of older plants. I planted them in the garden and in pots in the greenhouse. In every case, they sprouted tentatively, then died. Greg Tilford says "I wish I could give you an encouraging story about transplanting [crown divisions of] lomatium. We tried doing this exhaustively in the native habitat. They just bled to death and dried up . . ." (Tilford, 2001).

General care. Since lomatium thrives on abuse, there is little or no watering or fertilization required for plants in cultivation. They may require weeding during the first few years, unless they are planted in marginal areas where weeds will not grow. They may also require a side-dressing of sharp sand to simulate wild conditions, thereby increasing sun reflectivity around the plant and encouraging quick drainage away from the crown.

Yield. The fresh or dried root of lomatium is the part traditionally used. The aerial parts and especially the seeds may also have some application in medicine, an idea that is ripe for further research. Lomatium root is probably the most active antibacterial and antiviral herb indigenous to America. It is used for treating upper respiratory infection (whether caused by fungal, bacterial or viral pathogens), influenza and even hepatitis C.[1]

The average weight of a mature lomatium root is quite variable, but they can easily weigh in at 5 pounds (2.27 kg) or more (fresh weight). The average water content of the fresh root ranges between 60% and 65%. Therefore, 10 pounds of fresh root would dry down to about 4 pounds of dried root, and would be composed of only a few roots, maybe as few as 2.

Harvest, processing and storage. The cultivated root may be harvested any time during growth or dormancy. When a root is this long-lived, and filled with such pervasive latex, the tissue is unlikely to demonstrate much seasonal variation. Moore makes the sensible observation that the herb harvested earlier in the year is best for fresh extraction, while fall-harvested roots are better for drying (Moore, 1993).

---

[1] Lomatium root is a potent chemical stew, containing essential oils, gums, resins, tetronic acids and various active glycosides. Lomatium is best used at low dosage and combined with other herbs (such as dandelion) that move toxicity out of the bloodstream. Hypersensitivity to the herb, overdosage or failure to combine with mitigating companion herbs may result in the "lomatium rash" side-effect. This reaction is no fun, usually spreading in red, raised patches over sensitive areas of the body such as waistline, inner thighs or neck. Although the rash is transient and nonitchy, it is alarming, and may take weeks to resolve (even after discontinuing use of the herb).

149

Dig the cultivated roots with a bar or heavy spade, opening a wide hole around the taproot to avoid injuring it. It is difficult to extract the root without damaging it, and worth the time it takes to make sure you get as much of it as possible.

Wash the root thoroughly, removing all ingrown debris. If the root is bound for fresh extraction, it may be cut up immediately and processed. If it is bound for dehydration, then it is best set aside in a warm, dry and airy place for several days to wilt. Then, it may be sliced in 1 inch (2.54 cm) slabs. Dry the slabs by piercing them through and threading them on a string, hung high in a dry attic or convenient outbuilding. Slabs may also be dried in an herb dehydrator at the medium setting (95° F = 35° C) for a period of 2 or 3 days until they are internally dry. Dried lomatium root is oily, so no matter how long it is dehydrated, it will never feel exactly dry.

Store these aromatic pieces in plastic bags or in glass jars, in a cool room and out of the light. Packed in this manner, they retain their potency for up to 2 years. However, given the presence of oils that can become rancid with age, it is best to tincture the dried herb as soon as possible. The tincture lasts for years.

Lomatium seed is papery, oval and convex. It is bicolored, with a narrow beige wing surrounding a gray center. The dorsal surface bears 3 raised ridges, looking a little like a microscopic view of an onion cell undergoing mitosis. There are 60 seeds in 1 gram.

Seed collection, processing and storage. In insect-free areas, the seed may be allowed to ripen and dry on the umbel before collecting. The seed heads are turned upside-down into a plastic bucket or gourd and whipped against the edges until they detach. In areas heavily impacted by the Greya moth, the seed must be harvested while still green, by cutting the umbels and laying them out on sheets in the summer greenhouse or by putting them in large paper bags. They will mature and dry.

After the seed is completely dry, the small clusters of seeds may be gently broken apart by hand. Remove all foreign materials, bits of stem and especially any seeds showing insect damage.

The pure, dry seed is best stored in a closed plastic bag in the freezer. Stored in this manner the seed will remain viable for at least three years. However best results (highest germination rates and seedling vigor) are obtained by sowing the seed from the recent harvest.

Conservation status. The majority of *Lomatium dissectum* occurs in scattered patches throughout its wide range—plant groupings that have been in existence for millennia, living in broken, barely accessible, desolate country, often far away from human populations. If left undisturbed, these plants will probably remain until long after humans are gone. When I imagine a plant that could survive as long as the earth itself, it looks exactly like lomatium.

So why is the plant "at-risk," you might ask? Because when a lomatium plant is dug, it leaves a hole that cannot truly be refilled. Certainly the hole can be filled in with sand, loam, gravel and pinecones; but the plant *itself* cannot be replaced. Not for a hundred years. Maybe not for two hundred years. The security of a population of a plant like lomatium is not so much maintained by its ability to self-seed, but rather by the extended lifespan of its members. There is no such thing as sustainable harvest of wild lomatium. The plant is not renewable within our lifetime.

At the edges of its distribution, lomatium is less common. In these areas it needs full protection, with purposeful augmentation of existing populations whenever possible.

On the road between Williams and Provolt, where the steep hillside runs down almost to the chortling creek, I have for several years kept a fleeting eye on a small patch of *Lomatium dissectum.* There are three of them visible each spring—never more, never less—standing out greenly against the broken rock and oak duff of the roadbank. About the time the orchards are loaded with green apples, these plants seem to melt back into the rock. I have nearly driven into the ditch more than once, craning my neck to determine if they managed to set seed that year. On good years I am encouraged by one or more nodding umbels, heavy with their genetic load. If they can make seed here, I think, almost within reach of passersby, and yet remain invisible to almost everyone, then perhaps there is hope that lomatium everywhere will remain unnoticed by all except those who really care. May it be so.

Other species. Although *Lomatium dissectum* is considered official, an overview of the ethnographic literature brings to light several other species of *Lomatium* that have a history of use in medicine. These include *L. californicum* that was used by the Karok, Kawaiisu and Yuki tribes; *L. macrocarpum* that was used by the Thompson tribe; *L. nudicaule* that was used by the Kwakiutl and Thompson tribes; *L. nuttali* that was used by the Creek tribe; and *L. utriculatum* that was used by the Kawaiisu. These plants were used for a wide variety of purposes: cold remedies, emetics, reproductive aids, gastrointestinal medicines, febrifuges, poisons, orthopedics, etc. (Moerman, 1986). Further investigation into the utility of these species in modern herbal medicine is potentially valuable.

Among all these plants, one stands out. It is barestem biscuitroot *(Lomatium nudicaule)*. There a consistent and fairly extensive ethnographic literature documenting the use of the seeds of this plant in treating colds, rheumatism, infections, coughs—in short the same indications that are given for *L. dissectum* root (Moerman, 1986). My own experiments have shown that the plant is relatively easy to cultivate. Seeds thrown on fertile ground in the fall may germinate en masse the following spring, and well-tended plants flower dependably in the second year. Given that the seeds are a renewable plant part, and that harvesting them will not kill the plant, the possibility that the seeds of *L. nudicaule* could provide a renewable source of the same medicine normally derived from *L. dissectum* roots is at least a little bit exciting. The safety, practicality, environmental impact and economics of this potential remain to be revealed.

References

Adessey, A. 2002. Personal communication. Alan is a seed grower and wildcrafter (Wild Botanicals) who has a discerning eye for plant cycles and a long association with *Lomatium dissectum*. He served as a consultant during the writing of the "life cycle" section.

Lemaire, D. 2001. Personal communication. Darrell is a chemist living in the Great Basin. His work with lomatium includes experiments in seed germination and in situ cultivation in the natural habitat. He and others are also carrying on a long-standing tradition of saponifying and purifying lomatium root into a yellow powder that reportedly has the same effect as the raw herb, without the unwanted side effects (the rash). This product was first developed by Dr. Ernest Krebs in the early 1920s, following his observation that Native Americans survived without harm the influenza pandemic of 1917 by taking lomatium root.

Moerman, D. 1986. *Medicinal Plants of Native America.* Ann Arbor (MI): University of Michigan Department of Anthropology, Vol. 1, 534 pp.

Moore, M. 1993. *Medicinal Plants of the Pacific West.* Santa Fe (NM): Red Crane Books, 359 pp.

Tilford, G. 2001. Personal communication. Greg is herbalist/CEO of Animals Apawthecary in Hamilton, Montana. He is the author of *Edible and Medicinal Plants of the West.* The book is highly recommended, and contains a nice photograph of yellow-flowered *Lomatium dissectum.*

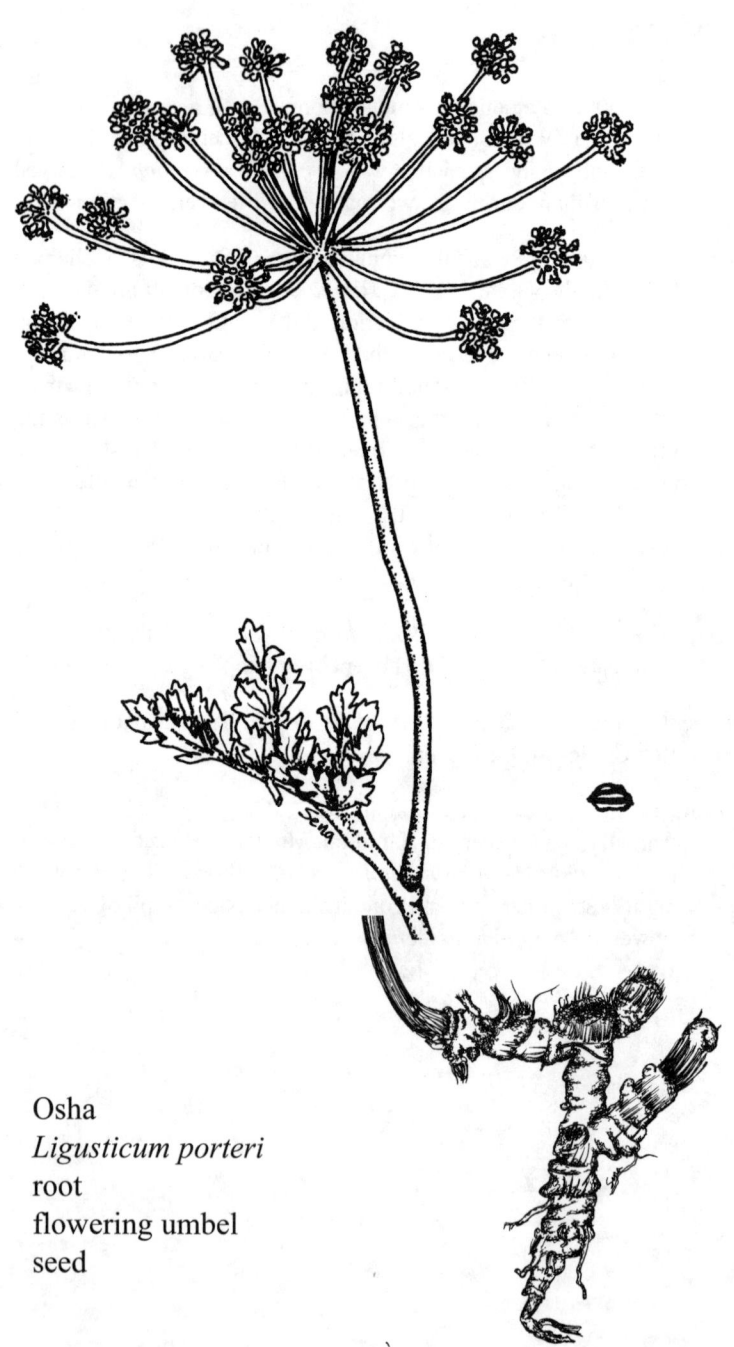

Osha
Ligusticum porteri
root
flowering umbel
seed

Osha

Ligusticum porteri L.

Family: *Apiaceae*

Ligusticum is a wide ranging genus of 11 species of lovage-like plants native to the high country of North America. Many of these aromatic herbs have been used in native herbalism, and are still in use to this day. *Ligusticum porteri* is the most famous of all, a greatly respected respiratory medicine that has gathered many names: bear medicine, Porter's lovage, licorice root, cough root and *chuchupate*. Probably the most universally recognized common name for this cross-cultural herb is "osha" (with the accent on the second syllable). In herbal vernacular the name "osha" is often used for other members of this genus (discussed here under the heading "other species"). In this book the name "osha" refers specifically to *Ligusticum porteri*.

The osha root is dark-skinned and convoluted, showing characteristic yearly growth rings below the crown, each ring rimmed with upturned, hair-like fibers that are a vestige of the leaf stems of previous years. The presence of these fibers is a feature shared by all *Ligusticum* species, helping to differentiate osha from poison hemlock *(Conium maculatum)* that sometimes shares the same habitat and is as poisonous as its name implies. Osha root is spongy, storing water during the wet season and becoming quite dessicated during drought. When broken, the root reveals its yellow interior, richly endowed with cavities and vascular bundles that are filled with yellow oil. The aroma is characteristic—intensely celery-like and smoky. Simply smelling the herb opens the respiratory passages.

The pithy crown gives rise to a basal rosette of finely divided compound leaves. Smaller leaves clasp the stems. Mature plants produce several stems that are ridged, segmented and hollow, rising to a height of 1 to 3 feet (30 to 90 cm). The largest flowers are white, flat-topped umbels occurring at the apex of the stem, with smaller flowers occurring on secondary branches. These flowers give way to the paired seeds. The aerial parts of the plant (including the seeds) smell very pleasantly like celery.

Range, hardiness and adaptability. Osha occupies high elevation sites, mainly in the central and southern Rocky Mountain Range, extending from southern Montana to the states of Sonora and Chihuahua in Mexico. The plant also occurs sporadically in southern Idaho, Utah and Arizona. The areas of highest concentration include the Bighorn Mountains of Montana and Wyoming, the Wind River Range of Wyoming, the *Sangre de Cristo* and *San Juan* mountains of southern Colorado and northern New Mexico and the *Sierra Madre Occidental* of northern Mexico (Moore, 1993).

Osha demonstrates a strong winter dormancy and is not injured by cold winters. In nature, it often experiences nighttime frost *during* the growth cycle. However, this does not necessarily mean that the plant will adapt to cultivation at low elevation sites, even in cold winter areas. In the wild, true osha is not seen at elevations under 7,000 feet (~2,135 m). It is difficult to determine what combination of high-altitude factors—whether it be the intensity of the alpine sun, the low oxygen content of the atmosphere, the temperature and purity of the water or the composition of the rocks and soils—is most directly responsible for the health of these plants at altitude, and may in turn present limiting factors for their adaptation to lower elevation sites.

Current Range of *Ligusticum porteri* in the U.S.

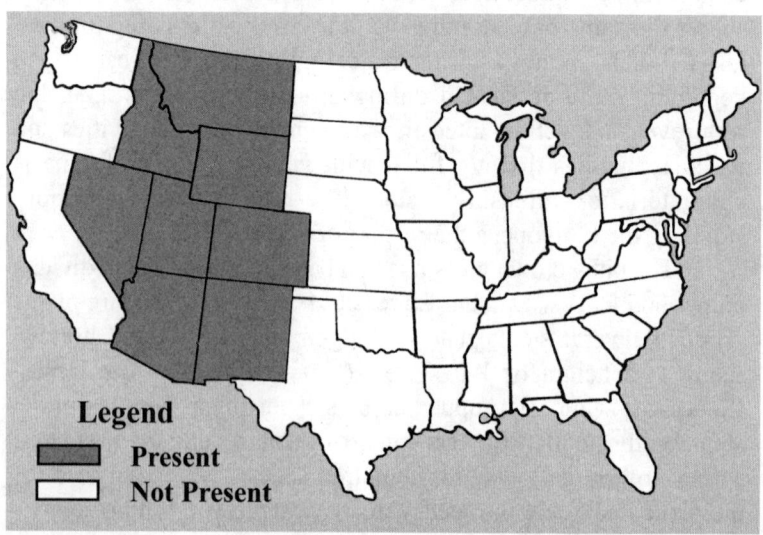

Legend
- ▨ Present
- ☐ Not Present

Growing osha at elevation in the western states will probably give the best results. Other potential areas would be higher
elevation sites in the east, especially in localities where other
Ligusticum species already grow. Attempting cultivation at low
elevation gardens in the Great Plains, Louisiana and Florida,
where no *Ligusticum* is found, is not likely to give good results.
However, given the combination of some small altitude (perhaps
a minimum of 1,000 feet = 305 m), a partially shaded and moist
site and a typical mountain seasonal cycle (cold in winter, moist
in spring and dry in summer, with cold nights), my experiments
indicate that domestication of osha is quite possible.

Ecology and plant community. Osha occurs most abundantly
in moist, subalpine areas (9,500 to 11,500 feet = 2,895 to 3,505 m),
a region dominated by mature stands of spruce, Douglas fir and
aspen. Osha prefers the aspen groves. In this habitat, the plant
grows in luxuriant patches in the partial shade. Water is supplied
from melting snow, and is consistently available throughout the
short growing season (usually May to August).

Aspen is a shallow-rooted tree that effectively builds soil and
prevents erosion, creating deep soil pockets in the rocky landscape.
The understory in aspen stands is generally dominated by tall,
perennial herbs and not grasses (Langenheim, 1962). Plants
occurring in common association with osha in such areas are cow
parsnip *(Heracleum* spp.), meadow rue *(Thalictrum fendleri),* aspen
sunflower *(Helianthella quinquinervis)* and delphinium *(Delphinium
barbeyi)* (Rivas, 1999). Other medicinal plants that may be found in
the general region preferred by osha would be likely to include
angelica *(Angelica grayi),* arnica *(Arnica* spp.), green gentian
(Frasera speciosa) and valerian *(Valeriana edulis).*

Osha also occurs in montane habitat (7,000 to 9,000 feet = 2,135
to 2,745 m) that is dominated by ponderosa pine, Douglas fir and aspen
forests. Here it may be found in association with toxic look-alike
poison hemlock *(Conium maculatum).* In marginal areas, patches of
osha will often be of smaller size or the plant may occur singly. Osha
will sometimes survive in a more open exposure. I have encountered
dried seed heads on stalks emerging from thin duff against dry,
limestone cliffs at 9,000 feet in the Sandia Mountains, New Mexico.

Life cycle. Osha plants begin to emerge during the spring thaw, running rapidly to flower in the early alpine summer (usually during the month of June). Cold-tolerance, rapid growth and early maturation of seed are traits that assure survival of alpine plants. By late August, the foliage of the plant turns bright yellow, and the seed heads are fully formed. Much magic and mystery has been woven around the story of how osha replicates in the wild, but in truth the cycle of seed maturation, dissemination, over-wintering and germination in the following spring is typical for high altitude species. There is little evidence to suggest that the seed must remain in contact with the radiating stems of the seed head in order to germinate, although in nature the umbel may bend over and present the seed to the earth in a cogent grouping. Furthermore, germination tests in controlled conditions have shown that the orientation of the individuated seed has little or no affect on germination (Cech, 2000). Dissemination occurs as the seed head shatters in the fall, midwinter or very early spring. Melting snow, the movements of mammals and wind are respon-sible for spreading the seed to a distance. The fact that much seed germinates in close proximity to the parent is partially responsi-ble for the patch-like growth habit of osha. Germination occurs in cold soils, but is inhibited by freezing temperatures. Recorded rates of emergence indicate that the germination period is around 12 weeks at 42° F (5.5° C) (Cech, 2000) and may be reduced to 6 weeks if the soil temperature is slightly warmer (50° F = 10° C) (Sigstedt, 2000).

Osha is a long-lived plant, but the maximum life expectancy has not been accurately established. Osha roots grown at Horizon Herbs Seed Farm averaged only 10 grams fresh weight after the second year, indicating a very slow-growing plant. Examination of the growth rings of older plants in the wild indicates that they live for at least 16 years. However, when an osha root matures, the root system often convolutes and presents multiple crowns. On an old plant, it is difficult to disprove the possibility that the original crown has rotted away, the plant living on by relying on newer growth. Native Americans respect "bear medicine" as if it were an elder, and science can do little to disprove the possibility that osha lives for many decades.

Cultivation from seed. Sow newly harvested and dried osha seed in the fall, midwinter or early spring, outdoors in the shade garden, in shaded nursery beds or in deep flats. I have found that the seed germinates most reliably if the soil is amended with organic compost and especially peat moss. Good drainage is not necessary. Make a shallow furrow about ¼ inch (0.64 cm) deep, sprinkle the seed sparingly, cover with soil and tamp firmly. Natural rainfall and snowfall will leach out germination-inhibiting compounds. The seed will germinate as the soil warms slightly in the spring, in conjunction with the oscillating temperatures caused by sunny days and cold nights. Under these conditions, and barring natural or unnatural disasters, the expected germination rate of recent seed is 70%. However, the seed does not germinate all at once. Rather, it takes several weeks to complete the first flush of germination. Some seed may remain dormant to germinate a year later. Germination is epigeal, with 2 seed leaves followed by the first, deeply divided true leaves within a few weeks.

Alternatively, the seed may be sown in deep flats in a cold greenhouse in the late fall or winter. The disadvantage of this method is that the flats will have to be hand-watered. Given the lack of natural, leaching precipitation, residual germination-inhibiting compounds may delay germination or give a low germination percentage. However, cultivating in the greenhouse makes it easier to protect the seed against birds, rodents, and (if you have a tight door on the greenhouse) cats.

Osha *(Ligusticum porteri)* germination

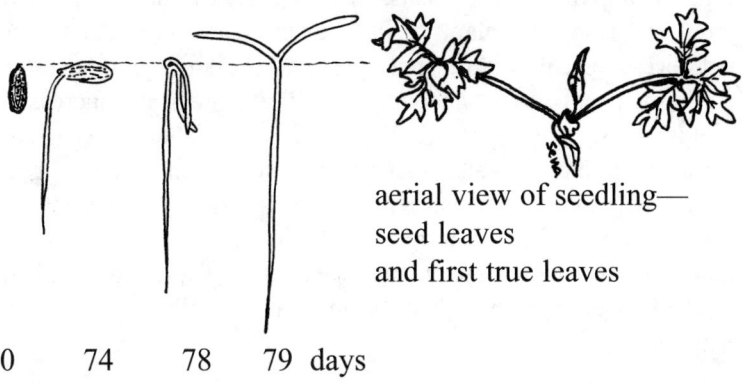

aerial view of seedling—
seed leaves
and first true leaves

0   74   78   79 days

Normally, taprooted plants do not transplant very well, but osha transplants without difficulty. This may be attributed to the structure of the root of the osha seedling, which consists not only of a stubby taproot, but also a myriad of branching feeder roots that emanate from the taproot and from the crown. When the plant finds itself in rocky quarters, the taproot predominates, delving deep after water and nutrients. When the plant finds itself in heavy, moist soils, then roots are developed closer to the surface, collecting nutrients at the interface of the mineral soil and the living mulch of the forest floor.

Plants direct-seeded in the shade garden may be thinned to about 12 inches (30 cm) apart. Once they set their first true leaves, seedlings may be barerooted and transplanted to the shade garden or into deep pots. Growing the plants in pots for one or two years before transplanting is actually recommended, due to the slow growth of the plant during the early years. It is generally easier to coddle them along in pots than it is to keep the small plants weeded, and seedlings transplant to their final location more dependably if they are older and in a ball of soil. Suitable potting soil for osha is slightly acid (pH ~6.5) and rich in humus. Osha thrives in our shadehouse, which is covered in 66% shade cloth and watered from above with misters.

General care. The same factors that encourage healthy growth of seedlings (ie. fertile soil, partial shade and constant moisture) also apply to the growing plant. Garden beds located at elevation, in moist areas under the shade of conifers, alders or aspen will give the best results. If the summer turns hot and dry, then watering the plants will prevent early dormancy. A side-dressing of composted manure, organic compost or composted leaves will encourage healthy growth and increased yields. Once the plants are truly established, they will demonstrate much greater tolerance for drought and full sunlight. To a certain extent, these stress factors will also have a bearing on the production of active compounds within the root. Therefore, it makes sense to give the young plants lots of attention, and to gradually remove the plants from human influence as they naturalize and mature.

Cultivation from crown division. Although some harvesters report success with replanting cuttings in the wild (Enos, 1999), others report that "crown divisions transplanted to the site of the original plant quickly rotted" (Tilford, 2001). Crown cuttings of taprooted plants generally fail unless they include enough feeder roots to keep the cutting alive. The stressed plant may eventually produce new roots and aerial parts, and a balanced plant may result after a year or two of growth. An examination of the crowns of mature osha roots does not give much confidence that they will make effective divisions—at this stage they are generally bare of feeder roots. However, more study into the potential of this methodology in creating viable clones as a positive spinoff of harvest activities is definitely warranted.

Yield. The dried root of osha is the part traditionally used in herbal medicine for treating upper respiratory infection, sore throat and cough. Taking osha in quantity will cause copious sweating and elimination of toxins. It is the herb of choice for smokers with compromised mucous membranes of throat, bronchi and lungs.

The average weight of a mature osha root is extremely difficult to gauge. There is a vast range of root size depending on growing conditions and the age of the plant. When digging, it may be difficult to determine where the root system of one plant stops and another begins. Similarly, in examining a commercial shipment of osha roots (consisting of broken pieces and crowns), it is difficult to determine how many plants are represented. Average wild-harvested roots probably exceed 50 grams dry weight.

The average water content of osha root is also difficult to gauge, due to the fact that the root absorbs water like a sponge, and dehydrates like a sponge if there is no water to be had. A small voucher specimen weighed 65 grams fresh weight and dried down to 40.5 grams, indicating a water content of 38%.

The dried leaf and especially the seeds of osha are used as a flavoring agent and carminative. Actually, seeds of many plants fix and concentrate the same compounds found in the rest of the plant (e.g. angelica, burdock and motherwort). This is also true of osha, as chewing the seed has a positive respiratory effect as well as a digestive influence. More study into the chemistry of osha seed in comparison to the root may bring to light the possibility of using the renewably harvested seed as a substitute for the root. The plant is a copious seed producer.

Harvest, processing and storage. By the time osha plants produce large rosettes with several flowering stalks, they are sufficiently mature to harvest. The root is usually dug when the leaves turn golden (in the fall, after the maturation of the seeds). Tools of choice are a sturdy spade, garden fork and/or digging bar, depending on how many rocks and tree roots are likely to be encountered.

Traditionally, the roots are kept as entire as possible during digging. They are then washed, and dried in the sun. Care is taken to turn the roots to promote even drying, and they are protected from rain and from dew. An herb dehydrator is very helpful in drying osha root. Dry for 1 day at low temperature (70° F = 21° C) and high air flow, then turn up the temperature to medium (95° F = 35° C) and dry them until they snap, making certain that the larger pieces are dehydrated all the way through. Once they are thoroughly dry, the roots may be consolidated for storage by breaking into pieces. One of my favorite "herbal tricks" is to bisect a dry osha root with a pair of snips, then squeeze the face of the cut with the snips and observe the yellow oil pouring from the vascular system. This is also a bench test for determining the quality of the dried roots (the more they bleed, the better; if they do not bleed, they are not much good). Osha is best stored in glass jars or plastic bags in lightproof sacks or drums, in a cool, dark and dry location. Stored in this manner, they maintain useful potency for many years.[1]

---

[1] In 1998, Margaret and Bryce Patterson discovered a bundle of dried leather containing roots and basketry materials. The bundle had been cached in antiquity by a Native American under a rock ledge in the Book Cliffs of southern Utah, and was subsequently dated by C-14 analysis to 400 to 600 years before the present. An herbal practitioner named Merry Lycett Harrison further investigated the bundle contents and painstakingly identified the plants that were represented. One herb was easily recognizable, though, due to the characteristic leaf fibers ringing the crown. It was osha. After reading the report of this research, I was left with only one question. After 600 years, was the osha still good? (Harrison, 2000).

Osha seed is golden brown when fresh, aging to reddish-brown. The seeds are boat-shaped, with 1 central ridge on the ventral surface and 3 prominent, raised ridges on the dorsal surface. The seed measures about 6 mm long and about 3 mm wide. In 1 gram of ripe, plump osha seeds there are about 300 seeds. Poor quality, under nourished seed may contain as many as 600 seeds per gram.

Seed collection, processing and storage. Osha seed is best harvested when it is completely mature and dry on the umbel. At this stage the seed is easily detached by hand-rubbing or by inverting the seed head into a plastic bucket or gourd, and whipping against the sides. Further dehydration is usually not necessary.

However, if the seed is slightly green, or if it is collected during a time of atmospheric dampness, then it will have to be dried. Spread the seed on screens or cloth, in a warm, dark and airy place, and stir often until it is thoroughly dry to the touch. Drying temperatures must not exceed 90° F (32° C).

The seed may be further processed to purity by picking out fragments of leaf and stem by hand, and by screening (to remove immature seeds, small debris and dust). Wind-winnowing will also help separate the plump, viable seed from empty seed coats, and will also rid the seed of light debris and dust. The cleaned seed is best stored in plastic bags or glass jars in a cool, dark and dry location. Normal seed life is one to two years, but best results will be obtained by sowing the seed within a few months of harvest.

Conservation status: At this writing, the Federal Department of Fish and Wildlife is considering *Ligusticum porteri* for a CITES, Appendix II classification (Federal Register/Vol. 66, No.113/ Tuesday, June 12, 2001). Such a classification would prohibit export of osha plants and dried roots. However, osha is a strictly regional herb, consumed almost exclusively by Americans and by Mexicans. There is something vaguely inappropriate about any ruling that would disallow export of osha to a Tarahumara Indian in northern Mexico (a native person who has used osha as part of an intact herbal tradition that stretches back into antiquity), but sets no restriction on the inclusion of osha as an ingredient in a cough medicine produced by a domestic herbal product manufacturer for sale to the public.

This would not be an issue if the mountains of northern Mexico were well-endowed with native osha, but in actuality there has been a longstanding flow of osha trade from the southern Rockies (where osha is more abundant) across the border to Mexico (where the herb is less abundant, and in greater demand). In Mexico, native stands are depleted from overharvest, and populations suffer when forests are cleared and arroyo heads erode. Cultivation of *chuchupate* is a priority among native interest groups, although there will be many horticultural hurdles to leap before the first viable alpine plantations are established (Felger, 2002).

Osha is not listed as a protected species by either state or federal government, although populations in state and national parks may benefit from park policy that disallows removal of natural resources. In many wild and relatively inaccessible places, osha has been left alone, and there it thrives. But osha is loosing ground in other areas where it was once abundant. According to a recent survey, 28,500 pounds of dried osha roots (equivalent to approximately 259,000 plants) were harvested from the wild during the years 1997 to 1999 for use by domestic herb companies. The quantity of trade is "increasing significantly" (McGuffin, 2001). It makes sense to protect remaining wild populations of this herb. By unlocking the secrets of cultivating osha, we can assure that bear medicine will continue to be available as an integral part of an intact tradition of herbal use that stretches from olden times through the present age and into the future.

Other species. Most of the 11 species of *Ligusticum* native to North America have been used in native medicine for treating gastric complaints and upper respiratory infection.[2] Given the botanical and medicinal similarity of all these plants, many herbalists lump them together as (basically) the same herb, and use them interchangeably. So the conservation of osha really involves assuring the sustainability of wild populations of *all* members of the *Ligusticum* family.

---

[2] A survey of the ethnographic literature reveals early accounts of the use of *Ligusticum apiifolium, L. filicinum, L. porteri* and *L. scoticum* by native peoples (Moerman, 1986). *L. californicum, L. grayi* and *L. canbyi* are sometimes used in the sweat and in the peyote ceremonies.

Canby's licorice root *(Ligusticum canbyi)* is found in montane habitats in the northern Rocky Mountains of Montana and Wyoming, ranging across to the Blue Mountains of Oregon and Washington. It is strongly taprooted, not convoluted like *L. porteri.* Native and current uses of this plant are synonymous with those of osha (Tilford, 2001).

Gray's licorice root *(Ligusticum grayi)* grows at elevations as low as 2,000 feet (610 m), occurring sporadically in Montana, Idaho, Washington and Nevada, but most abundantly in the Cascade, Coastal and Siskiyou Mountain ranges of Oregon, and the Sierra Nevada range of California. The plant is perhaps better known by its native name "kishwoof." Like *L. canbyi,* this plant is strongly taprooted, and the root is intensely aromatic and warming in its effect. Kishwoof generally occurs singly or in sparse patches in association with conifers, rooting into soil pockets on the mountainside or soils wetted by snowmelt in the highland meadows (Hobbs, 2002).

Other species native to the western states include *L. apiifolium, L. filicinum* and *L. tenuifolium.* Species that occur in western Canada and Alaska include *L. calderi, L. scoticum* and *L. verticillatum.* Species that occur in the eastern states include *L. canadense* and *L. scoticum.* These various plants have adapted to local conditions, and they demonstrate a preference for specific altitudes. This diversity is actually an advantage for those who live in the mountains and choose to cultivate *Ligusticum*—the local plant will grow best in local gardens.

Gardeners who live at sea level or in the great plains, or those who are daunted by the task of domesticating a wild plant like osha have a good alternative. I would suggest cultivating simple lovage *(Levisticum officinale)* instead. The plant is easy to grow from seed and adapts readily to lowland gardens. If you dig a fresh root from this fast-growing and forgiving plant, and hold a little in your mouth, it does not take a creative imagination to taste—osha.

References

Cech, R. 1999. *New Findings on Germination of Osha.* United Plant Savers Newsletter, Vol. 3(2), p. 23.

Enos, T. 1999. *Another Perspective on Osha.* United Plant Savers Newsletter, Vol. 2(1), p. 16.

Felger, R. 2002. *The Apachian/Madrean Region of Southwestern North America.* Tucson (AZ): Drylands Institute. http://nmnhwww.si.edu/botany/centres/apachmad.htm

Harrison, M. 2000. *The Botanical Parts of the Patterson Bundle.* Salt Lake City (UT): Utah Native Plant Society.

Hobbs, C. 2001. *Bioregional Herbalism: Healing Plants of the Western U.S.* Journal of Medicinal Plant Conservation, Fall.

Langenheim, J. 1962. *Vegetation and Environmental Patterns in the Crested Butte Area, Gunnison County, Colorado.* Ecological Monographs, 32, pp. 249-285.

McGuffin, M. 2001. *AHPA's Tonnage Survey Results.* United Plant Savers Bulletin.

Moerman, D. 1986. *Medicinal Plants of Native America.* Ann Arbor (MI): University of Michigan Department of Anthropology, Vol. 1, 534 pp.

Moore, M. 1993. *Medicinal Plants of the Pacific West.* Santa Fe (NM): Red Crane Books, 359 pp.

Rivas-Martínez, Sánchez-Mata and Costa. 1999. *North American Boreal and Western Temperate Forest Vegetation: Syntaxonomical Synopsis of the Potential Natural Plant Communities of North America, II.* Itinera Geobotanica, 12, pp. 3-311.

Sigstedt, S. 2000. Personal communication. Shawn lives on a ranch near Steamboat Springs, Colorado. He has dedicated himself for decades to the study and conservation of osha, and served as a consultant for the "life cycle" section.

Tilford, G. 2001. Personal communication. Greg is herbalist/CEO of Animals Apawthecary in Hamilton, Montana. He is the author of *Edible and Medicinal Plants of the West.* The book includes excellent photos of *Ligusticum canbyi* flowering umbel, root and leaf.

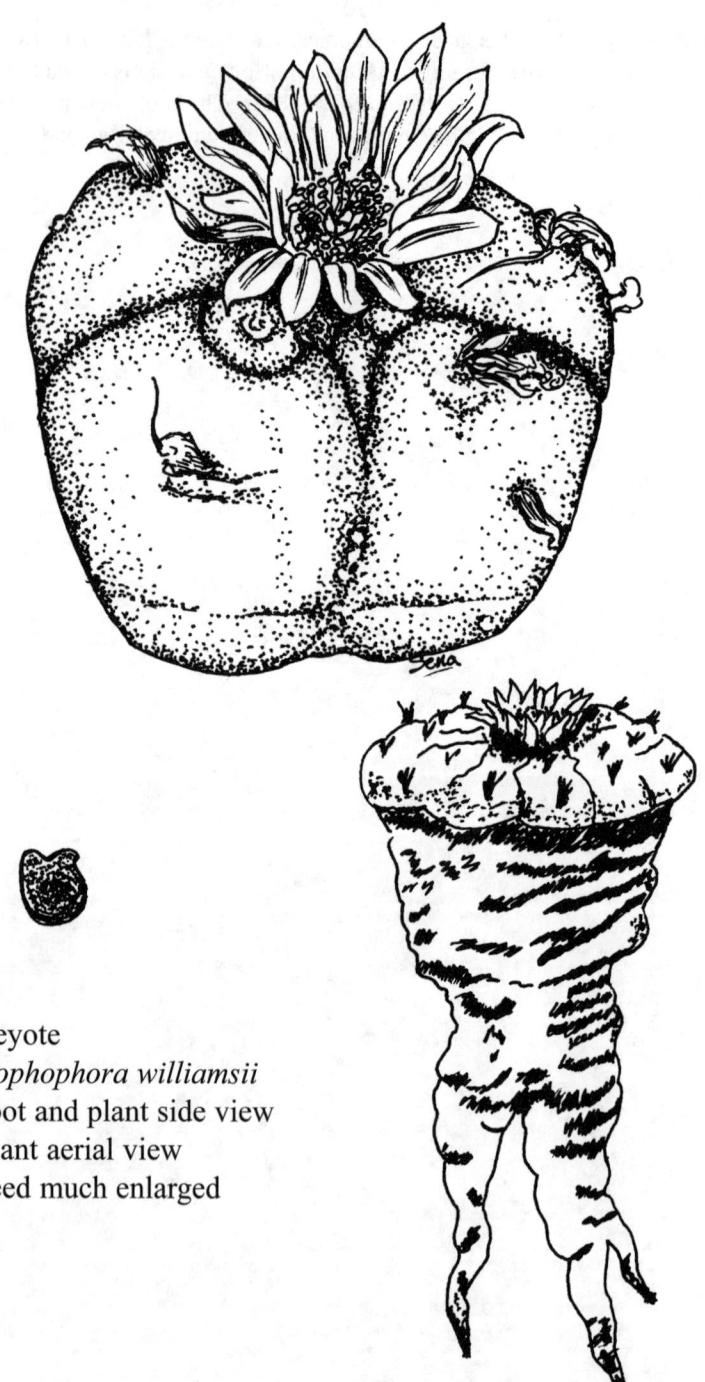

Peyote
Lophophora williamsii
root and plant side view
plant aerial view
seed much enlarged

Peyote

Lophophora williamsii

(Lem. ex Salm-Dyck) Coult.

Family: *Cactaceae*

Peyote is a long-lived cactus native to the Rio Grande Valley of southern Texas and the Chihuahuan Desert of northern Mexico. This blue-green, waxy-skinned succulent settles like a fat hen on a nest, atop a branching taproot that resembles the root of a giant molar. The root is conical and horizontally fissured, actually comprising a greater proportion of the mass of the plant than the aerial part . The root generally gives rise to one cactus, but with great age or as a response to harvest or other injury, a single root may support a poly-headed colony. The plant is composed of a leafless, thickened stem, evolved over millennia as a response to arid conditions. By dint of its reduced surface area, and by controlling the opening and closing of the many microscopic stomata that occur on its surface, peyote has the ability to regulate transpiration. The plant can store water for long periods of time, thereby preventing complete desiccation. During drought periods the aerial part shrinks and flattens. During times of rain the cactus becomes more succulent—swollen and rounded. Older individuals attain a diameter of 3 inches (~8 cm) or more. This ability to expand is enhanced by the morphology of the cactus itself, which is composed of accordion-like, vertical ribs (tubercles) that are fused into the shape of a button, the part used in medicine and ceremony. Young plants usually consist of 4 ribs; older plants may exhibit 14 ribs or more, and in this there is a wide range of variation. Each mature tubercle is topped by a bud-like feature (known as the areole) that gives rise to a wooly tuft of hair which is characteristic of peyote. The lack of spines differentiates peyote from other cactus look-alikes. The flower arises from within an apical depression in the center of the plant, with scale-like sepals ringing the larger inner petals that are colored light pink or perfectly white. The sweet fruit of peyote is red and club-shaped. The seeds are black, about the size of poppy seeds, with a concave, whitish hilum. Under magnification the seeds reveal their warty surface (Anderson, 1980).

Range, hardiness and adaptability. Peyote is native to the Mustang Plains of south Texas and the Chihuahuan Desert of northern Mexico. The area of distribution covers more than 60,000 square miles (150,000 km). The plant occurs at elevations ranging from the Rio Grande Valley (slightly greater than sea level) to a maximum height of 6,000 feet (1,830 m) at the southernmost extent of its range in the state of *San Luis Potosi* (Rzedowski, 1978).

Peyote prefers temperatures ranging from 45° to 100° F (7° to 38° C). During dormancy, if the soil is very dry, the plant may survive temperatures as low as 30° F (-1° C), but it will not tolerate freezing weather during the growth cycle or in conjunction with wet weather. Many sacred and/or specimen plants have been cultivated at Native American churches, university botanical gardens and private homes in the temperate North. The plants adapt very well to culture in pots or specialized greenhouses, as long as they are kept well-lighted and warm during the summer. During the winter dormancy the plants are best kept quite dry and must also be protected from freezing.

Current Range of Peyote in the U.S. and Mexico
(Lophophora williamsii and *L. diffusa)*

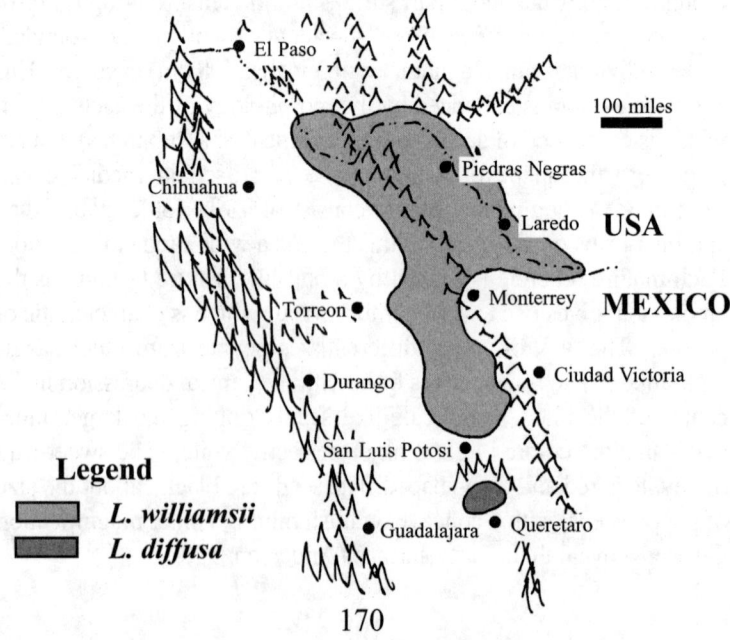

Ecology and plant community. The Chihuahuan drylands are considered a "warm to temperate" desert, encompassing a fairly wide range of soil types, rainfall patterns and vegetative covers (Rzedowski, 1978).

Peyote grows in alkaline soils. Preferred habitats include: silty flood plains, fissures between rocks on cliffs, low hills, the foothills of mountains and elevated plains. Typical desert soils are limestone-derived and rich in calcium, with a pH ranging between 7.5 and 8.5.

In Peyote habitat rain falls mainly during the spring and summer monsoons, and yearly rainfall may vary widely between 7 to 22 inches (18 to 60 cm). Rainfall during the warm months is beneficial, while rainfall and cold temperatures during the winter dormancy of the plant are not very well-tolerated.

Peyote occurs most frequently under the shade of neighboring shrubs and cacti, although it can also grow in the full sun. The main companion plant associated with peyote is actually another potent medicinal—chaparral *(Larrea tridentata)*. However, not all chaparral will harbor peyote, and peyote also is found *away* from chaparral. Chaparral itself does not fully cover the peyote regions, as it is a plant that tends to band its growth along specific boundaries of elevation and soil type. Mesquite *(Prosopis laevigata)* and various *Acacia* species are also frequent associates (Anderson, 1969). All of these plants serve a nursery-like function for young and developing peyote—shading it, providing physical protection and improving the soil with a thin mulch that is rich in carbon and nitrogen.

This detritus balances the pH of the soil substrate, improving nutrient assimilation to the cacti by "unbinding" nitrogen once locked in the soil in an alkaline death grip. This nitrogen stimulates development of the seedling, improving overall health and vigor. Nitrogenous compounds become the basis for the production of bitter alkaloids. These alkaloids provide protection from browsing or gnawing vertebrates. They are also involved in the medicinal activity of the plant, as well as its entheogenic effects. Mescaline, which is the main psychoactive alkaloid found in the plant, occurs at a level of 3% to 6%. Once the plant matures, the alkaloid concentrations slowly increase, especially in response to stress or prolonged dehydration (Gottlieb, 1997; Schultes, 1980).

Other frequent associates are the large, rosette-forming plants like agave and yucca. Agave is the source of an alcoholic beverage known as "mescal," and yucca is an incredibly useful medicinal and fibre plant. Other cacti, including *Echinocereus, Echinocactus, Mammillaria* and *Flourensia* also occupy the same environs (Anderson, 1969). These provide some mutual protection and shade, but they are mainly cohabitants, not symbionts. To a certain extent they may compete for available resources, including water, nutrients and elbow room.

Life cycle. The adult peyote cactus flowers throughout the summer, and is fertilized as pollen transfers from stamen to stigma, assisted by the activities of flies, ants and wind. The plant may self-pollinate or outcross, but seed production, seed fertility and genetic diversity is enhanced when cross-pollination occurs. The following year, the fertilized ovule quickly elongates into a red, club-shaped fruit that bears in its upper portion up to 30 rough, black seeds. As the fruit matures, dries, and deteriorates, the seeds drop into the apical cavity that once held the flower. Most are buried within a mass of wooly fuzz, but some are disseminated by gravity, ants and wind. During the subsequent rainy season, this cavity may flood, thereby washing seeds out into the environment. Seeds germinate immediately, or they may remain dormant until conditions are favorable. Germination usually occurs during rainy periods in the spring and summer, and is enhanced by high atmospheric humidity. Germination is epigeal, although the emergent seed leaves are fused together, and so small as to be nearly invisible. The small seedling benefits greatly from shade and humus provided by associated shrubs. The seedlings are spiny, but as the plant matures these spines give way to the wooly tufts. Often during the first few years of growth, aerial development is delayed as the plant puts much energy into establishing the necessarily deep and resilient taproot that is its true strength. Development is extremely slow. A four-year-old seedling is as small as a dime. In nature the plant takes about 13 years to reach maturity. Given this slow growth, as well as the preservative effects of the desert climate, I estimate that mature individuals live for a century or more.

Cultivation disclaimer. Cultivation of peyote cactus in the United States is currently an illegal practice. Cultivation in other countries may also be illegal; or it may be legal or unregulated. In the U.S., even plants grown in highly esteemed botanical gardens, as well as dried voucher specimens in university herbaria are considered technically illegal. Federal law prohibits possession of peyote except by persons who are both members of the Native American Church and can prove at least 25% Native American ancestry. Wild peyote is legally harvested and traded by "peyoteros" that are licensed by the Texas Department of Public Safety and the Federal Drug Enforcement Agency (DEA). However, there is no legal provision made for cultivating the plant inside the U.S. (a singularly nonecological stance). *The following information is provided for use by individuals in countries where peyote cultivation is legal, and should not be construed to condone, recommend or instruct illegal cultivation of the plant. United Plant Savers and the author accept no responsibility for the use or misuse of any information contained in this book.*

Cultivation from seed. Peyote normally germinates in nature during the spring and summer, and successful seeding of the plant in cultivation follows the same seasonal pattern. This allows the seedling to establish itself before the winter dormancy, when the growth medium is allowed to go dry. Peyote also germinates in response to humid atmospheric conditions, and for this reason the seeds are best started in a greenhouse or in a smaller plastic germinating chamber such as a tented flat or a pot covered with plastic.

Potting soil for germination and subsequent growth of peyote must be a coarse medium that drains with exceeding rapidity. The best starting material is "coarse sharp sand." This can be purchased from a nursery supply store, or it can be made at home from sand purchased by the truckload from a local quarry. The fine sand and silt that prevent rapid drainage in regular sand must be removed by wet screening. Introduce a small amount of regular sand into a hand sieve or wooden framed screen. The screen needs to have at most 17 strands per inch (~7 strands per cm) in order to create a sufficiently coarse product. Immerse the screen in water and agitate. The fine sand and silt will go through the screen and wash away, leaving the coarse sharp sand behind. A fine table screen may also be used. In this case, several shovelfuls of sand are put on the screen, and the fine sand and silt is washed out with a pressure hose. Regardless of your method of separation, the finished product is very coarse sand that will not pass through the screen mesh. This material serves as a basis for growing most desert plants (e.g. chaparral, datura, maravilla and Mormon tea). Good drainage promotes fast drying of the surface, which protects the plant from fungal infection and rot.

Many peyote growers agree that coarse sharp sand should make up the majority of the potting soil, but individual recipes vary hugely, reflecting both the diversity of the localities where the plant is found, and the fact that the plant itself has a tolerance for a wide range of substrates. A pH value ranging from 6.5 to 7.2 is recommended. Potting soils are not usually fertilized, as most growers prefer to give liquid fertilizer at the same time as watering.

Recipe 1: 100% coarse sharp sand

Recipe 2: ⅔ coarse sharp sand and ⅓ peat

Recipe 3: equal parts coarse sharp sand, perlite and peat

Recipe 4: ⅔ coarse sharp sand and ⅓ leaf mold

Recipe 5: ⅔ coarse sharp sand and ⅓ crushed limestone

Recipe 6: ⅔ "limestone soil" and ⅓ gypsum (crushed drywall)

Recipe 7: 100% gypsum (crushed drywall)

Recipe 8: equal parts coarse sharp sand, crushed limestone and desert soil

Recipe 9: commercial potting soil for cacti

Seeds are planted very near the surface of the medium and tamped in. The propagation flat, pot or growing bed is kept evenly moist and in a humid environment. The temperature may fluctuate slightly, but a good target temperature is 80° F (27° C).

174

Germination occurs between 3 and 21 days after sowing the seed. The seedlings may be left at close spacing for 1 or 2 years, at which time they may be transplanted to a finished spacing of 4 to 6 inches (~10 to 15 cm) apart. A typical grouping is 4 plants in a gallon pot.

Seedlings prefer partial shade conditions and long daylight hours. This may be accomplished by covering a solar greenhouse with 30% to 50% shade cloth. Many growers keep the plants indoors, training fluorescent grow lamps on the cacti for 13 to 14 hours per day. Small-scale cultivation is sometimes effectively carried out on a sunny windowsill.

Peyote grows faster if watered on a regular schedule. However, the surface of the growing medium must be allowed to go completely dry between waterings. In order to avoid over-watering, some growers water with a spray bottle, wetting the cactus and the soil surface only. During hot weather, the seedlings may be watered as often as twice per week.

Liquid fertilizer is best given once every month during the growing season. The best fertilizer for this application is probably a liquid seaweed preparation. This can be made at home by mixing ⅓ cup of ground, dried kelp in a gallon of water, agitating and allowing it to sit overnight before use. Or liquid seaweed can be purchased by the gallon from a nursery supply store. Fertilizer must be used at a very low concentration—dilute to 25% of label recommendations.

General care. Peyote has a long taproot, so the growing bed or pot needs to be at least 8 inches (~20 cm) deep. The bottom of the pot is layered with coarse gravel and charcoal. The surface of the soil can be covered with ¼ inch (0.6 cm) of aquarium gravel or coarse pumice, which helps keep the crown dry. Like the soil prepared for germinating the seedling, the soil provided for the growing plant must be coarse-structured so that it drains very rapidly. Besides coarse sharp sand, other additives such as ground limestone, aquarium gravel, coarse pumice and perlite are recommended. As long as these coarse materials predominate, it is a good idea to also include carbon-rich ingredients (organic compost, leaf mold, loamy soil and/or peat moss) in the mix. This will provide the plants with nutrients and a more substantial soil structure.

Growing plants, like the seedlings, are best watered regularly during the hot months of the year, and fertilized on a monthly basis. Too much water, too much fertilizer and in general too much attention will have negative effects. The plants should be ignored and allowed to stress occasionally, in order to help build resistance to pathogenic organisms (especially mold) and to encourage root development.

During the winter months, the plants must be allowed to dry out completely. Fertilization is discontinued. Above all, the dormant peyote requires protection from freezing weather. In desert climates, it may be possible to leave the cacti outdoors and completely dry. In mellow temperate climates, an unheated and unwatered solar greenhouse may provide adequate protection. In cold winter areas, the plants must be maintained in a heated greenhouse, or they may be brought indoors, to be left alone until spring again calls them into activity.

Cultivation from lateral offshoots. Mature peyote may produce small, clonal individuals from the lateral areoles. These are known as "pups." When fully formed, the pups may be broken off from the mother, then allowed to sit in the open air for several weeks in order to form a callus. The callus is a hard cuticle that forms over the raw surface, protecting the cactus from dehydration, protecting the damaged tissues from mold and preparing the area for the emergence of new roots. Once callused, the pups may be settled into the potting soil, and they will eventually form a taproot. Many propagators simply leave the pups (unplanted) on the surface of the growth medium until aerial roots begin to emerge (which may take as long as a year). Then, the cactus is settled into the surface of the potting soil, with the root pointing down. Watering is minimized until the root system becomes well-established.

Grafting. The growth of peyote cactus may be enhanced by grafting onto larger cacti. Fast-growing, single-column cacti such as *Trichocereous* are preferred rootstock. First, the areoles that occur near the tip of the rootstock are sliced off in order to prohibit regrowth near the graft. Then, the tip of this larger cactus is sliced through horizontally with a sterile, sharp knife or razor blade, leaving the cap piece on to keep the surface sterile and moist. Then, the tool is resterilized (by rubbing with alcohol or passing through a gas flame) and a small peyote is sliced from its root, or a small offshoot is sliced from the mother. The cap piece is removed from the rootstock, and the peyote scion is rapidly and smoothly transferred to the center of the exposed surface of the rootstock. The scion is then held in place with a large rubber band or by draping weighted strings over it. In a few days, the exposed surfaces of the rootstock will callus, the peyote graft will heal to the rootstock, and the vascular systems of the two plants will connect. Such a plant will grow and flower at an accelerated rate (Gottlieb, 1997).

Medicine. The part used in herbal medicine or in the peyote ceremony is the fresh or dried (aerial) cactus, often referred to as a "button." The use of peyote as a psychoactive sacrament in native healing ceremony is well-documented in the works of Richard Evans Schultes, and more recently in the scholarly and detailed work of Dr. Edward Anderson (Schultes, 1937; Anderson, 1980). The plant also has a history of use among the Huichol and Tarahumara Indians as a medicinal herb. Peyote is applied as an external poultice for wound healing and is taken in small dosages for combating hunger, thirst and exhaustion. The plant also has a history among native tribes as a treatment for rheumatic pains, colds, fevers, tuberculosis, intestinal maladies, venereal disease, pneumonia and scarlet fever (Vestal and Schultes, 1939).

Yield. The fresh weight of a mature button averages about 8 grams. The water content is about 75%, therefore the dry weight of an average button is about 2 grams. There are approximately 57 fresh peyote buttons per pound, and 227 dried peyote buttons per pound.

Harvest, processing and storage. The mature cactus is harvested during dry weather, usually in the summer or fall, by cutting the button from the taproot. Alkaloid content is highest during hot and dry weather. The cut is best made with a machete or sharp shovel at a slight angle so that ensuing rain will

177

be shed from the surface, thereby promoting rapid formation of callus and discouraging rot. The cut should be made high enough on the button to leave a little green all the way around the root. This is the root-stem juncture, which is rimmed with tiny, adventive buds. When harvested, these buds are activated, and one or several new cacti are formed, often within two months of harvest. Within about five years they grow large enough to replace the one that was taken. Development is relatively rapid, due to the existence of an already established taproot, and there is a strong tendency toward the creation of polyheaded individuals.

The harvested cacti may be used fresh. They do not spoil easily, and may be stored for several weeks at room temperature or under refrigeration without much change. Cold and *damp* conditions will cause rapid deterioration of the tissues and will seriously alter the medicinal effects.

To dry the cacti, they are placed on screens or on the rooftop in the open sun and protected from dew and rain. They can also be dehydrated in a forced-air dehydrator set to 110° F (43° C). It takes up to 10 days to dry a peyote button, due to the plant's innate mechanisms that slow dehydration.

The dried peyote buttons may be stored in plastic bags or in glass jars, out of the light, in a cool and dry location. According to Schultes, they "store indefinitely" (Schultes, 1937).

Peyote seed is rough-surfaced, tiny and black, rounded, but with a concave, whitish hilum (see illustration p. 168). There are approximately 2,000 seeds per gram seed weight. The seed is contained in the reddish fruit. As the fruit ripens and dries, it can be removed from the apical depression where it is camouflaged by the wooly tuft. Once located, the dried fruit is then teased apart by hand, and the seeds deposited on a sheet of white paper or in a bowl. They are then separated from the chaff by hand. Dried peyote buttons may carry viable seed within the apical depression, even if the fruit has long since deteriorated and dispersed. This seed may be removed by rapping the dried button upside-down on a sheet of white paper. The seeds retain their viability for several years, but best results are obtained by using recent seed.

Conservation status. Possession of peyote in Mexico is illegal, and in 1991 the plant was further listed by the Mexican government as "endangered." It is difficult to determine whether this conservation listing was motivated by a decline in native populations of the cactus and concern for its conservation, or simply as a means to further regulate illicit trade in a "drug plant."

In the United States, all cacti (including peyote) were given a CITES listing in 1975. This law disallows export of live, wild-harvested cactus plants and cactus raw material, but has little or no impact on trade in cacti (including peyote) within the boundaries of the United States. Since most peyote is consumed domestically, the CITES listing may not have much power to protect native stands of peyote cactus.

The legal harvest of peyote in the United States is strictly regulated by both the state of Texas and the Federal government. Approximately 2 million plants per year are legally harvested in south Texas (Anderson, 1995). Although there is provision made for legalized wild-harvest, it remains unlawful to cultivate peyote. Legalizing cultivation would significantly improve the sustainability of remaining wild populations of the cactus.

According to Anthony Davis, the yearly consumption of peyote by members of the Native American Church in the United States and Canada is at least 5 million plants. This means that at least 3 million plants are harvested illegally each year, either in the United States or in Mexico.

This level of harvest might be sustainable if a careful system of rotation were employed throughout the range of the plant, but this is far from the case. The majority of the peyote fields in the United States are on private land. Only certain land owners are willing to give permission for peyoteros to collect, and therefore these areas are overharvested, while other areas are not harvested at all. This might seem a bit reassuring in a way, except that land use practices are not consistent with the conservation of peyote. Most landowners make their living with cattle. In order to prepare for grazing they routinely plow the arid land and plant grasses, a practice that completely erases peyote from the picture.

179

Other species. There are two species in the *Lophophora* genus. The well-known *L. williamsii* has already been described in detail. In 1967, an investigator named H. Bravo discovered, near the Mexican state of Queretaro in the drylands of south-central Mexico, another species which came to be known as *L. diffusa* (see map p. 170). The plant is more succulent and softer than *L. williamsii,* and its color is yellowish-green, not blue-green. *L. diffusa* lacks ribs, although in other respects it resembles true peyote.   There is one other rather significant difference— *L. diffusa* contains little or none of the psychoactive alkaloid mescaline . . .

References

Anderson, E. 1980. *Peyote, the Divine Cactus.* Tucson (AZ): University of Arizona Press, 248 pp.

Anderson, E. 1969. *The Biogeography, Ecology and Taxonomy of Lophophora (Cactaceae).* Brittonia, Vol. 11(4), pp. 299-310.

Anderson, E. 1995. *The Peyote Gardens of South Texas: A Conservation Crisis?* Cactus and Succulent Journal, Vol. 67.

Gottlieb, A. 1997. *Peyote and Other Psychoactive Cacti.* Ronin Publishing, 96 pp.

Rzedowski, J. 1978. *Vegetation de Mexico.* Limusa, 432 pp.

Schultes, R. 1937. *Peyote and Plants Used in the Peyote Ceremony.* Harvard University Botanical Museum Leaflets, Cambridge (MA): Botanical Museum Press, IV(8), pp 129-152.

Schultes, R and A. Hoffman 1980. *The Botany and Chemistry of Hallucinogens,* 2nd Edition. Springfield (IL): Charles C. Thomas Publisher.

Vestal, P. and R. Schultes. 1939. *The Economic Botany of the Kiowa Indians.* Cambridge (MA): Botanical Museum.

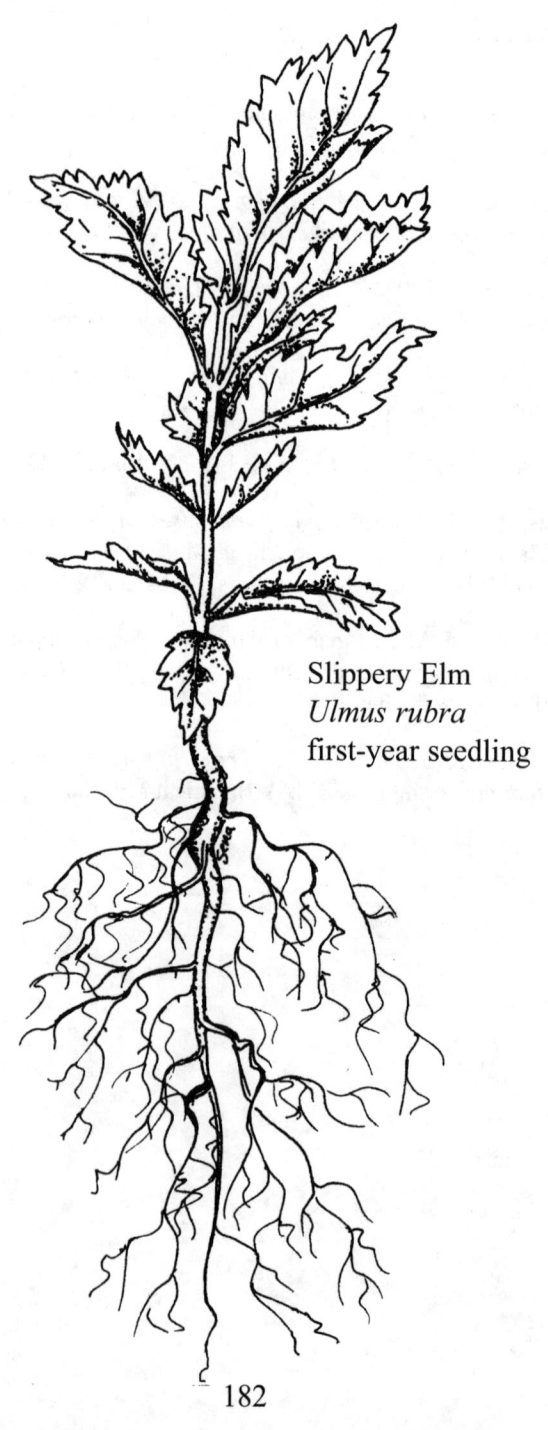

Slippery Elm
Ulmus rubra
first-year seedling

Slippery Elm
Ulmus rubra Muhl.

Syn. *Ulmus fulva* Michx.

Family: *Ulmaceae*

Slippery elm is a medium-sized deciduous tree native to the eastern forest biome of the United States and Canada. The tree shades smaller forest-dwelling plants, also providing a home for squirrels and a source of food for birds, rabbits and deer. The wood of the tree makes excellent firewood and long-lasting fence posts. Perhaps most importantly, the inner bark of slippery elm is the source of a nutritious and healing mucilage, much appreciated throughout the natural world.

The root system is shallow but wide spreading, and the tree also sends out rhizomes near the soil surface that produce multiple trunks or even other trees, known as "ramets" (Davis, 1998; Chapman, 1990). Whenever viewing the magnificent aerial spread of a large hardwood, it can be astonishing to think that a mirror image root system exists underground (as above, so below).

The dark greyish-brown outer bark of slippery elm is thick and rough, with deep, perpendicular fissures. The inner bark is buff white, fibrous and aromatic; it is mucilaginous when fresh or rehydrated. The wood is heavy, hard, strong, close-grained and relatively easy to split; it is colored dark reddish-brown with a lighter sapwood. The branches occur at a considerable height on the trunk; in open ground they spread irregularly, while in the forest they may grow very tall and straight. In both cases they describe a more erect profile than does American elm *(Ulmus americana)*. The twigs of a healthy tree are upright, stout and give a zig-zag appearance from the side; they are blanketed with a reddish pubescence that also covers the swollen, scaled dormant buds. The tree sends forth its reddish-purple flowers in the late winter to early spring. Then the leaf buds unfurl, expanding rapidly and forming the characteristic leaves that are uneven at the base, broadly lance-shaped and pointed, with a doubly serrated margin. The leaves are washboarded by prominent, very

183

straight, alternating, parallel veins; rough and sandpapery above and either smooth or hairy below. The seeds form not too long after the leaves, hanging down in large clusters. The individual seeds are papery, winged disks, with a dense central germ plasm. Both the disk and the germ plasm look like a wide droplet in profile.

Growing up in the midwestern woods, I knew the elms. They had leaves not friendly to the touch, and the few times that I got into their seeds (almost without exception because an authority had requested that I do some sweeping of driveway or porch), I ended up feeling pretty itchy. The seeds were not as interesting as those of associated trees, the Ohio buckeye *(Aesculus glabra),* black walnut *(Juglans nigra),* shagbark hickory *(Carya ovata)* and the many species of oak *(Quercus* spp.). Buckeyes had a prickly pericarp (suggesting numerous mischievous possibilities) surrounding the greatly treasured, mahogany-smooth, swollen nut. These were good luck. I carried them in my pockets, and they often ended up rolling around in my top dresser drawer along with the balled-up socks. The pericarp of black walnut stained my hands a ghoulish greenish-yellow that no amount of parental scrubbing could remove. I thought this nicely complimented the bright yellow of my school pencil. I dutifully practiced my penmanship on the coarse-textured paper, my colorful hands exuding a faint odor of iodine, all the while longing to be in that much larger classroom, the wooded banks of the Iowa River. Hickories remained edible for a year or two on the forest floor and could be smashed between rocks to divulge their tantalizing, sometimes rubbery, brain-like interior. Much work in cracking and picking resulted in a very little morsel, usually accompanied by fragments of the shell, but the taste was the best of all the nuts. Acorns were always abundant. They made functional, multipurpose marbles, especially when recent, green and heavy. So I kept myself busy playing with seeds, and even noting from time to time how they were collected and consumed by the woodland creatures. As a natural extension of this, I noted what seasons and local conditions were conducive to their germination and development. I will never forget bringing sprouted acorns to school for show-and-tell, then realizing with a shock that not everyone was as impressed as I by their long, naked, mousetail-like taproots!

It was not until after the Dutch elm disease passed through that I realized how many elms there had been. Whole street sides, once shady avenues during the summer and in the winter dark, fascinating, sleeping, naked skeletons against the snow-washed sky were reduced to rows of stumps cut low to the ground. In the woods, the dead trees were often left standing, their rotting bark harboring beetles that further spread the malady. The disease attacked the imported English elms and the native slippery elms alike. Once the fungus attacked one tree, it could pass underground through the interconnected roots to bring down other trees. Much later in my early adulthood, coming back from Africa and looking for ways to make a living and stay warm through the frigid winter, I cut firewood for a time. The best wood came from slippery elms (we called them "red elms") that were dead and standing, weather-beaten and barkless, smoothly reddish-grey in contrast to the frozen white and brown, snowy fields, hillsides and ravines. They were thick-trunked and often proved to have hollow boles. Big ones that were solid made almost unmanageably heavy rounds. Counting the growth rings, you could tell that some had lived up to 150 years before they died. Their heavy branches (what was left of them at least) were solid, hard and dry. A neighbor said he didn't like to burn red elm because it made too much creosote in the chimney. But I knew better—that wood was the distilled essence of a whole life under the Iowa sky, and it would keep you warm like nothing else.

Range, hardiness and adaptability. Slippery elm ranges throughout the eastern United States and Canada, from the Atlantic Coast to the Rocky Mountains. The tree never crossed this formidable barrier into the western states. The areas of highest concentration include the woodlands surrounding the Great Lakes, as well as the ravines and limestone hillsides of the midwestern states. The tree is less abundant in the southern states.

Slippery elm is perfectly cold-hardy. The early flowering and maturation of its fruit, in conjunction with the ability to reproduce by means of creeping rhizomes, allows the tree to adapt to areas where the growing season is very short (with as few as 90 frost-free days).

Given the presence of sufficient water, good drainage and a limestone soil, slippery elm may be successfully grown in temperate areas outside its natural range. An added advantage of this may be the development of disease-free stands in the western states.

Current Range of Slippery Elm in the United States

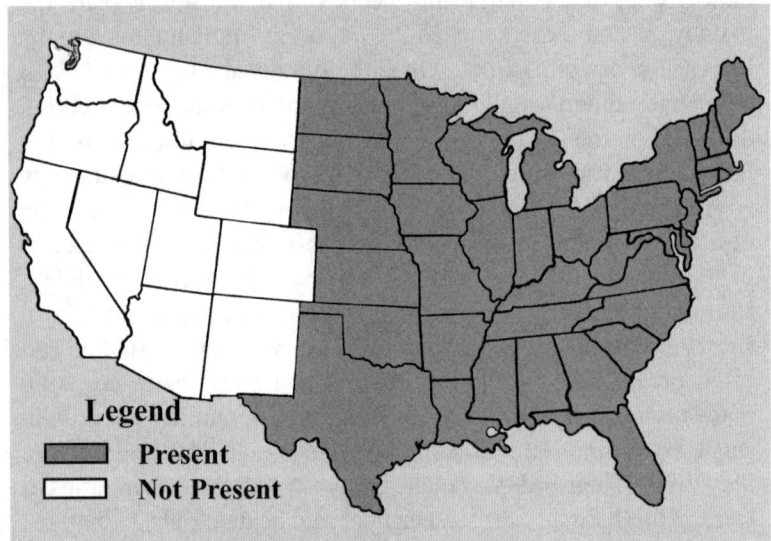

Legend
- Present
- Not Present

Ecology and plant community. Slippery elm is a highly adaptable tree, prospering both in the full sun and as a shade-tolerant member of the climax hardwood forest community. However, reproduction of new individuals by seeding or by underground rhizomes is most successful in areas where there is plenty of light. The growth rate of slippery elm is accelerated when it is located away from other trees, due to increased availability of light, nutrients and water.

The tree prefers to grow either in deep, rich, bottom land soils or in sloping soils of limestone origin (Scholz, 1958). The preferred pH value is slightly acid to neutral (pH 6.5 to 7). The root system has evolved to make use of surface nutrients, and therefore the tree does best in areas where there is a well-developed topsoil with a natural leaf mulch.

186

Although slippery elm generally prefers to grow in moist places, it is not fond of flooding. Periodic short-term floods may be tolerated, but prolonged flooding will kill the oxygen-dependent roots. Therefore, natural stands of the tree are found most commonly on alluvial terraces at the edge of the flood plain, on stream banks or on upland slopes. The tree also prospers in the Ozarks and other places in the midwest on drier upland soils or in rocky woods and on open, wooded bluffs (Steyermark, 1963).

Walnut, hickory, Ohio buckeye and oak have already been mentioned as woody companion species to slippery elm. Other common associates on upland sites include American elm *(Ulmus americana),* basswood *(Tilia americana),* black gum *(Nyssa sylvatica),* box elder *(Acer negundo),* hackberry *(Celtis occidentalis),* honey locust *(Gleditsia tracanthos),* maples *(Acer* spp.) and white ash *(Fraxinus americana).* Common associates on flood plains might include cottonwood *(Populus deltoides)* and sycamore *(Platanus occidentalis).* In all, over 60 species of hardwoods are commonly found growing with slippery elm, which is clearly not too picky about its companions and vice versa.

Smaller woody or vining species found in association with slippery elm include bittersweet *(Celastrus scandens),* black haw *(Viburnum prunifolium),* flowering dogwoods *(Cornus* spp.), hydrangea *(Hydrangea arborescens),* Virginia creeper *(Parthenocissus quinquefolia),* wahoo *(Euonymus atropurpureus)* and witch hazel *(Hamamelis virginiana).*

Slippery elm provides protection to an equally large array of delicate forbs. Literally all of the eastern forest-dependent species covered in this book (e.g. American ginseng, black cohosh, bloodroot, blue cohosh, goldenseal, etc.) are associates.

Life cycle. The flowers of slippery elm are among the first to bloom in the forest overstory, and they are an important source of nectar and pollen for the bees that pollinate them. Large seed sets occur only once every 2 to 4 years, starting when the tree reaches about the age of 15 (Brinkman, 1974). By early summer (May or June) the mature, winged fruits are already dropping from the tree. They are dispersed by gravity, rain and wind to a distance from the parent. Seeds will germinate in the full shade, in the forest duff or in association with other tree seedlings, herbaceous plants or grasses. However, seedling survival is augmented when the seeds come into contact with mineral soil in an area that receives at least partial sun. My experiments indicate that some seed (approximately 30%) will germinate within 30 days after contact with moist, warm soil. The majority of the remaining seed will lie dormant until the following spring. Delayed germination is a survival tactic that increases species flexibility in the face of environmental challenges, including late frosts and drought. Slippery elm may also act as a pioneer species, populating areas of disturbed soil or abandoned pastures.

Development of the sapling is moderately fast. Given plenty of light and freedom from competition, the sapling will attain a diameter of 1 inch (2.54 cm) diameter at breast height (d.b.h.) in seven years time. The fastest growth occurs from this stage up to a d.b.h. of about 8 inches (20 cm). The average yearly increase in diameter of mature trees is approximately 0.4 inch (1 cm) d.b.h.. Mature trees attain a height of at least 50 feet (15 m). An old growth slippery elm tree growing in the Shell-Marl Ravine Forest that overlooks the Potomac River in Charles County, Maryland measured over 6 feet (1.8 m) in circumference (Simmons, 1997). The tree is estimated to be at least 200 years old.

Cultivation from seed. In keeping with the natural seeding cycle, it makes sense to plant newly gathered and dried seed in the early summer. The best potting soil to use for growing slippery elm is rich in humus, with a little ground limestone, dolomite or stove ashes thrown in to sweeten the pot.

It is best to sow in deep containers or plug trays, as planting in deep flats would involve barerooting at transplant. Barerooting tends to shock and stunt the seedlings. Sow 3 or 4 seeds in each pot. This way you can be assured that each pot will eventually harbor at least 1 seedling. Place the seeds (along with their papery wing) flat on the soil, then cover with about ¼ inch (0.6 cm) of soil and firm down. Keep the pots evenly moist and shaded. Experiments at Horizon Herbs Seed Farm showed first signs of germination at day 20, with 23% germination on day 24, and 30% germination by day 30. Optimal temperature for germination is about 70° F (21° C). Germination is epigeal, with large, rounded seed leaves followed by the serrated true leaves.

After germination, thin the seedlings to 1 tree per pot. Grow the trees in the partial shade, and keep the soil moist. They attain a height of about 6 inches (15 cm) in the first growing season. By autumn they set new buds, then drop their leaves and go dormant. At this point, the trees may be transplanted to their final growing place, or they may be overwintered in the pots and transplanted in the spring. If the trees are to be held for another growing season before setting out, it makes sense to transplant them first into gallon pots. Since slippery elm is not strongly taprooted, this method of growing in pots until the trees are large enough to survive the rigors of the open environment is quite effective.

General care. Slippery elm does best in full sun or partial shade, planted in rich topsoil that has been amended with organic compost and lime. Space the trees at least 20 feet (6 m) apart. If Dutch elm disease is a concern, they should be spaced 50 feet (15 m) apart. Regular watering will help assure optimum growth, and during the first few years the trees must be kept weeded (or mowed around) so that they are not overcome by grasses. If the trees develop slowly or show signs of malnutrition, then they may require a side-dressing of organic compost or rotted manure.

Slippery elm is liable to damage from a formidable array of parasitic and/or pathogenic organisms. I was present at the UpS botanical sanctuary in Ohio when our little open plantation of three-year-old slippery elm seedlings was visited by a seven-year plague of locusts. The large, iridescent creatures mercilessly oviposited the receptive bark of the seedlings, which were seriously affected. In all, over 100 insect species have been identified that feed on elms (Baker, 1972).

Bark beetles and wood borers appreciate the nutritious bark and sapwood of the tree, and many are attracted to and live in rotten or damaged wood or bark. One of these, the European elm bark beetle *(Scolytus multistriatus)* is the primary vector for Dutch elm disease. The first sign of this fungal disease shows up in the spring, with wilting and yellowing of peripheral leaves. The symptoms may progress rapidly or slowly, but normally result in complete browning of the leaves and death of the tree within a year or two. The fungus simply clogs the vascular system of the tree, thereby interrupting water flow to the extremities. Given a healthy tree with an innate resistance to the fungus and the right climatic factors (oddly enough, damage is reduced during drought) the tree may recover.

Preventive measures to avoid Dutch elm disease (and indeed the several other major diseases among elms) include: spacing the trees at a distance greater than 50 feet (15 m) in order to limit the possibility of root contact that can carry the disease from one tree to another; sanitation—that is, removing and burning dead wood from growing trees and cleaning up piles of dead wood in the forest that might harbor beetles; pruning away infected wood at the first signs of disease; planting clones of trees that have demonstrated resistance to the disease; and planting trees by seed in areas isolated from the current range of the disease.

Medicine. The part used in herbal medicine is the inner bark, collected from the larger branches and/or trunk of trees that are at least 12 to 15 years old. The older the tree, the better, because with age the inner bark thickens, and greater quantities of mucilage are produced. The inner bark may be used fresh, but it is usually dried. Direct consumption is the easiest way to use it. Simply bite off a piece and chew it like gum. It is the chaw that keeps on giving. When the bark finally *stops* giving, spit out the fibrous wad and take another bite. Slippery elm is a survival food, as nutritious as oatmeal and easily digested. It is one of the best foods for convalescence, improving appetite and bolstering strength by degrees. It is one of the herbs of choice for treating urinary or gastric irritation and especially gastric or duodenal ulcer. The mucilage not only soothes the digestive and urinary tract, but will have a positive moistening and healing influence on the lungs and upper respiratory tract, as well.

More refined methods of preparing the inner bark may be called for. Many recipes have been published recommending addition of *boiling* water (see Grieve, 1931). This I do not understand. Boiling precipitates the mucilage and damages it. A better method is to prepare an infusion by soaking pieces of dried inner bark in *cold* water overnight. By morning, the water will have jellified, and may be taken throughout the day as needed. The powdered inner bark (which is widely available) may be mixed with cold water into a thin slurry and taken by the spoonful.

Externally, a poultice of the masticated inner bark or the dried, ground and wetted inner bark provides a cooling and healing treatment for old burns, abrasions and inflammations.

Yield. The amount of inner bark produced by a single tree is highly variable, depending largely on the expertise of the harvester and the size and age of the tree. If harvest is carried out in a sustainable manner, then only a limb is taken from the tree, and this of course will produce much less of the inner bark than if the entire tree were taken down and stripped. In the latter case the yield of dried bark could be many pounds. The water content of fresh, autumn-harvested inner bark was measured at 46% to 50% (Strauss, 2001). This means that every 10 pounds of fresh inner bark will yield approximately 5 pounds of dried bark.

Harvest, processing and storage. Harvest takes place in the spring or in the fall, when the sap is up and the inner bark "slips." This means that it peels easily from the sapwood. Renewable harvest is from branches and twigs. Twigs can be gathered whole, dried and ground into powder. They make a product that is slightly inferior to the inner bark, but useable. In the case of cutting off a limb, it is very important to make the cut a few inches back from the trunk, and to paint the wound over with a thick coat of latex paint or a special, elastic "tree-surgeon's paint" available from nursery supply stores. This will help the tree heal the wound by closing the door to infection. Trees that must for some reason be cut down will yield useful inner bark from the trunk. Trees cut down to the stump will tend to resprout, or "coppice." Therefore, if the entire tree *must* be sacrificed, it makes sense to cut it with a tall stump. If the entire bark is stripped from the standing tree, it kills the tree.

Another way of "harvesting your tree and having it too" is to "pollard" the tree. This is a method that was developed in England, where trees are generally held in very high esteem, but wood is still required for carving and for manufacture of tool handles, barrel staves, etc. (Mabey, 1998). The tree is cut very high, perhaps at a height of 30 feet (9 m) on the trunk and then allowed to resprout and grow, thereby creating a remarkable, giant, often humanoid profile. Sometimes this is done in America, too, but

191

usually because the trees are "interfering with electric lines." The advantage of pollarding is that the tree trunk is maintained closer to its original form, and given that the cut is made far from the ground, there is a greater chance the tree will resprout and grow, and a lesser chance that it will contract a soil-mediated infection or disease.

The outer bark is removed with a knife, a draw knife, a machete or a hatchet, depending on how coarse the bark is. This process is known as "rossing." After the outer bark is removed, then the inner bark can be peeled off in soft, delightful strips. If conditions are perfect, it can be stripped off with the fingers. Otherwise, use the draw knife or a regular knife, and try not to include too many quills of sapwood with the bark . . .

The strips of slippery elm inner bark are best dried immediately. If using a forced-air dehydrator, dry for 1 day at low temperature (70° F = 21° C) and high air flow, then turn up the temperature to high (110° F = 43° C) and dry them all the way through. Sun-drying is also fine. The strips may be laid out on screens or on sheets on tables and left in the sun, then covered at night to ward off the dew. If they rehydrate, they will be likely to mold. (The mucilage is a perfect environment for molds to form, a shortcoming of the harvested medicine which is related to the tree's susceptibility to disease, as well.) An unused solar greenhouse is also a great place to dry slippery elm. The herb can handle plenty of heat and positive air movement. Under these conditions, it will dry in 4 days' time (Strauss 2001).

Seed. The slippery elm fruit is 1-seeded, a papery, greenish-brown, winged disk measuring about 2.5 cm tall and 1.5 cm wide, the germ plasm like a bull's-eye covering only ⅓ of that distance. There are between 90 and 120 seeds in a gram, depending on the robustness of the seed and the care taken in harvest and handling.

Seed collection, processing and storage. Slippery elm seed is best harvested when it is mature, but still slightly green. The seed hangs high in the tree, and it is often feasible to collect only from a few select lower branches. At any given harvest, only a fraction of the mature trees in an area will bear fruit. Ladders, ropes, climbing spurs or (this is the Strauss method) lifting a jittery apprentice into the air with a front-end loader on a tractor will all serve. Squirrels and certain birds will be contenders for the crop. It seems that everyone likes this combination of mucilage and astringent tannins as a source of medicinal food. The seeds are picked by hand and put into baskets.

Returning home from the harvest, the seeds are laid out on screens or on tables covered with sheets, in a mildly warm, dry and slightly ventilated area. These conditions will promote slow dehydration and will allow the seeds to finish the maturation process and slowly harden off. During this time, the seeds must be turned several times a day to promote even drying. Throughout this process, it is possible to pick out foreign detritus such as twigs, mosses and leaf fragments.[1] After a few days of this attention, the seed should be pure, crinkly dry and ready for storage. The seeds last longest if kept in a paper envelope or bag, which is then enclosed in a plastic bag or jar and either stored in a cool, dry area or refrigerated at 40° F (~4.5° C). Stored under these conditions, the seed will retain its viability for up to a year. Best results are obtained by promptly planting recent seed.

Conservation status. I think none of the herbs on the UpS at-risk list have been so hotly contended as this one. To be frank, I have heard many personal opinions expressed by botanists, scientists and government employees that slippery elm is some-what of a weed species, and that it does not require or somehow even *deserve* our efforts in conservation. So I was really interested to look deeper into the general information that has been published on the plant, and in so doing I found the tree to be much more highly esteemed than I had anticipated (Allison, 1979; Chapman, 1990; Elias, 1970; Scholz, 1958; Steyermark, 1963). Furthermore, herbalists in general are voicing a plea for conservation and rehabilitation of this useful indigenous species. After all, the effects of the Dutch elm disease were and still are severe. From the 1930s when the disease was first brought to this continent, through the 1960s which saw the full effects of the catastrophe, over 42 million elms were killed in the midwest alone.

---

[1] Given the nature of the seed, it cannot be screened with any effect, and wind winnowing would only cause dispersal, because the seed is designed to float on the air.

During the years 1999 to 2001, about 265,000 (dry) pounds of slippery elm inner bark were harvested for herbal medicinal purposes (McGuffin, 2001). This might equate to a total of 88,000 trees that were cut down, trimmed or otherwise compromised by this practice. Surprisingly perhaps, 3 years of harvest for herbal purposes would thus be equivalent to only about 0.2% of the historical devastation caused by Dutch elm disease in the midwest. By practicing renewable harvesting techniques, the impact of obtaining this medicine from the forests can be minimized. In time, supplying this many trees through cultivation would not be very difficult. Cultivation on a moderate scale has already been initiated and will no doubt increase. We can look forward to a time when herbalists will use organically grown slippery elm inner bark from sustainably harvested, cultivated trees.

Other species. Slippery elms from various land races native to different parts of the country exhibit a wide degree of variation. This diversity has served the continued survival of the tree in the face of wholesale disease. Certain individuals will demonstrate disease resistance and propagate themselves by producing ramets that are also disease resistant. This diversity also applies to the mucilage content of the inner bark. Certain species or races within a species are mucilage-rich, while others are not so well-endowed. American elm *(Ulmus americana)* is the indigenous tree most commonly substituted for slippery elm. There is good ethnographic evidence that this tree was used by native Americans of the Cheyenne, Choctaw, Delaware, Fox, Houma, Iroquios, Koasati, Mohegan, Ojibwa, Penobscot and Pottawatomie tribes (Moerman, 1986). American elm is also mentioned as an alternative to slippery elm in *King's Dispensatory* (Felter and Lloyd, 1898). The inner bark of American elm is not as thick, aromatic and mucilaginous as slippery elm, but it serves the same medicinal purpose.

References

Allison, J. and G. Gregory. 1979. *How to Save Dutch Elm Diseased Trees by Pruning.* USDA FS publication NA-GR-9.

Baker, W. 1972. *Eastern Forest Insects.* Washington (DC): U.S. Dept. of Agriculture, misc. publication 1175, 642 pp.

Brinkman, K. 1974. *Elm,* in *Seeds of Woody Plants in the United States,* Schopmeyer (ed.). Washington (DC): U.S. Dept. of Agriculture, Agriculture Handbook 450, pp. 829-834.

Chapman, W. and A. Bessette. 1990. *Trees and Shrubs of the Adirondacks.* Utica (NY): North Country Books, 131 pp.

Davis, R., R. Larimore and J. Ebinger. 1998. *The Occurrence of Slippery Elm (Ulmus rubra Muhl.) Root Sprouts in Forest Understories in East-Central Illinois.* Transactions of the Illinois State Academy of Science, Vol. 91(1 & 2).

Elias, T. 1970. *The Genera of Ulmaceae in the Southeastern United States.* Journal of the Arnold Arboretum, 51, pp. 18-40.

Felter, H. and J. Lloyd. 1898 (Reprinted 1985). *King's American Dispensatory.* Portland (OR): Eclectic Medical Publishing, Vol. 1 & 2, 743 pp.

Grieve, M. 1931 (Reprinted 1971). *A Modern Herbal.* New York (NY): Hafner Publishing Company, Vol. 1 & 2, 888 pp.

McGuffin, M. 2001. *AHPA's Tonnage Survey Results.* United Plant Savers Bulletin.

Moerman, D. 1986. *Medicinal Plants of Native America.* Ann Arbor (MI): University of Michigan Dept. of Anthropology, Vol. 1, 534 pp.

Scholz, H. 1958. *Slippery Elm (Ulmus rubra Muhl.),* in *Silvics of Forest Trees of the United States.* Washington (DC): U.S. Department of Agriculture, Agriculture Handbook 271, pp. 736-739.

Simmonds, R. 1997. *Ancient Trees of the Old Growth Forest at Chapman's Landing, MD.*

Steyermark, J. 1963. *Flora of Missouri.* Ames (IA): Iowa State University Press, 1724 pp.

Strauss, P. 2001. Personal communication. Paul lives in Meigs County in southeastern Ohio. He knows the land, the creatures and the plants because he is a good observer, a hard worker and a natural *experiencer.* Paul served as a consultant during the writing of this chapter. He also provided the dry-down figures for the fall-harvested inner bark, and gave valuable information for the section on harvesting, processing and drying. His chapter on slippery elm in *Planting the Future* is a great source for more information on this tree.

Stillingia
Stillingia sylvatica
root
root cross section
flowering top
fruiting top
seed and seed chaff
(dorsal and ventral
view, actual size)

198

Stillingia
Stillingia sylvatica Garden ex. L.
Family: *Euphorbiaceae*

Stillingia is a sun-loving, leathery-leaved herbaceous perennial. Fleshy and tuberous, the root delves straight down through the hot, dry and sandy soil of its natural habitat. The branching taproot is reddish-brown and drum-like, designed for gathering and storing water and nutrients in order to nurture the somewhat scraggly aerial parts through the long summer. A cross-section of the root reveals a characteristically thick outer bark studded with numerous pockets of dark yellow resin, encircling diminishing rings of pink-brown, porous, inner tissue. The root is malodorous and tasting is not recommended, as the juices are seriously acrid. Several round, smooth stems arise at angles from the crown to a height of 2 to 3 feet (60 to 90 cm), bearing the alternate, lance-shaped, leathery leaves. The leaves are dark green and thick, with a prominent central vein and a minutely serrated edge. The base of the leaf is firmly fused to the stem, showing two hair-like glandular stipules near the point of juncture. The stems and the leaves exude a milky latex when broken. The flowering spike extends from the center of the plant, a blunt stalk beset with the yellow, concave cups that are the male flowers. The female flowers are less numerous, hidden among the leaves at the base of the flowering spike. Once fertilized, the ovaries quickly expand to form the swollen, three-lobed green fruits. The fruits are attached to the plant by means of an odd, characteristic, triangular platform that is ejected along with the seeds in the late summer. Each seed is about the size of a sweet pea, grey and white, fissured like a tiny brain. The seed is thin-shelled with a prominent hilum and a soft, bean-like endosperm. They are a favorite food of weevils, being fatty and nutritive. Unlike the rest of the plant, the seeds taste mild and sweet, but their parentage is revealed by the acrid aftertaste.

The stillingia plant is really most unusual in an inconspicuous sort of a way. Although the individual parts are quite fascinating, the growing plant may well fail to impress the casual observer. That is, unless the plant is ingested, in which case stillingia never fails to elicit a reaction.

Range, hardiness and adaptability. *Stillingia sylvatica* is native to the pine flatwoods and sand hill country of the coastal Piedmont stretching from Virginia south to Florida and across the gulf coast to the gravely or sandy flood plains and deserts of Texas, New Mexico and even Colorado. Distribution is generally sparse, but the plant may be found in local abundance (e.g. around the margins of the Okefinokee Swamp).

Stillingia is a plant of very specific environs, preferring sandy, acid soils and long, hot, dry summers. It is not very frost-tolerant, and we grow it in southern Oregon only in the greenhouse. Gardeners living in maritime regions and in the deep South are well-advised to try growing this plant outdoors. Otherwise, it may be greenhoused throughout the temperate U.S., and as long as it is kept dry and planted in sandy soil, it will probably overwinter in a cold greenhouse.

Even within the general area of its natural distribution, stillingia will gravitate to specific areas, sometimes producing almost monotypic stands in one likely area, while it is completely absent from another. Therefore, it is not considered to be a highly adaptable plant, and will probably require trial and error to discover the exact microniche that best supports its healthy growth.

Current range of *Stillingia sylvatica* in the U.S.

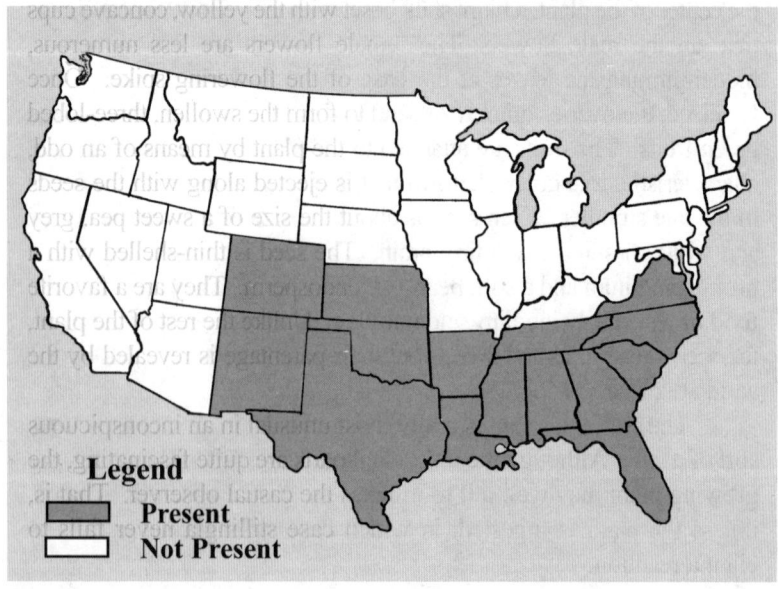

Legend
- Present
- Not Present

Ecology and plant community. Stillingia prefers growing in dry to desert areas, in the full sun or under the sparse shade of pines and oaks. Although the plant generally grows in very well-drained, sandy soils, it also grows in red clay soils. The optimal pH value of these nutrient-divested soils ranges from 5.5 to 6.5. Stillingia also occurs in black, humus-rich soil, but high nutrient levels stimulate aerial growth to the detriment of root yield. The dry to moderately dry pine flatwood is maintained by periodic fires, which keep the flatwoods from succeeding into hardwood dominated forests. These fires are critical to the germination of pines and saw palmetto, and they eventually result in the increased vigor of certain flowering plants, including stillingia. Tree species that may occur in close association with wild stands of stillingia include Arkansas oak *(Quercus arkansana)*, bayberry *(Myrica cerifera)*, bluejack oak *(Q. incana)*, fringe tree *(Chionanthus virginicus)*, loblolly pine *(Pinus taeda)*, longleaf pine *(P. palustris)*, sand post oak *(Q. margarettia)*, sandhill oak *(Q. inopina)*, shortleaf pine *(P. echinata)* and turkey oak *(Q. laevis)*.

Shrubby, vining and herbaceous associates may include Carolina buckthorn *(Frangula caroliniana)*, farkleberry *(Vaccinium arboreum)*, saw palmetto *(Serrenoa repens)*, small-flowered paw-paw *(Asimina parviflora)*, true unicorn *(Aletris farinosa)*, yaupon *(Ilex vomitoria)*, yellow jessamine *(Gelsemium sempervirens)*, wild indigo *(Baptisia tinctoria)*, wild Job's tears *(Onosmodium virginianum)* and witch hazel *(Hamamelis virginiana.)*. Of these, true unicorn, wild Job's tears and wild indigo are vital herbal medicines that are also conservation priorities.

Life cycle. Stillingia flowers starting in March and will continue flowering in many localities until as late as June. Flowering occurs in cycles, where the primary terminal flowering raceme is borne on a stem, which then splits and produces two or three more branches, each then producing another flowering raceme. This results in a protracted period of seed production and dispersion, which is of survival advantage to plants that live in arid environments. In such a place, good conditions for germination may occur unpredictably and perhaps as infrequently as once per year. Another advantage of this extended period of seed production is that it provides a kind of insurance against insect damage. Weevils have cycles of greater and lesser

201

activity, and as long as some seed is matured during a time when weevils are infrequent, then undamaged seed has a chance of entering the seed bank. The seedpod dehisces on the plant and the seeds are ejected into the environment where they may easily be covered by sand. The plant enters dormancy as the days grow shorter, and cooler temperatures prevail. The leaves and stalks turn from deep green to a bright, mottled crimson, and the leaves then fall from the stalks. The stalks subsequently die down to the crown. Meanwhile, the seeds remain quiescent in the sandy soil. Moist, warm spring or summer conditions promote germination. Germination is epigeal, with two rounded seed leaves followed by the finely serrated, true leaves. The plants develop a sturdy, branching taproot during the first year, and usually flower for the first time in the second year. Mature plants of at least three years of age may produce many stems and consequently numerous flowers and seeds. Thus the cycle repeats. The maximum life span of stillingia has not, to my knowledge, been determined, but given the slow-growing nature of the plant and the preservative effects of the dry environment where it lives, the plant probably lives for decades.

Cultivation from seed. Sow recent seed of stillingia in a sandy, acid soil in the summer, or sow in pots in the greenhouse when temperatures may be expected to reach at least 80° F (~27° C). The seed is a heat-dependent germinator, and germination rate may be improved by fire treating.[1] Recent, undamaged seed germinates, without scarification, after a period of about 30 days in a warm greenhouse. The normal rate of initial emergence is about 20%. This germination rate is dependent on careful seed selection, including exclusion of seeds that are drilled by weevils and exclusion of empty seed coats. After the initial germination, ongoing germination may occur in the ensuing months.

---

[1] Fire treating. The seed is planted about ¼ inch (0.6 cm) deep in a wooden flat of sandy, moist potting soil. Wet down the sides of the flat so they do not burn. Place a pile of dried kindling (dry pine needles and cones work best) right on top of the soil of the flat. Light the flash fire and let it burn until the fuel is gone. Water the flat daily. The seedlings will emerge within two or three weeks, directly through the charcoal and ashes. Amazing!

Stillingia seedlings may be transplanted (about 1 foot apart) after the development of the first true leaves. Since the seedlings are slow growing at first, and because they are not self-thinning, a labor-saving method is to leave them for an entire growing season in the flat, spaced closely and gaining strength. The healthy dormant roots may be transplanted in the autumn or in the spring to the final location. The branching taproot only reaches a depth of about 4 inches (10 cm) in the first year, is not sensitive to transplant, and as long as the right conditions are maintained (ie. well-drained, coarse sand or sandy soil, acid pH value, full sun, infrequent watering and high temperatures), transplant survival is usually 100%. Roots are best placed high in the soil, with the crown lifted above the soil surface. This placement discourages crown rot. Stillingia must be kept weeded for the first year or two, at which point the plant becomes a healthy contender and may be allowed to naturalize.

Medicine. The fresh or very recently dried root is the part used in medicine. This plant is usually used in combination with other herbs (e.g. licorice, marshmallow) in order to ameliorate its acrid nature and to augment the glandular effects. Stillingia is a classic alterative and a stimulant to the lymphatic flow, used historically for treating some very serious conditions including syphilis and cancer. It is one of the very active ingredients of the much-maligned Hoxsey anticancer formula (Ausubel, 2000).[2]

---

[2] **The Hoxsey Formula.** This version of the famous Hoxsey anticancer formula is adapted from the label of an antique bottle that was manufactured at the original Hoxsey Cancer Clinic in Dallas, Texas.
56% potassium iodide (KI)
8% licorice root *(Glycyrrhiza glabra)*
8% red clover blossom *(Trifolium pratense)*
8% buckthorn bark *(Rhamnus frangula)*
4% burdock root *(Arctium lappa)*
4% stillingia root *(Stillingia sylvatica)*
4% barberry root bark *(Berberis vulgaris)*
4% poke root *(Phytolacca americana)*
2% cascara amarga *(Sweetia panamensis)*
2% prickly ash bark *(Xanthoxylum clava-herculis)*
Note 1: these would be the preextraction percentages by dry weight.
Note 2: Cascara amarga is not generally available and is best substituted with another bitter wood of the tropics (e.g. quassia *(Picrasma excelsa)*).

Small doses of the herb (again almost always in combination) are used in treating any condition involving swollen lymph nodes or eruptive dermatitis. Chronic allergies, recurring upper respiratory infections (especially tonsillitis and bronchitis) and eczema are likely to yield to this herb. Stillingia contains phorbol esters that may seriously irritate the mucous membranes. Larger doses of the herb or extreme sensitivity to the herb will result in loose stools, nausea or emesis.

Yield. At Horizon Herbs Seed Farm, 2-year-old cultivated (green-housed) plants averaged 20 g each (fresh root weight). By year 3, they had attained an average weight of 70 grams. Wild-harvested roots generally weigh between 100 and 150 grams each, but may weigh as much as 1 pound (454 g) or more. On the basis of 3-year-old cultivated plants, 1 pound of fresh stillingia roots would represent the yield of 7 plants, while 1 pound of dried stillingia roots would represent the yield of about 16 plants. The average water content is 60%. Therefore, 10 pounds of fresh roots would dry down to 4 pounds of dry roots.

Harvest, processing and storage. Stillingia roots are traditionally dug at any time during the yearly cycle, but it probably makes sense to dig them in the late summer or in their early dormancy, after they have matured their seed and after they have generated and fixed active constituents. The roots are dug around with a spade, and pulled up by means of grasping the smooth stems. Take care not to damage the roots, as points of injury become inroads for mold.

Stillingia root is best used fresh, and the material is liable to deteriorate in storage. If the roots are to be shipped while in the fresh state, keep them entire, dry and dirty. They can be washed and cut in pieces just prior to extraction. If the roots are to be dried, wash them thoroughly and cut in diagonal, approximately 1 inch (~2.5 cm) slices. The sliced roots are traditionally dried in the sun (protected from nighttime moisture and rain) which takes several days, especially in the humid southern states. Blue mold is likely to invade the roots when they are dried in this manner, so a forced-air herb dehydrator is really a better choice. Dry at medium temperature (80° F = 27° C) and high air flow until the roots are dehydrated all the way through. The root pieces are best stored in plastic bags in lightproof sacks or drums, in a cool, dark and dry location. The roots begin losing their potency as soon as they are dried, and last in storage for only about six months.

Seed. Stillingia seed is ovate, with a pronounced, fleshy hilum. The seed measures approximately 5 mm long by 3.5 mm wide. Depending on the robustness of the seed and the percentage of empty testa in the sample, 1 gram of seeds contains anywhere from 30 to 50 seeds. Healthy plants produce large, solid seeds in a good year, but may generate only marginal germ plasm in a bad year. Larger seeds give a better germination rate.

Seed collection, processing and storage. Stillingia seed is matured on the plant and ejected into the environment on an ongoing basis, throughout the latter part of the growing season. Therefore, it is difficult to obtain much stillingia seed at any given time. The most effective method of collection is to keep an eye on the developing plants, and begin harvesting in earnest when the plants have nearly matured the main seed flush for the year. The plants are upended into a bucket or gourd and shaken vigorously to help release the seed. Alternatively, the nearly ripe seedpods are picked by hand from the plant and sandwiched between screens, then laid out in the sun to finish the maturation process. The seedpods will split apart, and the seeds will dry and harden.

The seed may be cleaned of foreign debris (especially fragments of the pod) by spreading it out on a table and sorting by hand. At this time, all damaged or drilled seed must also be removed and discarded. This will prohibit weevils from hatching and continuing to feed on the seed in storage. Seeds are best stored in plastic bags or glass jars, in a cool and dry location. Seed cleaned and sorted in this manner will maintain its viability for two years, but best results will be obtained by using seed from the recent harvest.

Conservation status. Stillingia was uplisted from the UpS watch list to the at-risk list in the year 2001. The reason for this change of status is clear—this not-so-common plant requires very specific growing conditions and is therefore confined to a spotty and limited range. Existing stands of stillingia are under pressure from development and from ongoing herbal harvest. The renewable parts of the plant are not used, and stillingia does not regenerate effectively from portions left in the ground. Digging the root kills the plant.

A survey of state conservation lists reveals that various state governments are aware of the decline of this interesting plant. For instance, the Virginia Department of Conservation lists *Stillingia sylvatica* as "extremely rare." This designation is assigned to plants represented by five or fewer populations or occurrences in the state, and is also reserved for plants that are especially vulnerable to extirpation.

Other species. There are seven species of Stillingia native to the United States, Mexico and the Baja. *Stillingia sylvatica* is the most wide-ranging and is considered official, but the majority of stillingia species are probably harvested and used by local herbalists. In folk practice, all species are considered to be medicinally interchangeable. Here is an overview, starting in the southeast and working across to California.

Water toothleaf *(Stillingia aquatica)* is found in moist environs in South Carolina, Georgia, Florida and Alabama. The plants prefer to grow in coastal swales (these are marshy areas located behind beach dune systems). According to Howard Horne, in these areas the plant is often abundant and forms nearly monotypic stands. Sawgrass is a common associate. Inland, *S. aquatica* occurs in freshwater swamps or in depressed, moist areas in wet pine savannah habitats. Herbaceous sedges *(Rhynchospora)* are common associates (Horne, 2001).

Seaside hotels and condominiums are a major contender for the coastal habitat of *Stillingia aquatica*. Inland distributions of the plant are challenged by logging activities and the drying up of swamps. This plant is commonly found in commercial herb shipments as an adulterant to *Stillingia sylvatica*. The admixture is sold to local brokers as "queen's delight." The average root digger knows that queen's delight occurs both in sand hill habitat and in the swamp, but fails to realize that plants found in these diverse areas represent different species.

Texas toothleaf *(Stillingia texana)* is found in Texas, Oklahoma and New Mexico. The morphology of *S. texana* is similar to

206

S. sylvatica, and in some sandy flood plains they cohabitate. In commerce, *S. texana* root may be found as an adulterant to *S. sylvatica*. *S. texana* is considered by Michael Moore to be "a preferred species" and he uses it interchangeably with *S. sylvatica* (Moore, 1989).

There are three arguably endemic species of stillingia. One is Trecul's toothleaf *(S. triculiana)* that occurs in the deserts of Texas. The other is the Mojave toothleaf *(S. paucidentata),* that is limited to the Mojave desert in Arizona and New Mexico. The annual toothleaf *(Stillingia spinulosa)* sometimes acts like a perennial. This species occurs in deserts and flood plains of Arizona, Nevada and California.

Queen's root *(Stillingia linearifolia)* occurs very sporadically over a wide range of territory, including gravely or sandy, seasonal washes and high flood plains in Colorado, New Mexico, Arizona, Nevada, California, Baja and Mexico. The plant is shorter than *S. sylvatica,* with a truncated, woody taproot (Moore, 1989).

References

Ausubel, K. 2000. *When Healing Becomes A Crime: The Amazing Story of the Hoxsey Cancer Clinics and the Return of Alternative Therapies.* Healing Arts Press.

Horne, H. 2001. Personal communication. Howard is a learned expert on *Stillingia aquatica.* He confirms that *S. sylvatica* and *S. aquatica* occupy distinct habitats and asserts that they probably do not intergrade, because their chromosome numbers differ. Howard generously contributed to the "life cycle" section on *S. sylvatica,* and provided the majority of habitat information and associations for *S. aquatica.*

Moore, M. 1989. *Medicinal Plants of the Desert and Canyon West.* Santa Fe (NM): Museum of New Mexico Press, 184 pp.

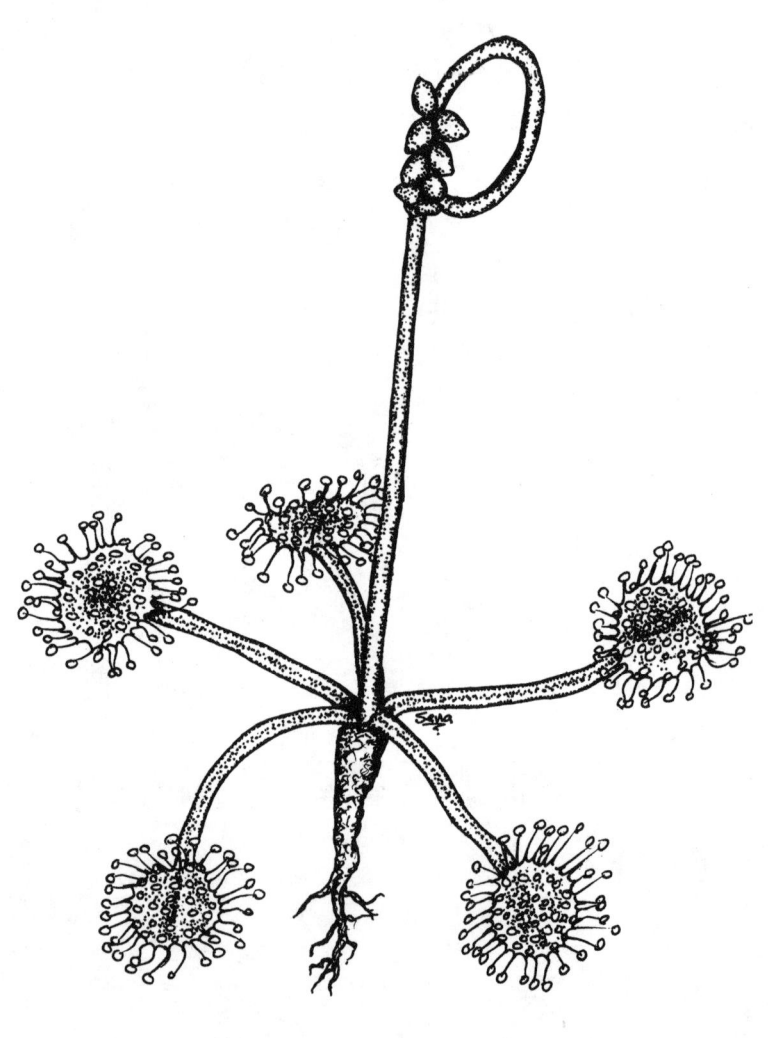

Sundew
Drosera rotundifolia
root, leaves and immature flowering stalk

Sundew

Drosera rotundifolia L.

Syn. *Drosera longifolia*

Family: *Droseraceae*

The round leaf sundew is an herbaceous perennial, insectivorous plant of cold, open fens, bogs and waterways. The young plant forms a short, branching taproot. This root dies in the autumn, but continues to anchor the dormant bud (the hybernaculum) through the winter. In the spring, new roots are formed, and these are hair-like and horizontal. The hybernaculum opens, pushing out a tiny basal rosette of leaves, each measuring at the maximum 1.25 inches (3 cm) in diameter. The leaves are borne on flattened petioles; they lie against the moist peat substrate, or rise up toward the sun. The leaves are like a reddish-green, circular section of mucous membrane reflexed outward, supporting a myriad of red tentacles, each tipped by an oozing gland that exudes a glistening drop of glutinous, proteolytic enzyme. The drops enlarge as the sunlight intensifies.

The slender, smooth flower stem arises from the center of the rosette to a height of 2 to 6 inches (5 to 15 cm). A single plant may bear anywhere from 1 to 7 stems. The flower buds occur on one side of the stem only, forming a scorpioid coil that unfurls as the flowers open. This occurs around midday on a sunny day, revealing the self-fertile, white or pinkish-white inflorescences. The flowers last only one day, giving way to partitioned capsules that eventually swell with seed. The ripe seed is black, attaining about the size and shape of a nit.

Sundew catches insects in order to augment the scant nutrients supplied by a nearly sterile environment. Sticky tentacles trap the insect and bend down to transport it inward as the digestive depths of the leaf rise up to engulf this helpless victim. The droplets also catch, magnify and reflect the sun's rays, and even given their ghastly function, the droplets are still quite beautiful. They also gave rise to the common and the Latin name of the plant. *Droseros* is Greek for "dew."

Range, hardiness and adaptability. Round leaf sundew has a wide distribution throughout the eastern, northern and western United States. The plant is more common in the northern reaches of North America, ranging from Greenland and Newfoundland across the boreal forests of Canada to Alaska (Johnson, 1995). Sundew also occurs in Europe, Asia, South Africa and South America.

Sundew is a survivor of cold conditions. The plant has learned to mature quickly—even first-year plants are capable of flowering and making seed during the short summers at elevation or in cold, northern fens and bogs. The plant has also evolved a unique feature—the hybernaculum—which minimizes its need for nutrient resources during the winter and reduces the surface area exposed to cold temperatures by packing the life-force of the plant into a resting bud.

Sundew is also an adaptive plant, and is capable of living in a fairly wide range of climatic conditions as long as winter dormancy is provided, and as long as the growing medium is properly prepared (acid pH value, sandy peat substrate and low nutrient levels). The plants must also be kept constantly moist and in the sun. Therefore, it is not too unusual to find sundew kept as a curiosity in the cold greenhouse or in the backyard bog.

Current Range of Round Leaf Sundew in the U.S.

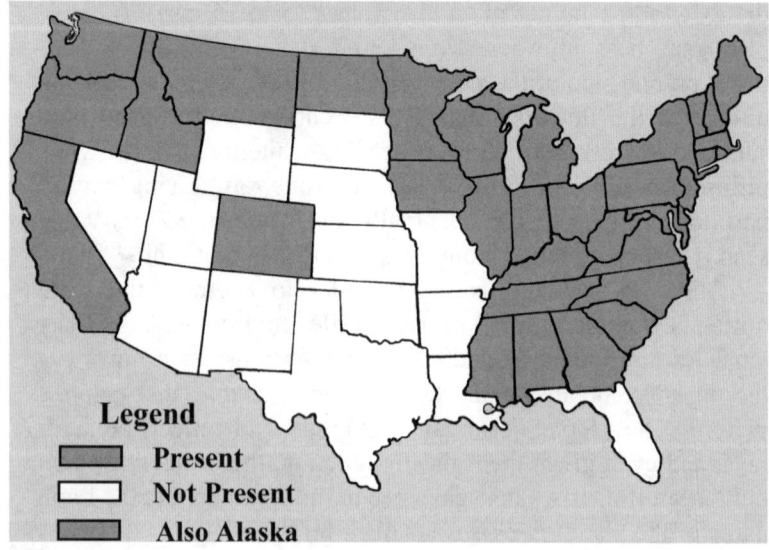

Legend
- Present
- Not Present
- Also Alaska

Ecology and plant community. In its northern range, sundew is most commonly found growing in freshwater peat lands. Peat lands are classified either as "fens" or "bogs." Both habitats are made up of accumulations of living and decomposing bryophytic[1] plants known as "sphagnum moss," represented in North America by about 20 closely allied species of the genus *Sphagnum*. In peat lands, the moss decays very slowly due to waterlogged, anaerobic conditions. Dead and decayed sphagnum moss is known as peat moss, a large-celled, relatively sterile, nutrient-free medium that retains its spongy, hydrophilic character almost indefinitely.

Fens are shallow depressions in the landscape that are kept wet by an elevated water table. There is a wider diversity of plants and trees in fens than in bogs, because nutrients are supplied in the form of dissolved minerals from the ground water. These minerals also have an alkalinizing effect. Fens range in pH value from 4 to 9.

Fens develop into bogs when the peat accumulates to a great depth (up to 24 feet thick = 7 m). Bogs are actually *raised* over the level of the surrounding landscape, and they receive the majority of their water from rainfall. Therefore, bogs usually have a very acid pH value of 3.5 to 4.5, and contain even less nutrient reserves than fens. Nitrogen, phosphorous and calcium occur at very low levels or are completely lacking.

The surface of the bog is pitted by wet hollows that are dominated by bryophytes, but sometimes harbor lesser lady's slipper orchids *(Cypripedium parviflorum),* pitcher plants *(Sarracenia purpurea)* and buck bean *(Menyanthes trifoliata).*

The bog is also punctuated by drier, raised hummocks covered by shrubby species such as blueberries *(Vaccinium* spp.), bog rosemary *(Andromeda glaucophyllum),* Labrador tea *(Ledum groenlandicum),* leatherleaf *(Chamaedaphne calyculata)*, small cranberry *(Vaccinium oxycoccos)* and swamp laurel *(Kalmia polifolia).*

Sundew itself prefers the interface between hollow and hummock, usually growing in the full sun. The encroachment of trees (such as eastern hemlock, maples, quaking aspen, tamarack and white cedar) will tend to force out the sundew.

---

[1] Bryophytes are nonflowering plants—the mosses and liverworts.

In its more southern range, sundew is usually found in the mountains (e.g. the Sierra Nevadas of northern California), growing at the edge of rivulets of water in alpine marshes and wet meadows. These are areas fed by snowmelt, resulting in an elevated water table. The sundew may be visible from a distance as a reddish rime at water's edge, growing among sphagnum mosses or in sandy or mucky soil. Pitcher plants, grasses, sedges and willow are common associates.

Sundew demonstrates a great deal of adaptability and has even been recorded growing on vertical, clay seepages on the banks of the Blackwater River in Virginia. This microniche occurs at the river's bend where deep sand deposits overlay an impermeable layer of clay. Springwater seeps continuously over the clay surface. Here rogue populations of sundew thrive, along with associated species including canebrake *(Arundinaria gigantea),* laurel greenbrier *(Smilax laurifolia),* summersweet *(Clethra alnifolia),* sweet bay *(Magnolia virginiana),* tag alder *(Alnus serrulata)* and the common denominator—sphagnum moss (Sheridan, 2002).

Life cycle. Sundew flowers in the first year and perennially thereafter. Flowering occurs from early summer through September. The flowers open only in full sunlight, and only for one day, starting at the base of the raceme and continuing to the tip. Ironically and sometimes fatally, pollination is accomplished by the same insects that are commonly trapped by the plant (mosquitoes and gnats). In the absence of insects, the flowers may self-pollinate, and outcrossing is also effected by wind-carried pollen.

Seed requires about 60 days to mature and is released in the autumn or winter as the multichambered capsule fractures or decomposes. This "edge-of-the-water" plant has evolved a unique method for seed dispersal. The germ plasm is contained in an inflated testa, which is capable of floating to a distance. Therefore the aforementioned snowmelt and cold rivulets of the native habitat are largely responsible for dissemination.

Once seeds find purchase in peat moss or sandy muck, they rest quiescent through the cold months and germinate in the spring. The seeds germinate most efficiently after this natural cold stratification, in a moist medium and in the light.

Cultivation from seed. The ideal medium for growing sundew is peat moss mixed with coarse sharp sand. The method for producing coarse sharp sand is detailed in the peyote chapter (under "cultivation from seed" p. 173). The quantities used may vary according to various factors, including: whether the plants are to be kept potted or cultured in situ, the source of the water and the permeability of the bottom substrate. A good rule of thumb is to start by mixing 1 part by volume of coarse sharp sand with 2 parts by volume of screened peat moss. Given the questionable environmental implications of using peat moss, coconut fiber may serve as a substitute.

In coordination with the natural cycle, the seed may be sown on the surface of the medium in the fall, midwinter or very early spring. If sowing directly into pots in a greenhouse or sunny windowsill, the seed needs to be prechilled in moist medium in the refrigerator for 30 days at 40° F (~4° C). Tamp the seed in firmly, and make sure that the medium stays continuously damp with soft (rain, snow, pond, river or stream) water. Chlorinated water destroys sundew, having also a negative effect on germination. Bottom watering is much preferred over aerial sprinkling, which may dislodge the seed. Providing partial protection from drying winds and pounding rain is helpful. Partial shading of the seedbed or newly seeded pots is also fine— actually preferred over a full sun exposure—but the seed must receive several hours of sun per day in order to germinate. Seed sown in this manner in the spring usually takes 35 or more days to germinate.

When sowing seed in pots, it is best to use plastic pots filled almost to the top with the peat-sand mix. It is humiliating, but plastic is preferable to ceramic pots, which tend to drink up the water and dry out the precious seed. The pots may be placed in a nonmetallic tray in the partial sun. The tray must be kept filled with soft water, which will keep this very absorptive medium (and consequently the seeds and developing plants) moist.

The backyard peat bog is also an excellent place to grow sundews. The peat bog is made by digging a 3 foot (1 m) deep hole or trench and lining the edges of the hole with the backdirt. Remember that true bogs (as a result of long deposition and slow decomposition of the mosses) are actually raised *above* the level of the surrounding landscape. The resulting raised crater may be lined with a (commercially available) pond liner or smeared with a thick layer of clay slurry to keep the bog from leaking. Then, the crater is filled with peat moss, right up to the top. This minibog is best wetted with soft water and left to settle for a few weeks before planting. Situating the bog in such a way that it receives a natural water supply (e.g. seepage from a pond or water from rain gutters) helps assure that the bog surface will not dry out. It also makes sense to create an overflow to drain off excess water which could otherwise breach the walls of the bog and send the plants "floating downstream." The backyard bog can be very useful for growing semiaquatic medicinal plants such as calamus *(Acorus calamus)*, blue flag *(Iris versicolor)*, brahmi *(Bacopa monniera)* and watercress *(Nasturtium officinale)* as well as insectivorous plants (see also the chapter on Venus fly trap). Acid-loving bushy species (e.g. blueberries and uva ursi) can be planted on, or around, the berm.

The Backyard Bog

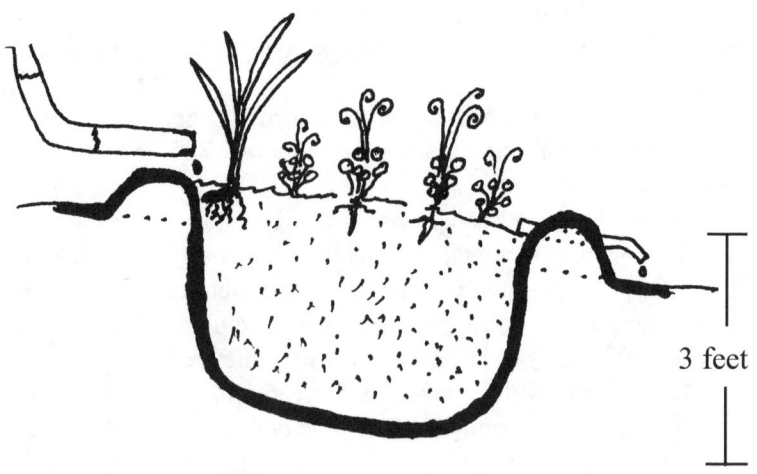

3 feet

Propagation by leaf cuttings or division. Sundews can be cloned quite easily. The leaf cutting consists of an entire leaf and its stem. The crown division consists of an adult plant with large leaves removed, squeezed or cut into several pieces at the crown, each containing a few rootlets and immature leaves. The leaf cutting is laid out on the surface of the moist peat and partially covered with chunky, broken peat or pieces of sphagnum moss. The crown division is shallowly replanted and the medium firmed around its base. Planting too deeply is a common mistake that may result in mold or rot. The idea is to stimulate the leaf cutting or division to root in on its own and create a new rosette. The preferred conditions include high humidity, even heat and filtered light. These conditions are best supplied by a greenhouse, ventilated propagation tray (plastic or glass covered) or a terrarium. Some growers set up propagation trays about 12 inches (30 cm) below full spectrum, fluorescent lights. Once the cuttings or divisions root in and begin putting out new leaves (which takes about 3 months' time), they may be carefully transplanted to new pots or to the backyard bog. Space transplants about 3 inches (~8 cm) apart.

General care. Sundew loves the light, and the plants must be kept in a sunny location if they are to thrive. Failure to do so will cause sundew to become very leggy, and if the shady conditions are combined with cool weather, the plants are liable to become covered with gray mold *(Botrytis cinerea)* which will kill them. The plants require little upkeep beyond the maintenance of the soil, moisture and light requirements that have already been discussed. There is no call for fertilizers. Indeed, applications of fertilizers may well kill the plants, which much prefer to self-feed on tiny insects. This form of fertilization is very successful in producing large and healthy plants (Shulze, 1990). There is no call for weeding—very little else will grow in a medium of pure peat and sand. If the plants are simply let be, they will attune to the seasons at their own pace, eventually flowering and reseeding. In very cold areas (with winter temperatures dipping below 28° F = -2.2° C) outdoor plants are best protected in the late fall by a thick layer of loose sphagnum moss. The moss is then removed come spring.

Medicine. Sundew is best prepared as a fresh plant extract (alcoholic). There is little enough of the plant to start with (in the fresh state) and once dried, there is almost nothing there. This applies both to the physical bulk of the plant, and to secondary constituents (naphthoquinones, mucilage and enzymes) that are responsible for its antitussive and immune-enhancing activity. Sundew is almost always taken in combination with complimentary herbs (e.g. elecampane root, marshmallow root or leaf, mullein flowers, thyme leaf and/or wild cherry bark). These augment the upper respiratory effect, and they also fill out the formula. Sundew itself is most effective at very low dosage, and should account for no more than 20% of any formula. Sundew is a specific for treating uncontrollable, dry, spasmodic coughing (sometimes diagnosed as whooping cough) that continues in fits for days and nights on end. Due to the violence of this coughing, and also because there is an insidious tendency for the attacks to become more pronounced when a person attempts to lie down and rest, this condition can be quite debilitating. The eventual state of exhaustion leaves the individual open to deeper complications, including life-threatening pneumonia. In my experience this condition responds better to sundew than any other herb.

Yield. The fresh or dried entire mature plant is the part traditionally used. Although extremely robust specimens may weigh as much as 3 grams, an average plant weighs 1 gram in the fresh state and dries down to 0.1 grams. The water content of fresh sundew is approximately 90%. There are about 454 fresh plants per pound, and about 4,540 dried plants per pound. Therefore, 1 pound of fresh plants would dry down to $\frac{1}{10}$ of a pound of dry plants. "Sundew tea" made of the dried plants is considered a current as well as a traditional remedy (Blumenthal (ed.) 1998; Gruenwald, 2000; Wichtl, 1994). The recommended maximum daily dosage of 3 grams would represent the yield of 30 plants, a substantial wastage over using sundew in tincture form as a part of a formula, where the yield of 1 fresh plant would suffice. Using sundew in the fresh state instead of dried is an excellent example of "conservation through good pharmacy" (Cech, 1999).

Harvest, processing and storage. The plants are harvested at maturity and ideally at peak of flowering. It is not difficult to extract the shallow-rooted sundew from the growing medium, but it *is* rather difficult to separate clinging pieces of the growing medium from the sticky sundew itself! This is basically a hand-cleaning process, and given the neutral and harmless character of sphagnum moss it is acceptable to leave some strands of it in with the herb. The issue of insects will arise. This is another good reason to process the herb in the fresh state, and by using that great antibacterial solvent—grain alcohol. In order to limit the number of fresh gnats in the medicine, it may make sense to harvest the plants early in the morning, before they have started their daily routine of capture and digestion . . .

The plants may be dried by laying them out on a piece of white sheet on a screen in a warm place with positive air flow, out of the light. The plants dehydrate to nearly weightless skeletons within a day or two.

When transporting the fresh plants, they are best packed in moist sphagnum moss and kept cool. They remain stable for several days in this state, but the fresh plant tincture is best made as soon as possible after harvest.

Seed. Sundew seed is shiny, black and inflated. Microscopic examination reveals fine longitudinal grooves on the testa, and a dark, centrally placed endosperm. The seed measures about 1 mm long by 0.25 mm wide. There are approximately 19,500 seeds in 1 gram of sundew seed.

Seed collection, processing and storage. Sundew seed usually ripens during the late summer and winter, between the months of October and January. Once the seed capsule is mature and dry, it may be hand-stripped from the plant and placed on a fine screen over a piece of clean sheeting. The capsule is broken apart and the tiny seeds fall through to be collected on the sheeting. They may then be captured in a piece of waxed paper, which is then folded into a little envelope and stored in a glass jar or in a plastic bag. Store away from the light, in a cool, dry place. Refrigeration extends seed life. The seed retains its viability for up to three years, but best results will be obtained by using seed from the recent harvest.

Conservation status. Sundew is listed by TRAFFIC (the wildlife monitoring program sponsored by the World Wildlife Fund) as a "species of concern." Over 100 different medical preparations (including homeopathic remedies) are manufactured from this tiny plant. There is an overall decline in the size and number of sundew populations worldwide, mainly associated with the loss of peatland habitat, and in many European countries the plant is listed as "endangered, vulnerable or rare" (TRAFFIC, 2002).

Due to the diminutive size of the plant and the continued tradition of utilizing the dried herb in medicinal preparations, sundew harvest statistics give cause for alarm. To my knowledge, there are no documented harvest figures available from the United States and Canada, but in Europe the harvest is controlled and documented. TRAFFIC reports that in the year 1994, in Finland alone, 2,100 kg of sundew plants were harvested and dried for the European phytopharmaceutical industry. According to their estimates, this equates to between 5.25 million and 33.6 million plants! (TRAFFIC, 2002).

The conservation of sundew is intrinsically linked to the conservation of its most prevalent home—the peat lands. According to the The World Conservation Union (IUCN),[2] peat lands are the predominant form of wetland ecosystems on a global scale. Boreal wetlands (the northern home of sundew) cover about 400 million hectares of the earth's surface and represent between 38% and 50% of the global wetland resource. The carbon stored in peat represents $\frac{1}{4}$ of the world's soil carbon pool, and between 44% and 71% of all carbon held in terrestrial biota. Despite this predominance of the peatland habitat, and the clear environmental advantage of wetlands as the most significant global catchment of water and carbon, there is a general cultural antipathy toward these areas. They are often considered

---

[2] IUCN: The World Conservation Union—a union of governments, government agencies, and nongovernmental organizations working at the field and policy levels, together with scientists and experts, to protect nature.

primary sites for both resource extraction and draining and "development." As a consequence, the current estimate is that on a global scale more than 50% of the peatland ecosystem has vanished from the face of the Earth. On a more positive note, the country of Canada leads the world in peatland conservation (North American Wetlands Conservation Council, 1996).

Other species. There are six species of the *Drosera* genus that are native to North America. Our round leaf sundew *(D. rotundifolia)* is considered official, but the other species are probably used as local medicines. All species of sundew will contain mucilage and proteolytic enzymes, but the profile of immune-enhancing and antitussive naphthoquinone constituents varies depending on the species (Gruenwald ed., 2000). However, the specific naphthoquinone constituent known as plumbagin is probably present in all species of sundew.

On a global scale, there is significant harvest of at least four species of sundew for medicine. These include *D. anglica, D. intermedia, D. madigascariensis* and *D. rotundifolia* (TRAFFIC, 2002). Of these, both spoon leaf sundew *(D. intermedia)* and round leaf sundew *(D. rotundifolia)* are native to the New World.

Dwarf sundew *(Drosera brevifolia)* is native to both the United States and Mexico. Pink sundew *(D. capillaris)* is an evergreen species distributed throughout the southeastern United States, Mexico, Central and South America. Slender leaf sundew *(D. linearis)* is found in the region of the Great Lakes and Labrador, inhabiting alkaline marl bogs. Spoon leaf sundew *(D. intermedia)* is native to the eastern United States. Thread leaf sundew *(D. filiformis)* is native to the eastern and southern United States. This plant is a popular horticultural variety, due to its strikingly thin, long leaves.

221

References

Blumenthal, Busse and Goldberg (eds.). 1998. *The Complete German Commission E Monographs: Therapeutic Guide to Herbal Medicines.* Austin (TX): American Botanical Council.

Cech, R. 1999. *Balancing Conservation with Utilization, Restoring Populations of Commercially Valuable Medicinal Herbs in Forests and Agroforests.* Herbalgram 45, pp. 58-60.

Gruenwald, J. (ed.). 2000. *PDR for Herbal Medicines.* Montvale (NJ): Medical Economics Company, pp. 740-741.

North American Wetlands Conservation Council. 1996. International Workshop on Global Mire and Peatland Conservation. Brisbane, Australia. http://ibs.uel.ac.uk/imcg/resource/papers/brisbane.html

Schulze, W. and E. Schulze. 1990. *Insect Capture and Growth of the Insectivorous Drosera rotundifolia.* Oecologia, 82(3), pp. 427-429.

Sheridan, P. 2002. *A Unique Habitat for Drosera Rotundifolia L. (Droseraceae) on the Blackwater River, Virginia.* Meadowview Biological Research Station report, Dept. of Biology, Virginia Commonwealth University.
http://www.pitcherplant.org/ Abstracts/UNIQUE-HABITAT.html

TRAFFIC. 2002. TRAFFIC is the wildlife monitoring program of the World Wildlife Fund for Nature (WWF) and The World Conservation Union (IUCN). TRAFFIC works in cooperation with the CITES secretariat.
www.traffic.org/plants/species-5.html

Wichtl, M. 1994. *Herbal Drugs and Phytopharmaceuticals.* Boca Raton (FL): CRC Press, pp. 178-188.

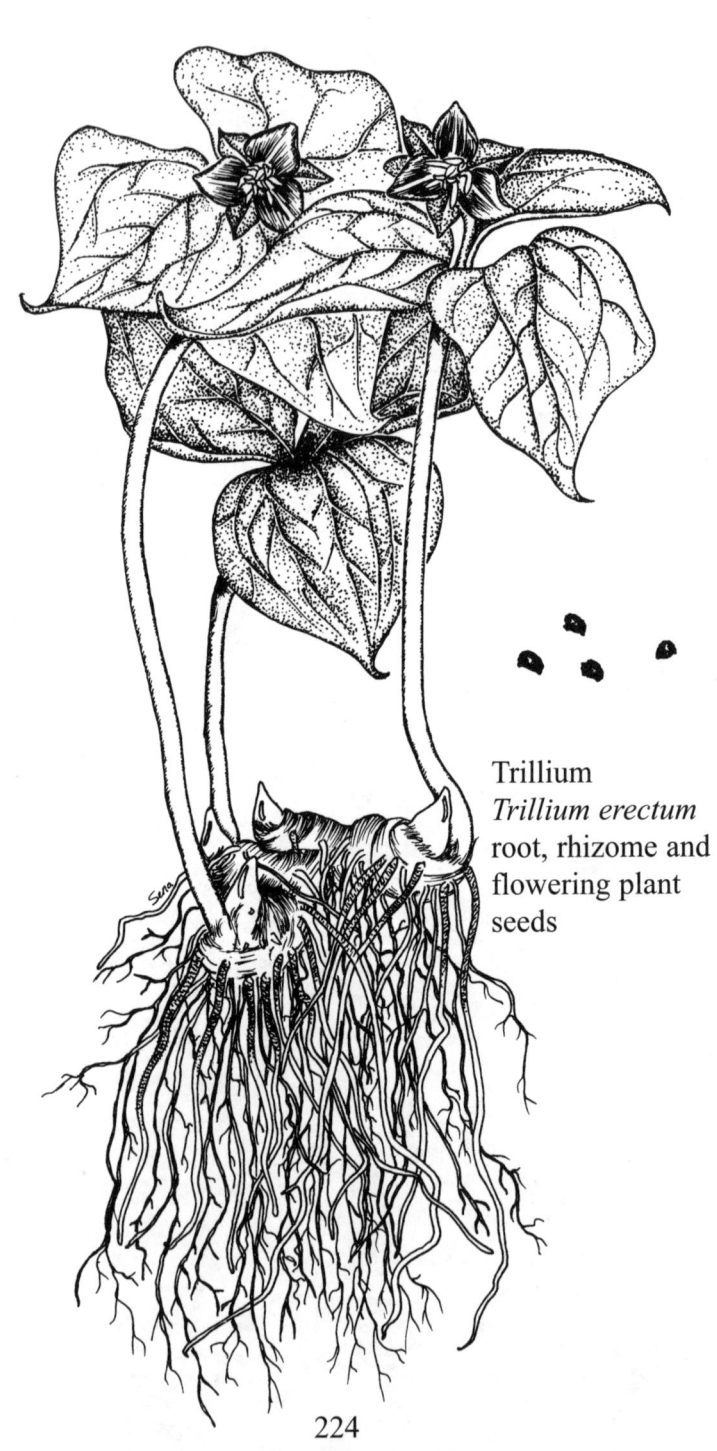

Trillium
Trillium erectum
root, rhizome and
flowering plant
seeds

Trillium (Beth Root)

Trillium erectum L.

Family: *Liliaceae*

Beth root is a long-lived woodland herbaceous perennial. The chubby rhizome lodges deeply in the soil, often formed in amorphous, horizontal or upright clumps, barrel-shaped with a truncated base. The rhizome is colored dark reddish-brown, showing numerous growth rings and pocked with spiraling, ledge-like stem scars that tell the story of the plant's age. Internally, the rhizome is starchy, cream-colored and milky on the freshly-cut surface. The taste is sweetish and a bit acrid. The flexible roots are wrinkled like the trunk of an elephant. They extend from the rhizome in great proliferation. In commerce the dried root and rhizome are known as the "root."

Each fleshy, terminal bud elongates hugely in the spring to produce the smooth, carbohydrate-rich stem and the characteristic, graceful whorl of three deeply-veined leaves. Plants are single-stemmed when young, becoming multiple-stemmed with age. The flower arises from the center of the leaves and is often hidden below them, nodding down toward the roots or looking out demurely into the forest. Classic beth root has a royal, dark maroon flower consisting of three sepals and three petals. This repeating theme of threes (leaves, sepals and petals) is a trait shared by all members of the *Trillium* genus and was the original inspiration for its name. The flowers are long-lasting, and they smell like semen. This explicit aroma is actually attractive to ants, bees, beetles and flies. If these pollinators do their job well, then the flower gives way to a ridged, pointed, reddish, sweet-smelling fruit. The fruit matures and swells with heavy, ripe seeds. The tip of the fruit begins to separate, often dropping clumps of sticky seeds to the soil. The base of the fruit softens, and the entire fruit may then drop to the forest floor where it begins to rot. Ants arrive, attracted to the fatty protruberance (the raphe) that jellies out from each reddish-brown, swollen seed. The ants then carry the seeds to a distance, consume the raphe and discard the seed in the backdirt of the anthill. This mode of dissemination (described previously in the chapter on bloodroot) is known as myrmecochery, or "ant farming."

Range, hardiness and adaptability. The current native distribution of beth root stretches from the Atlantic seaboard throughout the hardwood forests of the eastern United States and southeastern Canada (Ontario and Quebec), not extending west beyond the Mississippi River. The greatest concentrations still remaining are found in the Appalachian mountain range.

Beth root exhibits a long and complete dormancy, and the seed is dependent on cold conditions to enter into the process of germination and to complete development of the seedling. Therefore, cold winter temperatures do not bother it, and the plant may be successfully grown outside its native range as long as the gardener attends to the soil, shade and winter dormancy requirements. Areas already inhabited by other species in the *Trillium* genus are an obvious choice for introducing beth root.

Current Range of *Trillium erectum*

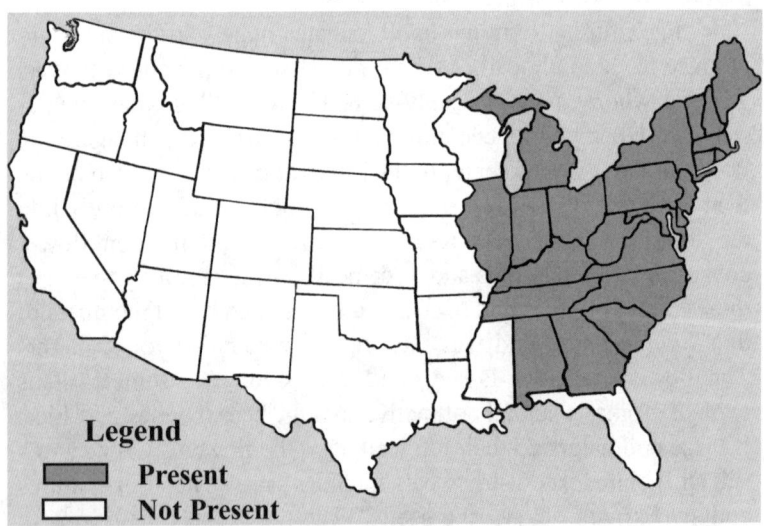

Legend
Present
Not Present

Ecology and plant community. Beth root prefers to grow in moist, cool woodland settings, under the shade of a mixed hardwood forest. It is often found singly or in patches in deep hollows or growing alongside a stream. The preferred soil type is slightly acid forest loam (pH 5 to 6). Muck, clay and sandy soils are tolerated, as long as there is sufficient organic content and a deep surface mulch.

The plant is sensitive to excess light, preferring to grow in areas of complete forest canopy. Occasional mottled light is excellent, but full sun exposure can be detrimental. Therefore, the plant does very nicely on northern facing slopes and in the shade of large forest features such as mature trees, rocky cliffs or watery clefts.

Beth root prefers to grow in moist soils. Occasional flooding does not harm the plant, which is relatively resistant to rot. The peculiar morphology of its rootlets, the crinkled "elephant trunk" appearance is shared by other plants that have an affinity for moist or mucky soils (e.g. skunk cabbage). Interestingly, both trillium and skunk cabbage are also very deeply seated in the soil, with the crown often occurring at a depth of 3 to 5 inches (~ 8 to 13 cm).

Common associates are other water-loving and shade-tolerant understory plants of the rich woodlands including American dog violet *(Viola consperoa)*, bloodroot *(Sanguinaria canadensis)*, cardinal flower *(Lobelia cardinalis)*, goldenseal *(Hydrastis canadensis)*, Jack-in-the pulpit *(Arisaema triphyllum)*, ramps *(Allium tricoccum)*, skunk cabbage *(Symplocarpus foetidus)*, Solomon's seal *(Polygonatum biflorum)*, spikenard *(Aralia racemosa)* and stoneroot *(Collinsonia canadensis)*.

Life cycle. Beth root is one of the earliest of spring ephemerals, often blooming during the first few weeks of April and maintaining its flowers as late as June. Despite the deep mulch of its habitat, heavy spring frosts sometimes damage the plant. This is one disadvantage of being such an early riser. As previously described, the plant is pollinated by carrion-loving flies and beetles, producing a succulent fruit and disseminating its seed in the late summer to autumn. The seed does not withstand dehydration, so it must find purchase in moist soil within a few days of leaving the fruit. Although the raphe is soft, the seeds themselves are very hard, and they do not germinate readily. They contain a substantial reserve of energy in their bean-like endosperm and can remain viable and vigorous for many years, quiescent in the rich soil. The longevity of the seed reflects the overall longevity of the plant. Trillium is not in a hurry.

The seed demonstrates two-phase germination. This peculiar germination habit is also shared by blue cohosh (see "life cycle," page 43). After overwintering for one or many years, the seed initiates the first phase of germination. This may be in response to an increased concentration of gibberellic acid[1] in the immediate substrate. During the first growing season, the seed forms a branching root system and a vegetative bud. There is no aerial expression at this time (Deno, 1996). The nascent plant overwinters in this state. In the second spring, responding to warming soils and the abundant light of the spring forest (before the majority of trees leaf out and shade the forest floor), the bud quickly extends into a single seed leaf. Germination is epigeal. This seed leaf photosynthesizes for a growing season, goes dormant in the winter and in the third spring the seedling produces its first true leaf. Depending on the resources available to the developing plant, including nutrients, light and especially elbow-room, the seedling may require two or more additional years before it produces the first characteristic whorl of three leaves. Progress is slow and steady, but may be interrupted if the seedling is damaged during the developmental stage. Deer relish this plant, and have been known to thin out or demolish entire hillsides. Ill-placed human footsteps can also cause irreparable damage. Once the plant actually produces a flower, which may take anywhere from 8 to 15 years after germination, it is still at-risk from deer, but most humans will know not to cause it any injury. Their mothers told them at an early age that if they picked a trillium, all kinds of bad things would happen in fairyland, and most of us don't want to be responsible for *that*. Trilliums in nature have been known to live for as long as 72 years (Klein, 1999).

---

[1] Gibberellic acid (GA-3) is a growth hormone that is usually produced within seeds when they first imbibe moisture. The hormone stimulates elongation of the radicle and development of the embryonic leaves. Some plants, trillium included, are unable to make their own GA-3, and thus are dependent on fungi to produce the growth hormone exogenously. GA-3 is one of the by-products of fungal life cycles.

Cultivation from seed. The seed must be kept moist in storage, and is ideally planted as soon as possible after harvest and cleaning. Germination is improved by washing and cleaning the seed with the mesh bag technique that was discussed earlier in the chapters on bloodroot, blue cohosh and goldenseal. The fresh seed is stored in a mesh bag (hung at the back of the sink) at room temperature and rinsed twice daily with cold water for a period of about two weeks. The seeds may be gently kneaded in the bag in order to help break down and wash away the raphe. This method helps leach out germination-inhibiting compounds, resulting in very plump and viable seed.

Soils used for starting beth root seed should be rich and humusy. Regular potting soil will serve, but it is best to inoculate it with some forest soil in order to supply mycorrhizae and gibberellins. Some growers actually presoak beth root seeds in a water solution of purified gibberellic acid, which definitely improves the germination rate. The GA-3 is produced by culturing and extracting *Gibberelia fujikuroi* fungus, and is commercially available. Kelp tea also contains gibberellins.

The preferred sowing location is a fine seedbed in a forested situation or in the shade garden. Deep flats are also potentially functional, but it must be remembered that the seed will not emerge aerially in the first year, and this represents a long period of time to keep a flat protected and moist. Flats kept on tables in a shadehouse may serve.

Seed is best sown in the autumn or very early spring. Sow the seed about ¼ inch (0.6 cm) deep and tamp down the surface, then cover with a generous layer of fine leaf mulch. This maintains even soil moisture and discourages emergence of many weed species. At Horizon Herbs Seed Farm, fresh seeds sown in outdoor conditions on 2/5/2001 emerged vigorously on 4/5/2002, a germination period of 424 days. The single leaves were sharply pointed, and the little colony seemed right at home in a gallon pot. Seedlings may be grown at close spacing until they are sufficiently developed for transplant.

Cultivation from root divisions and cuttings. Mature beth roots form an amorphous clump that gives rise to multiple stems and consequently many nascent buds. These occur at the base of each stem. The clump is readily broken or cut apart, and each piece containing a bud and rootlets is a prime division for replanting. In this manner several new clones may be produced from a single parent. These sometimes even flower in the first season.

The entire surface of the beth root rhizome is covered with tiny eyes (adventive buds) that have the capacity to produce growth buds and roots when held in the right conditions. Although pieces containing the large, vegetative bud make the best cuttings, transverse sections as narrow as ½ inch (1.2 cm) can also be convinced to produce a plant. Cuttings are made with a sharp knife or razor blade. They are left out overnight to callus and then planted in pots. The pots must be kept moist and shaded until the new plant, which is a clone of the mother, emerges. Plants grown from adventive buds may achieve maturity in 3 to 6 years' time.

General care. After 3 or more years of growth, it is best to transplant the small rhizomes to a distance of at least 12 inches (30 cm) apart. Root cuttings can also be placed at this spacing. Transplanting is best accomplished only during the dormant period, and preferably in the autumn. The rhizomes can be planted up to 5 inches (~13 cm) deep, with the rootlets spread out and down and the bud pointing straight up toward the surface. Once the plants are established, an application of organic compost or composted manure applied as a side-dressing in the fall or early spring will encourage rapid development and flowering. If forest beds are clearly delineated by paths, then it is easier to keep people from walking on the plants, which are especially vulnerable during spring emergence. The area should also be protected from deer if possible. If natural leaffall is not forthcoming, then the plants need to be deeply mulched with hardwood leaves or rotted sawdust each autumn.

Trillium is most at home in the woodland environment, where it will eventually naturalize and reseed on its own. However, the plant can also be grown in an unheated greenhouse. Beth roots planted in rich beds underneath the benches in my greenhouse are watered by warm, nutrient-rich drippings from the flats above. They thrive in this environment, which is shady and humid in the summer and cold in the winter. Greenhousing beth root substantially speeds sexual maturity and increases root yield phenomenally.

Medicine. Trillium is strictly indigenous to North America, and so we look to the early native uses of the plant as a guide to its medicinality. Native Americans used it for three basic functions: to promote childbirth and stem post-partum bleeding; as an internal remedy for upper respiratory, digestive or uterine malaise; and as a poultice for treating "putrid ulcers, tumors and inflamed parts" (Moerman, 1986). Beth root is still used in modern herbal medicine, despite the negative ecological connotations. The entire plant is active, including the rhizome, stem and leaves. Much of the activity can be ascribed to the presence of steroidal saponins and tannins, although it is the whole plant that does the work. Beth root regulates hormonal imbalance, tonifies the internal organs, stems excessive menstrual discharge, and in large doses will stimulate contractions while it reduces postpartum bleeding.

Other herbs (e.g. cultivated blue cohosh, partridge berry, raspberry leaf and motherwort) may serve as more common substitutes for our precious beth root. These are also considered to be of assistance in preparing the mother for birthing or variously used as uterine tonics. Shepherd's purse, yarrow, or a compound of erigeron and cinnamon essential oils in an alcoholic base are successfully used by midwives in treating heavy post-partum bleeding.

The native use of the fresh poultice of beth root plant in treating external ulcerations and tumors is a fascinating application. Since it contains no sanguinarine, trillium may well affect a change in abnormal tissues through a different mode of operation than the more commonly employed antimitotic herbs (e.g. bloodroot and celandine). Perhaps trillium offers a unique advantage. More investigation is definitely warranted.

Yield. I dug a mature, dormant beth root from our greenhouse in order to determine approximate yield and plant water content. The plant was nine years old, had been started from a sprouted cutting and grown in the aforementioned ideal conditions in the moist shade underneath the propagation benches. The fresh root and rhizome sported 11 nascent buds and weighed 187 grams. The root dried down to 54.6 g, indicating a plant water content of 70.8 %. On the basis of this cultivated sample, 1 pound of fresh roots would represent the yield of 2.4 plants, and 1 pound of dried roots would represent the yield of 8 plants.

Harvest, processing and storage. Beth root is best harvested during dormancy in the autumn or very early spring. However, traditionally the plant has been dug while in full flower. This is certainly the easiest way to find the plants in the wild, also to differentiate the dark maroon-flowered beth root from several other species that may have white or pink flowers, and that may share the same habitat. Cultivation makes possible an increased level of care and control, allowing growers to harvest properly identified roots during dormancy.

If harvesting for aerial parts only, it makes sense to pick the leaves and stem after the fruit is mature, thereby giving the plant one last chance to produce seed before it is compromised, and also allowing the plant time to set buds for the next season. Aerial parts should be kept loosely packed in a basket, thereby avoiding "sweating" the fragile herb and also keeping it from being crushed. The fresh plants are then transported as quickly as possible to the drying room or herb dehydrator.

Roots bound for fresh shipment are best left dirty, then covered in moist peat. Packed in this manner and kept relatively cool, the roots remain alive and stable for many weeks. Roots bound for dehydration are washed immediately and sliced in transverse sections about ½ inch (1.2 cm) wide. Dry the root pieces in a warm place with positive airflow, stirring often. A forced-air dehydrator may also be used. Dry for 1 day with low temperature (70° F = 21° C) and high air flow, then turn up the temperature to medium (90° to 100° F = 32° to 38° C) and dry the roots until they snap. The root pieces are then stored in plastic bags in lightproof sacks or drums, in a cool, dark and dry location. The dried roots retain their potency for up to two years.

Seed. Beth root seed is ovate, smooth-skinned and externally reddish-brown, with a thin testa and a hard, cartilaginous, milky-white endosperm. It tastes like an uncooked bean, but gives an acrid aftertaste. The fresh, live seed measures 3 mm long and 2 mm wide. The seeds are subject to dehydration and must be kept moist in storage. The raphe is a bit of ovarian tissue that adheres to the fresh seeds. This may be removed by washing and cleaning the seed as previously discussed (under the heading "cultivation from seed"). Once the raphe is removed, 1 gram of viable, moist seed contains about 180 seeds. Live, vital seeds can be easily differentiated from dead seeds. Live seeds are translucent, swollen and perky, with a firm endosperm. Dead seeds are dull, dark and filled with putrescent goo. The seeds dry out very quickly, and once dry may be considered to be dead.

Seed collection, processing and storage. Beth root seed is best harvested when the fruits are fully ripe and ready to fall from the plant. This usually occurs in the month of July. The fruits are hand-picked, and the seeds squeezed out and placed in a mesh bag. The seeds are then washed and cleaned as previously described, and may be put in cold storage (not frozen!) as soon as they are free of the clinging raphe. Seeds may be cold-stored in moist peat moss, or the mesh bag may simply be placed in a sealed plastic bag in the refrigerator. This bag must be removed and rerinsed from time to time in order to rehydrate and aerate the seeds. This will also keep them fresh and prohibit the spread of mold. The cleaner the seed, the less likely it will be to succumb to putrefaction. The seed may be stored in this manner for up to eight months, although it makes sense to plant it as soon as possible after harvest and cleaning.

Conservation status. Beth root *(Trillium erectum)* is listed as "rare" in Nova Scotia, as "endangered" by the state of Illinois, "threatened" by the state of Rhode Island and is "protected" in the state of New York (Marshall, 1993). Although several species of *Trillium* are both CITES and IUCN listed, *T. erectum* is not among them. However, the plant is currently under consideration for a CITES listing (Federal Register Vol. 66 #113, June 12, 2001). It is an unfortunate fact of conservation legislation that governments do not officially recognize the deterioration of native plant populations until the plants are nearly gone.

Wild trilliums face many challenges in the modern world. As a forest-dependent plant, trillium is adversely affected by even the least invasive of logging activities, and entire populations are extirpated in the aftermath of clear-cutting. In a strange twist of fate, waning populations of carnivorous animals in the increasingly tame forests of the United States and Canada have resulted in a burgeoning of deer populations. This in turn causes increased pressure on plant species that are browsed by deer. Deer prefer to eat soft and mucilaginous foods, and the bright green, turgid leaves and stems of trillium are considered a delicacy. The more wolves, cougars, and bobcats, the more trillium! Finally, this is a favored plant for shade gardens and there has been an ongoing trade, both local and international, in potted trilliums that are almost exclusively derived from the wild. Because the plant grows so slowly, and because the specific requirements for germinating trillium from seed prove daunting to most growers, attempts to cultivate the plant from seed have often failed. In the absence of local, state and Federal laws disallowing harvest of many species of this beautiful plant, the harvest continues, resulting in a shift of plants out of the wild and into the city. In an ideal world, we would see them independently propagated and prospering in both places.

Other species. Historically and currently, all species of *Trillium* are used interchangeably in herbal medicine. According to *King's Dispensatory,* "Nearly all the species of the genus *Trillium* are medicinal, and possess analogous properties . . ." (Felter and Lloyd, 1898). Historically, the root digger gave little thought to which species was being taken, not only because the plants could not be readily differentiated during dormancy, but also because the appearance of the roots of the various species was identical, and local brokers and druggists readily accepted them all as "beth root." Trillium was one of the original medicinal plants "discovered" in the new world, and was freely taken from the woods and exported to Europe during the days of wooden sailing ships. The herb was accepted into the European pharmacopoeia and integrated into European herbal practice, thus assuring a demand which continues to this day.

There are 39 recognized species of the *Trillium* genus native to North America, and the plant is found in every state of the union with the exception of Alaska, Arizona, Hawaii, Nevada, New Mexico and Utah. Differentiating the various species of the *Trillium* genus can be challenging. The color of the flowers will tend to change according to the season, often appearing snow white in the early spring and turning pink or reddish in the summer. The plants also intergrade and freely hybridize in the wild. The resulting taxonomic snarl is very difficult to pick apart, very much like yarn that has been arranged by a kitten, or a poem by Ferlinghetti. Unless one has a specific reason for the attachment, it really isn't worth trying to set straight.

Besides our beth root, several other species of *Trillium* were employed medicinally by Native Americans, and these are still most commonly used in medicine. The giant white wake-robin *(Trillium grandiflorum)* has a wide distribution throughout the Atlantic and midwestern states. These are actually more showy than beth root, and therefore easier to locate. They are truly awesome on a hillside above a running stream, or chanced upon in the deep forest, where they sometimes make monotypic patches, their flowers like stars in the night. The Pacific trillium *(Trillium ovatum)* has a wide distribution in the coniferous forests of the Pacific Northwest and was used extensively by the native peoples. The flowers are white or pink, and the plant demonstrates much variation. On a local hike, I once came across a patch in the mellow woods containing individuals with glossy, almost metallic, deep purple leaves. I considered for a moment the horticultural implications of digging these roots, then turned my back on the leering face of the profit ogre, bowed once to the plants and left them be. Fairyland rejoiced, and perhaps a tiny chip of bad karma dropped off in my wake as I waded home through the Oregon grape, avoiding the banana slugs, remembering the words of my Boy Scout leader that applied, I suddenly realized, both to poison oak and trilliums—"Leaves of three, let them be."

References

Deno, N. 1996. *Seed Germination Theory and Practice, First Supplement to the Second Edition.* State College (PA): Pennsylvania State University.

Felter, H. and J. Lloyd. 1898 (Reprinted 1985). *King's American Dispensatory.* Portland (OR): Eclectic Medical Publishing, Vol. 1 & 2, 743 pp.

Klein, R. 1999. *How Old are Our Medicines?* United Plant Savers Newsletter, Vol. 2(1), pp. 5-10

Marshall, N. 1993. *The Gardener's Guide to Plant Conservation.* Baltimore (MD): World Wildlife Fund, 186 pp.

Moerman, D. 1986. *Medicinal Plants of Native America.* Ann Arbor (MI): University of Michigan Dept. of Anthropology, Vol. 1, 534 pp.

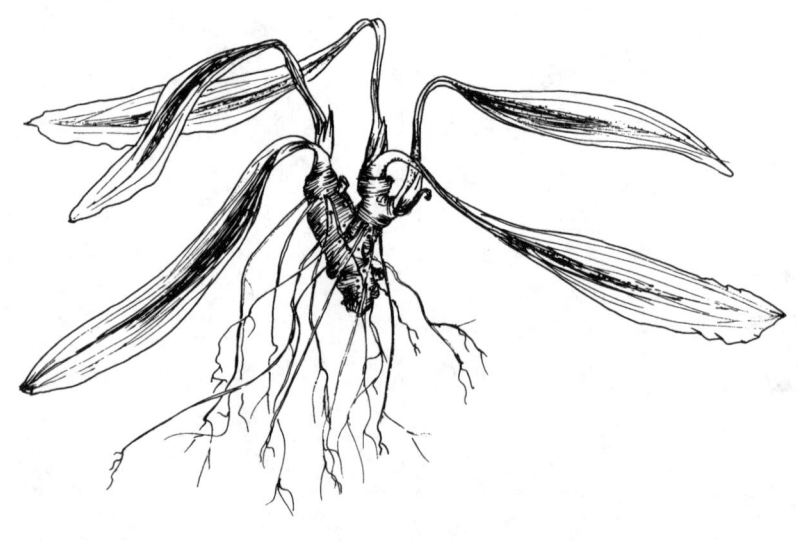

False Unicorn
Chamaelirium luteum
roots, rhizome and leaves

Unicorn, False
Chamaelirium luteum (L.) Gray
Family: *Liliaceae*

False unicorn is a slender, slow-growing and long-lived, dioecious woodland perennial. The rhizome is dark gray, transversely ribbed, sometimes shaped like a small unicorn horn and usually truncated (as if bitten off from below). It is as hard as bone. Wiry rootlets extend out from the rhizome, sparse above and thicker below. Some of the rootlets decay over time, leaving behind a fibrous core that extends out through an enlarged hole in the skin of the rhizome, eventually rotting away completely and leaving a perfectly round hole. These apertures resemble worm holes; they are a reliable identifying feature. The buddy crown gives rise to a flattish, evergreen basal rosette of spatulate leaves with longitudinal veins. The leaves advance in diminishing size up the flowering spike. The plant flowers only once in every three or four years, with male and female flowers occurring on separate individuals. The male plants are longer-lived than the female, and there are (as a consequence) more males than females in any given population of the plants (Meagher, 1982). The male flowering stalk measures about 18 inches (43 cm). The female flowering stalk rises to 30 inches (72 cm) and droops gracefully at the tip. The flowers are yellowish-white and crowd together on the stalk, giving way to oblong capsules that dry in the late autumn and scatter the seeds. The seeds are beige, irregular, flattened and ovate, encased in a papery sac, the "aril." In the early winter the leaves take on a purple hue. When the stem dies back it leaves behind a craterous stem scar. The presence of several stem scars on a rhizome indicates advanced age.

Plant explorers, botanists, wild-harvesters, herbalists and druggists have never been able to agree on a common name for this plant, and great confusion has resulted. I've heard it called many things, including Helonias root, fairy wand, devil's bit, false unicorn, true unicorn, blazing star and starwort. But, my favorite colloquial name combines the rare beauty of the flower with the resemblance of the pale root to a larva—folks call it "star grub root."

Current Range of False Unicorn in the U.S.

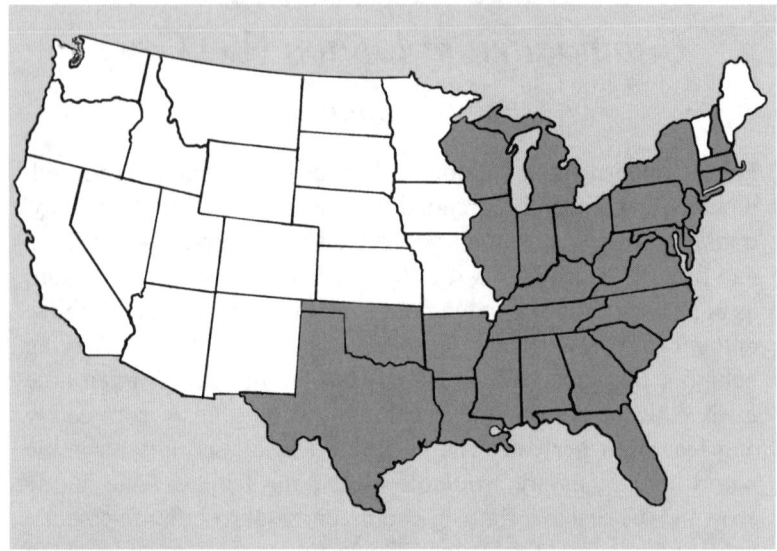

Native range, hardiness and adaptability. The current distribution of false unicorn root stretches from the Atlantic seaboard throughout the eastern hardwood forests, not extending much further west than the Mississippi River, including also the southern Ozark plateau. The greatest concentrations still remaining are found in the southern Appalachian Mountains.

The plant is cold-hardy, but sensitive to the extreme cold in the northerly reaches of its range. Therefore, in very cold areas, it is best to apply a thick mulch in the autumn, and pull it back again to encourage reemergence in the spring.

False unicorn is a member of the lily family, related to many native and ornamental flowers that are fairly tricky to grow and require specific growing conditions (e.g. camas, *Colchicum, Convallaria,* trout lily, fritillary and trillium). When the requirements of temperature, shade, moisture and acidity are met, and as long as the plants are protected from slugs, false unicorn may be grown successfully outside its native range. However, it is not an *easy* herb to grow. Even those cultivating this plant within the boundaries of its native range are obliged to pay careful attention to detail, employ perseverance, patience, and work under the light of their lucky stars if they are to succeed.

Ecology. False unicorn root grows on sloping land in rich, open woodlands, under the mottled shade of hardwood or coniferous trees and woody shrubs. Mature plants will actually withstand direct sunlight, especially morning sun or the brief sunlight available to a north slope, but full sunlight may be deleterious to plants and is likely to be fatal to seedlings.

In nature, the plant grows in soils with a high humic content, preferring acid soils that range between pH 4.5 to 6. Deep conifer or mixed hardwood-derived loam or sandy loam in the Piedmont[1] or bottom lands are ideal soil types. The plant prefers to grow in locations where leaf mulch does not accumulate.

False unicorn prefers moist to mesic (moderately moist) soils that drain quickly. The plant withstands drought conditions, often without damage, but sodden soils or swampy conditions are not well-tolerated (Hollis, 2002).

Natural stands of false unicorn consist of locally abundant groupings and scattered individuals; the plant does not make dense patches. The rhizome does not "creep," so the plant must rely on seed dissemination to further the species. Younger individuals occur in close association with the parent, growing slowly and poised to take over should the older plant die.

Community. Examples of herbaceous plants that may grow in association with native stands of false unicorn are: foamflower *(Tiarella cordifolia)*, galax *(Galax urceolata)*, hepatica *(Hepatica* spp.), lady's slipper orchid *(Cypripedium* spp.), partridge berry *(Mitchella repens)*, Solomon's seal *(Polygonatum biflorum)*, stoneroot *(Collinsonia canadensis)* and white snakeroot *(Eupatorium rugosum)*. Woody understory species that may shade false unicorn include elderberry *(Sambucus canadensis)*, black haw *(Viburnum prunifolium)* and spice bush *(Lindera benzoin)*. False unicorn often grows in clearings surrounded by mountain laurel *(Kalmia latifolia)* and rhododendron species, as well as other members of the heath family. These are also indicator plants for the preferred acid soils.

---

[1] The Piedmont is a plateau between the coastal plain and the Appalachian Mountains. Here false unicorn is "abundant in particular locations, but the locations are uncommon" (Hollis, 2002).

Certain forest soils in the West may prove conducive to growing false unicorn, even without the addition of soil amendments. This includes alder-maple forests, especially areas reclaimed from acid-loving blackberries. Other good choices would be Oregon coast alder-elderberry associations or forests harboring rhododendron and azalea in the Pacific Northwest. In my experience, oak-pine-madrone forests, and even the oak savannas of southern Oregon and California are amenable to cultivation of false unicorn. This is a significant departure from my normal environmental recommendation for other forest-dependent plants from the East (e.g. bloodroot, goldenseal and ginseng), but false unicorn is more tolerant of acidity, heat and sunlight. Regardless of soil type, growing false unicorn in the western forests requires summer irrigation.

Life cycle. In nature, false unicorn flowers in the spring and is pollinated by wind, bees and insects. The plants flower infrequently, and both male and female flowering individuals are necessary for fertilization, a combination of factors that is largely responsible for the rarity of the species. After fertilization and with age, the female flower turns from white to yellowish-white, slowly developing the seeds throughout the summer months and into the autumn. The seeds dry within the capsule and disperse by means of animal activity, wind and snowmelt. The seeds overwinter and germinate in the early spring in cold soils. Although false unicorn is a monocot, germination is epigeal, with immediate formation of a single, elongated seed leaf followed by two to five spatulate (spoon-shaped) true leaves. The leaves are very small (¼ inch = 0.6 cm) in width, arising from a fleshy base. A few rootlets are formed, thinner than threads, that nonetheless delve quite deeply, reaching up to 6 inches (14.4 cm) in the first year, establishing the water and nutrient carrying capacity of the tiny seedling. In the second year, additional sets of true leaves are formed, and the root system continues to develop. By the fourth year, the plant presents as a multiple-leaved rosette, with a differentiated, thickened rhizome. By year 7, under the best of circumstances, the rhizome will attain full size, and the plant will declare its sex by producing a flowering stalk. Plants in nature live as long as 30 to 80 years (Meagher 1984).

Cultivation from seed. Soils used for germination flats or for potting the false unicorn seedlings should be of high organic content and on the acid side. The recipe I like to use is: 2 parts regular peat moss, 1 part decomposed pine needles, 1 part perlite and ½ part sand. Decomposed pine needles can be collected from underneath pine trees. Pull aside the recent needles and go for the spongy layer that is turning into soil. Take a little here and there, and cover your hen scratches with pine needle mulch. If it is difficult to obtain decomposed pine needles, then rotted coniferous sawdust or bark mulch may be substituted. There are also prepared mixes available for acid-loving plants (e.g. rhododendron) at nursery supply stores. Although to my knowledge specific mycorrhizal associations have not been identified for false unicorn, given the sparseness of feeder roots on the rhizome, I would expect that mycorrhizal associations *do* exist. Therefore, it makes sense to inoculate the potting soil with a shovelful of forest-derived soil (well mixed in) as a means of introducing fungi. The rotted pine needles serve the same function.

Germination of false unicorn seed is not too difficult, although the seed must be allowed to after-ripen and overwinter to dispel inhibiting factors before germination is possible (Baskin, 2001). The best approach is to use newly harvested and dried seed and sow shallowly (1/8 inch = 0.3 cm) in shaded, outdoor propagation beds in the fall, midwinter (if conditions allow) or very early spring. Tamp the seed in securely, and keep evenly moist. Once the seeds are planted, freezing temperatures and snow cover are not a problem. In fact, natural precipitation will serve to leach germination-inhibiting factors from the seed and cause it to swell, and oscillating temperatures will evoke the germination response. At Horizon Herbs Seed Farm I sowed the same lot of seeds on 12/30/00 and also on 2/23/01 in outdoor beds, and the seeds in these samples germinated synchronously in April of 2001. The following year, seed sown in the (cooler) shadehouse on 11/15/01 germinated on 6/3/02, a germination period of 200 days.

Given plenty of seed, you can just sow the seed directly in shaded beds and thin the plants if they come up too densely. But there is almost never a surfeit of false unicorn seed. In the words of Joe Hollis, "Nonavailability of seed is a primary factor preventing the development of this species as a cultivated crop."

Artificial stratification may also give good results. The seed is placed in a moist medium (peat moss, vermiculite or sand) in the refrigerator at ~40° F (~4° C) for 8 to 12 weeks. The mixture is then sprinkled on the surface of a flat, tamped down and kept moist until germination. Ideally, the flats are then left outside in a shadehouse or in the shade garden, since subjecting them immediately to warm greenhouse temperatures is unlikely to give satisfactory results.

Average planting success with false unicorn seed is 60% to 80%. Higher germination rates may be achieved by selecting only the most mature seeds by wind-winnowing and discarding all but the heaviest fraction.

The new seedlings must be left undisturbed for at least 1 growing season, preferably 2 growing seasons, before they are large enough to transplant out of the propagation bed or out of the flat. It takes the new seedlings 4 months to fully develop their first set of true leaves. By the first autumn after germination, they may be large enough to tease apart and plant at wider spacing in prepared beds in the shade garden or forest. The seedlings can also be planted in small (4") pots in order to mature further in controlled conditions. Potting-up provides an advantage in that the plants are larger at transplant, with an easy-to-handle root ball instead of a tiny bare root. Since the plants are not taprooted they adapt nicely to life in pots. I find that our shadehouse, which is fitted out with 66% shade cloth and water-saving misters, is an ideal environment for germinating flats of false unicorn seeds and for holding the plants for extended periods of time. This is a tradeoff situation, since transplanting directly from shaded propagation beds to the final location saves human effort and resources, but growing in controlled conditions in pots for one or two years will reduce transplant mortality and help assure success.

Cultivation from rhizome cuttings. The entire surface of the false unicorn rhizome is covered with tiny eyes (adventive buds) that have the capacity to produce growth buds and roots when held in the right conditions. Because the rhizome is small, the cuttings must be made small in order to achieve much advantage. Transverse sections as narrow as ¼ inch (0.6 cm) are made with a clean, sharp knife or razor blade. The sections look like little toy wheels. They are left out overnight to callus and then planted in pots. The pots must be kept moist and shaded until the new plant, which is a clone of the mother, emerges. The piece with the crown can also be replanted, although splitting the crown itself is usually not a successful technique. Plants grown from cuttings may achieve maturity in five to six years' time.

General care. Transplant to the final location at a spacing of 6 inches to 1 foot (15 to 30 cm) between plants. If the soil is low in humic content, then it needs to be amended with organic compost or rotted manure before planting. Firm the roots down in, with the rosette well above the surface of the mineral soil, then fill in around the plant with a thick mulch of pine needles, bark mulch or rotted conifer-derived sawdust. In very cold winter areas, the mulch should be applied again in the early winter to cover and protect the plants, but in warmer areas it makes sense to let this evergreen plant photosynthesize its way through the winter. Care for the plants by weeding and watering when necessary. An occasional side-dressing of well-rotted manure or organic compost is well-tolerated and will speed growth and increase yields. Protect the plants from slugs and snails, both by mixing the planting with other shade-tolerant species that provide an alternate food source to pests, and by ridding the environment of slug habitat. Old boards left lying around in the damp are the preferred hotel of the gastropod.

Medicine. The fresh or dried false unicorn and rhizome (the root) is the part traditionally used. The fibrous rootlets do not amount to much, and the rhizome makes the vast majority of the medicine. This is a uterine tonic of great repute, used in treating sexual malfunction, abnormal discharge, menstrual irregularities, miscarriage and prolapse. The herb is generally used in small dosage, often combined with other herbs in formula to stretch it. False unicorn has secondary utility as a gastrointestinal tonic in treating loss of appetite, indigestion and malabsorption of nutrients. Although the uterine tonic aspects of this herb are quite unique and really irreplaceable, the digestive aspects are easily matched by using any of the bitter herbs (e.g. calamus).

245

Yield. An average rhizome with rootlets weighs 5 grams fresh and dries down to 1.6 grams. The water content of fresh roots ranges between 66% to 70%. There are about 90 fresh roots per pound, and about 284 dried roots per pound. Each pound of fresh roots would dry down to a little over ⅓ pound of dry roots.

The leaves of this plant, like the rootlets, do not amount to much weight. To my knowledge, the leaves are not purposefully used in medicine, but are sometimes included along with the root in commercial shipments—dried leaves and leafstalk fibers loosely attached to the desiccated crown. The growing plant is easily damaged by loss of leaves, and for this reason I do not foresee much advantage in attempting to develop medicine from the aerial parts of the plant—they are not really a renewable resource. Further study regarding the chemical structure and safety of the aerial parts may eventually give reason to recommend use of the entire dried plant.

Harvest, processing and storage. Because false unicorn is an evergreen perennial, the time or season of harvest does not much affect the quality or concentration of the medicine. The lack of dormancy and the slowness of development combine to produce a very hard root that is not much affected by the cycling of the seasons. Following traditional herbal practice, it is probably best to harvest the roots in the autumn or winter. This also allows one to collect the seed before digging the plant.

Dig the roots by hand or with a small digging tool, being careful not to injure the cortex, then shake them free of excess dirt. If the roots are to be used as planting stock, make sure to get all the fibrous rootlets, and remove only the largest leaves, retaining a healthy central leaf rosette. Also, do not wash the rhizomes, as the covering of soil will help protect them from mold during transport and replanting. If the roots are to be used for extraction, then remove the leaves and give the roots a brief washing in a nearby stream or with a pressure hose. False unicorn roots are easy to clean. Excessive washing may cause a diminution of water-soluble constituents. Do not chop up the roots, as they last much longer in storage if kept in the whole form. After they drip dry, they may be processed immediately in the fresh state or laid out on screens in a warm, dark place with positive airflow, turning often. An herb dehydrator is very helpful in drying false unicorn. Dry for 1 day with low temperature (70° F = 21° C) and high air flow, then turn the temperature higher (100° F = 38° C) and dry them until they are dehydrated all the way through. Once the roots are thoroughly dry, they are best stored in glass jars or in plastic bags in lightproof sacks, in a cool, dark and dry location. Stored in this manner, they retain useful potency for at least three years.

False unicorn seed is tan, elongated to approximately 4 mm, flattened and irregular in shape (sometimes shaped like an embryonic tadpole), each seed enclosed in an ephemeral, transparent, papery aril. In 1 gram of seed there are ~1,800 seeds.

Seed collecting, cleaning, storage and longevity. In keeping with its sedate growth habits, the plant requires several months to mature its seed. Pick the seed as soon as it is ripe, before the stem is flattened by wind and rain. You can even pick the seeding raceme and bring it indoors, placing it in a vase of water like a cut flower, to give extra time to mature the last of the seed, which then dries on the stalk.

The dry, seeded tops are then tapped on a table to release the seed, or the capsules are stripped from the stem and rubbed until the seed separates. At this point the seed may be placed on a fine screen and shaken to remove dust, or passed through a coarse screen to separate it from larger chaff, including pieces of the capsule and stem. Make sure to catch the viable seed on a piece of sheeting or on a fine screen! From this point on, wind-winnowing is really the only way (short of extremely tedious hand-separation) to attain higher purity. On a day when the breeze is gentle, but predictable, spread a large sheet on the dry ground and, standing upwind, release the seeds into the airstream, allowing them to fall on the sheet. This will result in a gradient of materials laid down on the sheet, starting with the heaviest and most viable seed and ending on the downwind side with empty seed coats, light chaff and dust. You can choose what to keep and what to discard, funneling the seed into a container such as a gourd or a bowl. This process may then be repeated until the seed becomes sufficiently pure.

I once winnowed false unicorn seed on a day that was a bit blowsy. A sneaky eddy of wind approached silently from behind, caught the seed as I dropped it and deposited it somewhere in the middle of the garden, a very expensive little seed twister. Needless to say, I retained the remainder of the sample, deciding on the spot that it was plenty clean enough for my purposes.

False unicorn seed withstands dry storage without immediately losing its viability, but it is not a long-lived seed. When stored at room temperature and humidity, the seed loses its viability within a year. If stored in plastic or in jars under refrigeration and at low humidity, longevity may extend to about two years. Highest germination will be obtained using recent seed.

Adulteration. Whether caused by similarity of common name, medicinality, relative rarity or perhaps by dint of contagious confusion, the plants *Chamaelirium luteum* (our unicorn, false) and *Aletris farinosa* (unicorn, true) have been consistently interchanged in herbal commerce (Felter and Lloyd, 1898), despite substantive differences in the appearance of the plant, the appearance of the dried root, their taxonomy and their distribution. Not wishing to contribute to this situation, I will not here reproduce the usual litany of shared common names, but instead refer the reader to the respective chapters of this book (since both herbs have found their way onto the United Plant Savers' at-risk list), for clear descriptions and botanical line drawings of each. They are simply not the same plant. False unicorn is primarily a uterine tonic, while true unicorn is used primarily for treating digestive disorders and is only secondarily a uterine tonic.

Analogous herbs. The so-called "swamp pink" *(Helonias bullata)* is an evergreen, perennial, native lily with a shrinking distribution that still includes the states of New Jersey, Delaware, Maryland, Virginia, North Carolina, South Carolina and Georgia. The plant consists of a rosette of long, smooth leaves that give rise to a thick, hollow stem bearing a strikingly purple, cone-shaped blossom. Swamp pink is forest- and wetland-dependent, growing at the headwaters of streams or in spring-fed wetlands. It is a clumping, rhizomatous plant that propagates only grudgingly from seed. It was listed under the United States Endangered Species Act in 1988 as a "threatened" species.

According to *King's Dispensatory,* the plant has analogous properties to false unicorn (Felter and Lloyd, 1898).

Motherwort has recently been posed as a possible alternative to the use of false unicorn for women's health (Gladstar, 2000). This recommendation is well-founded in regards to treatment of digestive disorders (both plants are bitter), female nervous debility, menstrual complaints and general lack of genito-urinary tone. Motherwort is easy to grow.

The tiger lily *(Lilium tigrinum)* plant has been suggested as a substitute for false unicorn in treating cases of uterine irritation and congestion, ovarian pain and/or uterine prolapse (Felter and Lloyd, 1898).[2] Although this is an antiquated reference, the possible interchangeability of these lilies (tiger lily and false unicorn) is a prospect worthy of further investigation. Tiger lily is fast-growing and gives a good yield, especially in comparison to false unicorn. Tiger lily is propagated either by division of the bulb or by planting the blue-black skinned aerial bulbils. The presence of aerial bulbils differentiates this original Chinese cultivar from fancy hybrids, which do not make aerial bulbils and may have lost much of their medicinality through selection for other traits (e.g. flower size, color). It is actually difficult to improve on the original cultivar, which is quite strikingly handsome, bearing velvety-orange flowers with distinct, maroon markings.

Conservation status. It is truly amazing to discover how many false unicorn products have been manufactured, historically and in modern times—virtually all of them made from the tiny roots of plants taken from the wild. Even Lydia Pinkham's famed female elixir purportedly contained false unicorn (Burton, 1949), although many renditions of this compound list true unicorn *(Aletris farinosa)* instead. False unicorn is like the showy pet of many herbalists—they wish they could substitute the herb in therapy, but are hampered by attachments to the old formulas and are afraid that substitutes will not work (or sell) as well as the original. The plant continues to be used at low dosage, but used

---

[2] This reference may be found with some difficulty on p. 1133 of King's Dispensatory, in small print under the heading "related species."

nonetheless. Such ongoing demand will very likely eventually extirpate this species in the wild.[3] In the case of false unicorn, loss of habitat is actually less threatening than overharvest, and there is truly no level of harvest that can be considered sustainable. The very longevity of the plant, a trait that assures its survival in the undisturbed wilds, works against it when populations are disrupted by harvest activities. It takes a long time for infant plants to reach seed-bearing age, and in the meantime, the compromised population may no longer be able to survive adverse events, whether caused by nature or by humans.

As a consequence, in various states at the outer margins of its natural range, false unicorn is already listed on state conservation lists. For instance, there is only one documented occurrence of wild false unicorn in the entire state of Delaware, where it is listed by the Delaware Natural Heritage Program (DNHP) as "extremely rare." In New Jersey it is listed by the state as a "species of concern," and the state of Indiana lists it as "endangered." Given the declining population of this demure forest beauty, states that still harbor local abundance of false unicorn will eventually be following suit, recognizing that this is a species needing careful monitoring and protection.

Home gardeners, farmers, conservationists and researchers will eventually bear the responsibility for keeping false unicorn alive. For a select few this will become the work of a lifetime, a work that could well bear fruit after we are long gone.

---

[3] According to Joe Hollis "A wildcrafter can easily exterminate an entire population in a few hours, and several of my best seed collecting locations [in North Carolina] have met this fate recently."

References

Baskin, C. 2001. *Morphophysiological Dormancy in Seeds of Chamaelerium luteum, a Long-Lived Dioecious Lily.* Journal of the Torrey Botanical Society, 128(1), pp. 7-15.

Burton, J. 1949. *Lydia Pinkham is Her Name.* New York (NY): Farrar, Straus.

Felter, H. and J. Lloyd. 1898 (Reprinted 1985). *King's American Dispensatory.* Portland (OR): Eclectic Medical Publishing, Vol. 1 & 2, 743 pp.

Gladstar, R. (ed.). 2000. *Planting the Future: Saving our Medicinal Herbs.* Rochester (VT): Healing Arts Press, pp. 139-149.

Hollis, J. 2002. Joe lives in Burnsville, North Carolina. He is a knowledgeable seedsman, plant explorer and gardener of native and exotic medicinals. His farm is known as "Mountain Gardens." Joe knows *Chamaelirium luteum* from long association and served as a patient consultant during the writing of this chapter.

Meagher, T. and J. Antonovics. 1982. *The Population Biology of Chamaelirium luteum, a Dioecious Lily.* Ecology, 63(6), pp. 1690-1711.

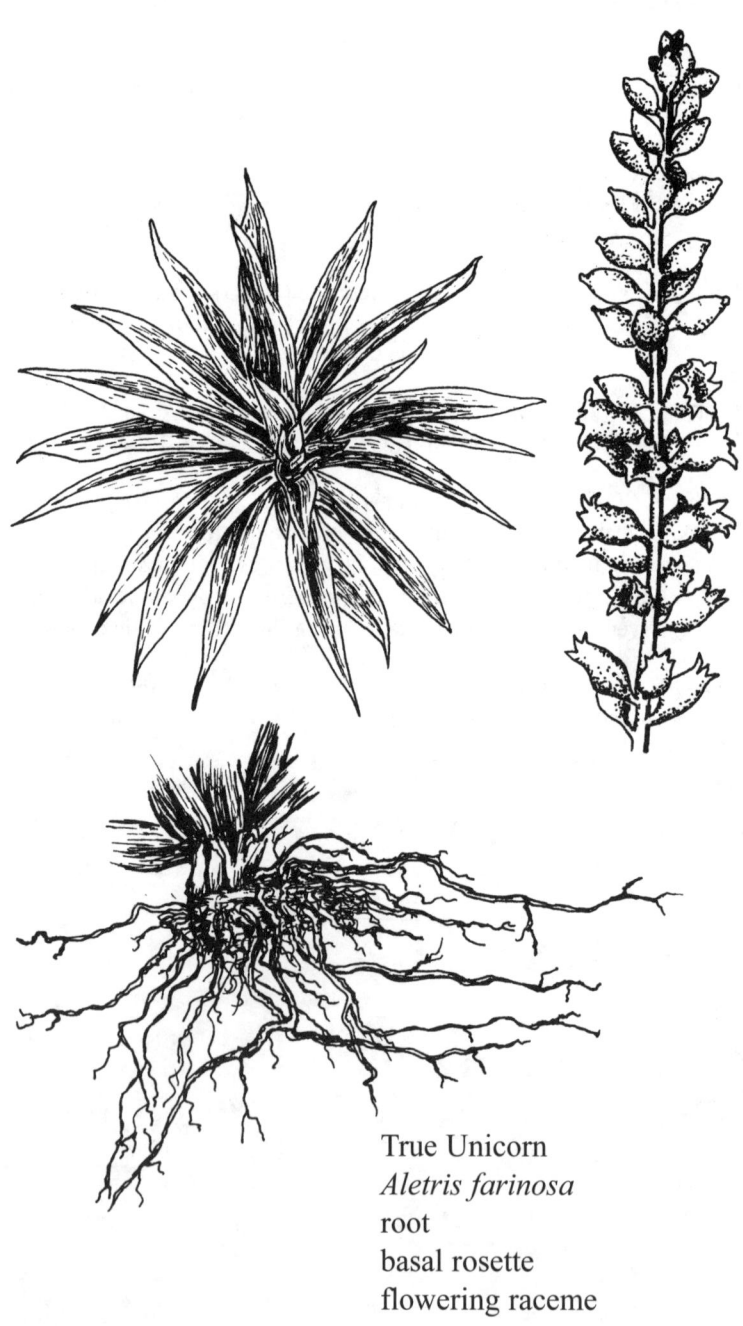

True Unicorn
Aletris farinosa
root
basal rosette
flowering raceme

Unicorn, True
Aletris farinosa L.
Family: *Liliaceae*

Aletris is a sparsely populated and dwindling genus of five species of handsomely flowering, herbaceous perennial plants indigenous to southeastern Canada and the eastern and especially the southern United States. Although it is the white-flowered *Aletris farinosa* that is considered official, all species of *Aletris* have been used interchangeably in herbal medicine and are grouped here under the name of "true unicorn."

The rhizome of true unicorn is rough and wrinkled by growth rings, firmly attached to the bulbous rosette of leaves above and usually terminating in a point below. The rhizome is not quite horizontal; it angles down from the crown. Turned upside-down, a typical rhizome does truly resemble a spiraling unicorn horn as depicted in much fanciful art. The rhizome is partially obscured by a mass of crinkled root fibers that emanate in all directions. Dead root fibers are colored brown. Live material is pure white and somewhat succulent, shrouded by many short, bristling feeder roots. The plant creates a yearly rosette of wide, lance-shaped, grassy leaves that die back during dormancy, leaving a messy garland of leaf fibers at the base of the crown. This material insulates the life-force of the root from environmental extremes of moisture as well as dryness that typify the sandy soil of the preferred habitat. The growing rosette arises from a bulb-like feature that is really comprised of the thickened, blanched bases of the leaves. New leaves are formed at the center while old leaves die out and return to the soil at the periphery. Some writers have likened the shape of the rosette to a star, giving rise to another common name "star grass." The leaves are yellowish-green and smooth textured, with prominent longitudinal veins convening to a sharp point. The flowering stem arises from the center of the rosette to a height of up to 3 feet (~90 cm). The stem is round at the base, becoming angular as it approaches the flower. The flowers contain both male and female parts, loosely clustering to form a terminal raceme. The urn-shaped flowers are white or yellow depending on the species, and they are dusted with a mealy, flour-like excrescence that inspired the species name of the official plant *(farinosa)*. The flowers give way to the three-valved pods, that dry and open in the shape of a beak. The seeds are reddish-brown and ovate, with a slightly pointed hilum; smaller even than those of *Lobelia inflata* and sized some-where between a dust-mote and fine redwood sawdust.

Common names. This relatively rare and unobtrusive plant has for some reason garnered more common names than (probably) any other herb. If these names were maritime exple-tives, a sailor would require a liter of grog, a bad case of saltwater bum-rash and two long breaths to spout them all: ague grass, ague root, aloe root, backache root, Bettie grass, bitter grass, bitter plant, black root, blazing star, cane leaves, colic root, crow corn, devil's bit, false unicorn, husk root, husk wort, maiden's relief, mealy starwort, miller's maid, rheumatism root, star grass, star wort, true unicorn, unicorn horn, unicorn plant, unicorn root and white tube star grass.

Range, hardiness and adaptability. True unicorn occurs sporadically throughout a wide range from southeastern Canada (Ontario and Quebec) south through the eastern states to Florida; west across the gulf states to Texas; then north and east through Oklahoma, Arkansas, Tennessee, Illinois, Wisconsin and Michigan. The plant is sometimes found in black sand prairies that are the preferred habitat in the northern portions of its range, and is a somewhat less rare inhabitant of acid, sandy soils in the pine barrens of the gulf states. Florida is the center of diversity—all five species are found in that state. I first came into contact with true unicorn in southern Georgia, on a moist, sandy roadside within a few meters of pines and within a few miles of the margins of the Okefinokee swamp.

Attempts to domesticate true unicorn outside this range are generally met with failure, probably because of the very specific soil composition, pH and water requirements of the plant. If these conditions can be matched with some precision, then the plant will grow in gardens in the northern, midwestern and western states.

Current Range of True Unicorn

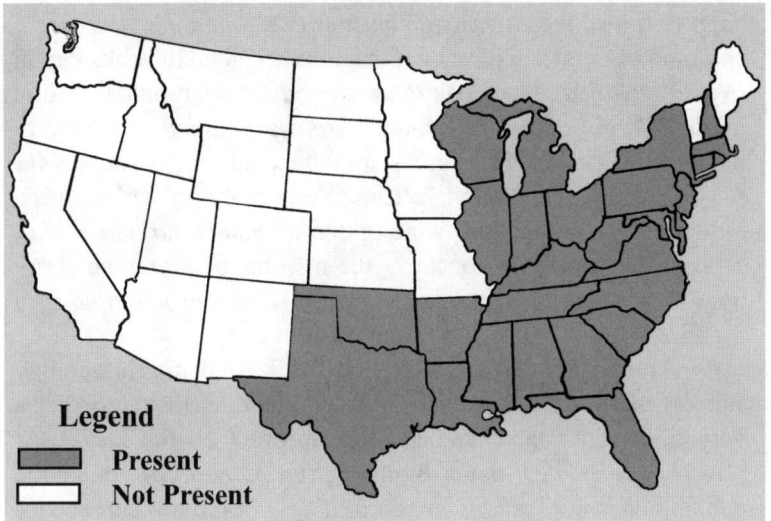

Ecology and plant community. The general habitats that support the growth of true unicorn include: pine barrens, moist open woodlands, meadows, edges of peat bogs and black sand prairies. The plant grows in full sun to partial shade, in sandy soils with a pH value that ranges from 5.5 to 6.5. True unicorn prefers areas that have a high water table, but still the surface may not remain moist during the entire growing season.

Tree species that may occur in close association with wild stands of true unicorn in the gulf states include loblolly pine *(Pinus taeda),* longleaf pine *(P. palustris),* sand post oak *(Quercus margarettia),* sandhill oak *(Q. inopina),* shortleaf pine *(P. echinata)* and turkey oak *(Q. laevis).* Shrubby, vining and herbaceous associates may include Carolina buckthorn *(Frangula caroliniana),* farkleberry *(Vaccinium arboreum),* saw palmetto *(Serrenoa repens),* small-flowered pawpaw *(Asimina parviflora),* yaupon *(Ilex vomitoria),* yellow jessamine *(Gelsemium sempervirens),* wild indigo *(Baptisia tinctoria),* wild Job's tears *(Onosmodium virginianum)* and witch hazel *(Hamamelis virginiana).*

Open, moist woodlands of the Appalachian Mountains sometimes harbor scattered populations of true unicorn. In happier times, the American chestnut *(Castanea dentata)* was a common associate. Current companions might include black gum *(Nyssa sylvatica),* black oak *(Quercus velutinas),* mountain laurel *(Kalmia latifolia)* and sassafras *(Sassafras albidum).* Understory plant associates in these areas might include moccasin flower *(Cypripedium acaule),* rattlesnake plantain *(Goodyera pubescens)* and spotted wintergreen *(Chimaphila maculata).* True unicorn may also occur at the margins of evergreen shrub bogs in association with Venus flytrap *(Dionaea muscipula)* in the Piedmont of North and South Carolina.

Around the Great Lakes, the black sand prairie ecology supports scattered occurrences of true unicorn. This region has a very high water table and is often forested by the black oak *(Quercus velutinas),* paper birch *(Betula papyrifera)* and/or the quaking aspen *(Populus tremuloides).* Common herbaceous associates in this habitat include the whip nutrush *(Scleria triglomerata),* Kalm's Saint John's wort *(Hypericum kalmianum),* gayfeather *(Liatris spicata),* purple milkwort *(Polygala sanguinea)* and meadowsweet species *(Spiraea* spp.).

Life cycle. True unicorn flowers in the summer and matures its seed in the autumn. In the southern portions of true unicorn's range, flowering starts in the month of May, and in the far northern reaches flowering may be deferred until as late as August. The flowers are self-fertile but may be assisted in pollination by gnats, small bees and by the wind. The seed develops within the three-chambered pod, which subsequently splits and spills its tiny load. Dissemination is by wind or water, and the seeds often do not travel far from the mother plant. Therefore, it is common to find a large plant surrounded by its progeny, poised to take over the prime growing position should the older plant complete its life span and die. Once the seed comes into contact with ideal conditions of temperature, soil, moisture, and light, then germination occurs within 5 weeks. The ideal temperature is about 68° F (20° C), and the seed must receive sunlight in order to germinate (Deno, 1993).[1] The seed may lie dormant for a short time until it comes into contact with the right conditions for growth, or it may eventually expire. Germination is epigeal, and true unicorn is a monocot. The tiny rosette develops throughout the later summer and autumn, establishing itself for the winter dormancy. The plants reawaken in the spring, developing a strong rosette and a clump of feeder roots during the first year. The plant usually flowers for the first time in the second year. Mature plants of at least 3 years of age may produce several stems and consequently numerous flowers and seeds. Thus the cycle repeats. The maximum life span of true unicorn has not to my knowledge been determined. Examination of growth rings on older individuals indicates that they live for at least 25 years. The rosette is durable and sand is a good preservative. Populations are sustained both by individual longevity and by vigorous self-seeding.

Cultivation from seed. True unicorn seed may be sown in warm soil in the spring or very early summer, sprinkled on the surface of the medium and pressed in, then kept damp and in the light. Because the seed is very tiny, it will be difficult to sprinkle evenly over the surface of the soil. Mixing the seed with a little sand before sowing will help prevent germination in clumps. The plant may be direct-seeded at the border of the backyard bog or in a sandy bed in the garden. If starting in the greenhouse, the best potting soil consists of 50% coarse, sharp sand and 50% peat moss, which helps maintain excellent drainage and an acid pH value. Once planted and firmed into place, the seed is best watered from below or by a very light misting. Many failures can

---

[1] This is what I call a "light-dependent germinator." Light dependency is controlled by a protein pigment called "phytochrome" that resides in the seed coat. The survival advantage of this adaptation is that in a dark place (which would be an unfriendly place for a photosynthesizing plant to grow), germination will be deferred. Furthermore, the seed is very tiny, and if buried too deeply will not be able to reach the soil surface before it exhausts its resources and dies. Therefore the seed bides its time until it arrives in a light place (and therefore away from other plants and near the surface of the soil), under which conditions it has a good chance of developing into an adult plant.

be traced to violent watering practices that float the seed or disorient its positioning at the critical stage where the radicle elongates and seeks gravity with all its tiny might. Seedlings are almost microscopic at first, and must be left undisturbed until they achieve sufficient size for transplant. Direct-seeded plants may be thinned or transplanted out to a spacing of 6 inches (~15 cm) apart. Seedlings grown in flats may be pricked into pots and grown out for several months until they reach sufficient size for transplant. In the southern or maritime states, the seeds may be started in the late summer instead of in the spring. This will allow them to establish a solid rosette, which then overwinters and may produce a flowering plant the following year. This would be in accordance with the natural cycle in mild winter areas, where flowering, seed production and germination take place in a single growing season.

Cultivation by division. The individual rosette itself cannot be successfully divided, but older plants sometimes produce two or more rosettes from a single rhizome. These may be twisted off of the rhizome. They will come free with lively rootlets attached, and may be transplanted individually.

General care. The preferred growing conditions include a sunny exposure, with well-drained, acid and nutrient-poor soil. Weeding will not be a difficult chore, because most weeds do not favor such soil. Furthermore, fertilization of true unicorn is actually contraindicated. The best results will be obtained by seeding the plant into the exact conditions of its native habitat and letting nature take its coarse, with the eventual goal of naturalization.

Yield. I dug a group of mature, dormant true unicorn plants from our greenhouse in order to determine approximate yield and plant water content. The plants were 3 years old, having been started from seed and grown in sandy gravel at the edge of the floor-level beds. They were fully mature, having flowered the previous year. The plants (consisting of fresh aerial portion, root and rhizome) weighed on the average 18 grams each. They dried down to an average of 3.75 g per plant, indicating a plant water content of 79%. On the basis of this cultivated sample, 1 pound of fresh roots would represent the yield of 25 plants, and 1 pound of dried roots would represent the yield of 121 plants.

Harvest, processing and storage. True unicorn is best dug in the autumn (Elliot, 1995) or early spring, when the power of the plant is in the root. The plant may be used fresh or dried, and although the *root* is often specified as the main active plant part, the *entire plant,* including leaves, rhizome and rootlets are similarly effective medicine. The plants are popped out of the ground with a shovel or garden fork. Plants bound for shipment in the fresh state are best left dirty and packed in moist sphagnum moss. Plants bound for fresh extraction or dehydration are shaken free of sand, briefly washed and allowed to drip until they are externally dry. The plant contains water-soluble saponins, so extended washing is counterproductive. Although some medicine makers use the fresh plant (Gruenwald, ed., 2000), the more traditional use is in the dry form. Drying the plant before use may prevent the occurrence of rare side-effects, which include emesis and catharsis. Traditionally, true unicorn is dried in the whole form, thereby limiting oxidation and loss of volatile oils. Dry the plants in a warm place with positive airflow. A forced-air dehydrator may also be used. Dry for 1 day with low temperature (70° F = 21° C) and high air flow, then turn up the temperature to medium (90° to 100° F = 32° to 38° C) and continue until the rhizome is internally dry. The dried plants are then stored in plastic bags in lightproof sacks or drums, in a cool, dark and dry location. The herb remains stable for about one year in storage.

Medicine. True unicorn is primarily a nourishing, digestive tonic: a mild bitter, a decent antispasmodic, a pronounced sialagogue, a stimulant to the appetite and a good remedy for treating upset stomach, excess gas or diarrhea. Therefore the folk name "colicroot."

The plant also has a special affinity for the female reproductive organs, and has been used for imparting strength to the uterus and ovaries. This activity is synergised by the concomitant improvement of digestive function. Therefore the folk name "maiden's relief." True unicorn (like wild yam) contains diosgenin, and has an antispasmodic effect on the uterus.

The plant also assists in regulating ovulation and the menstrual cycle. True unicorn has also been used as an adjunct therapy in treating prolapsed uterus and associated lower back pain.

Diverse opinions have been set forth concerning the *taste* of true unicorn root. I find it mildly bitter, with a saponin-like acridity that lingers in the back of the throat. One of the earliest investigators, Jacob Bigelow states in his early treatise entitled *American Medical Botany* that true unicorn has a "genuine, intense and permanent bitterness." In direct contrast, *King's Dispensatory* states that the root is "odorless, acrid to the taste, *not bitter*" [their italics] (Felter and Lloyd, 1898). The modern compendium *PDR for Herbal Medicines* states that "The plant has a sweet taste, becoming bitter and soapy" (Greunwald ed., 2000). Have all of these investigators actually tasted the plant? Perhaps this confusion may be attributed to the subjective nature of taste itself, where the degree of bitterness is actually relative to the experience of the taster. However, the discrepancy may also be caused by the herb itself, which is most bitter when fresh, retains its bitterness when newly dried, and loses much of its bitterness in extended storage (Grieve, 1971).

Seed, seed collection, processing and storage. There are about 24,000 seeds in a gram of true unicorn seed. The mature stalks may be upended into a plastic bucket or gourd and shaken vigorously against the sides. The mature, reddish seed will spill from the capsules and accrue on the bottom of the vessel. The seed capsule opens and closes in accordance with the humidity. If it becomes necessary to harvest in moist weather, then it is best to strip the capsules from the stalk and spread them out on a piece of sheeting in a very dry place or (briefly) in the sun. They will open, and may then be agitated in a container to convince them to spill their seed. The seed is best separated from larger chaff by screening. Since the seed is very small, a fine screen will function nicely, allowing the dust-like seed to fall through onto a piece of sheeting spread conveniently and with foresight below the screen. The seed can then be gathered up and stored in a sealed plastic bag, in a cool and dry place. Such tiny seed carries only nominal nutrient reserves and thus retains its viability for two years or less. Best results will be obtained by using recent seed.

Conservation status. True unicorn is rare throughout its range. I know dedicated botanizers who live within the native distribution of this plant but have never seen it in the wild. The preferred habitat is shrinking daily as a result of development and especially due to the draining of the wetlands. Among all the plants on the UpS at-risk list, this one has been most nearly rendered extinct by aggressive harvest for the medicinal herb trade. Private conservation agencies as well as various state governments consider true unicorn to be a conservation priority. In Canada, *Aletris farinosa* is listed as "very rare," in New York it is "imperiled," in Delaware it is considered "rare to uncommon," and the plant has been extirpated from the state of Maine.

Other species. *Aletris farinosa* is the most northern-hardy of all *Aletris* species. The remaining species are limited to the South and are mainly found along the gulf coast. These include the showy golden colicroot *(A. aurea),* yellow colicroot *(A. lutea),* southern colicroot *(A. obovata)* and bracted colicroot *(A. bracteata)* which is a Florida endemic.

References

Deno, N. 1993. *Seed Germination Theory and Practice, Second Edition.* State College (PA): Pennsylvania State University.

Elliot, D. 1995. *Wild Roots.* Rochester (NY): Healing Arts Press, 128 pp.

Felter, H. and J. Lloyd. 1898 (Reprinted 1985). *King's American Dispensatory.* Portland (OR): Eclectic Medical Publishing, Vol. 1 & 2, 743 pp.

Grieve, M. 1971. *A Modern Herbal.* New York (NY): Hafner Publishing Company, Vol 1 & 2, 888 pp.

Gruenwald, J. (ed.). 2000. *PDR for Herbal Medicines.* Montvale (NJ): Medical Economics Company, p 11.

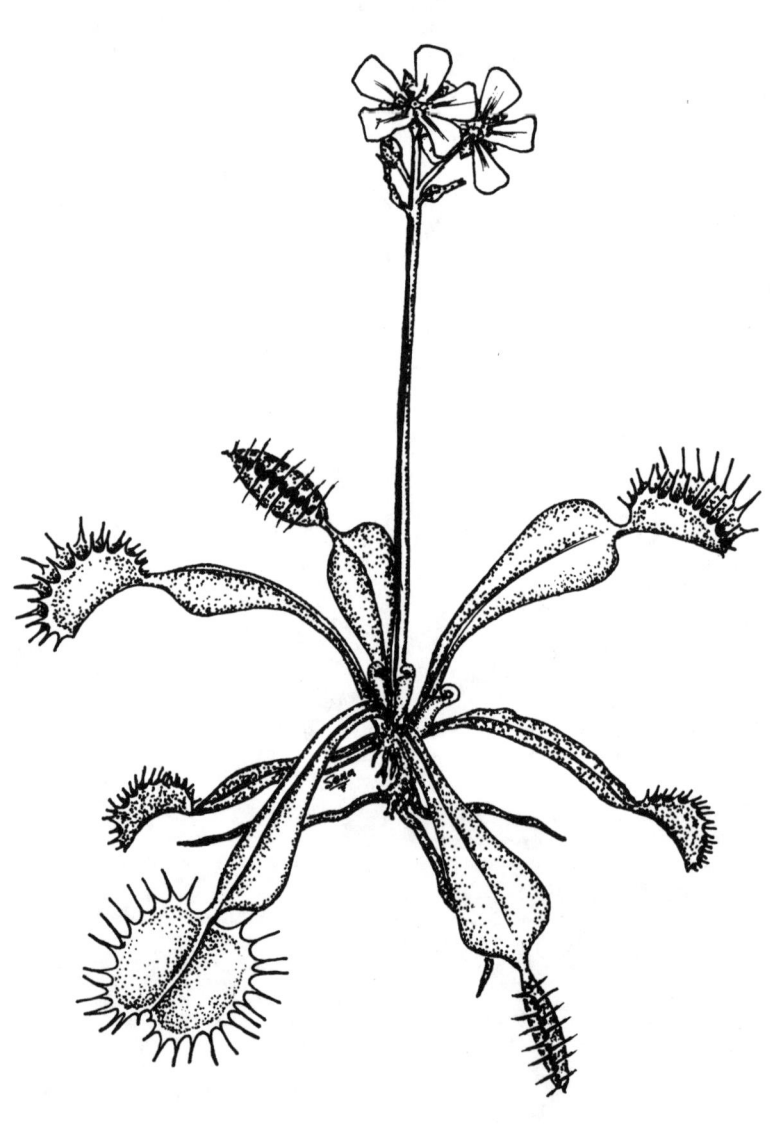

Venus Flytrap
Dionaea muscipula
root and flowering plant

Venus Fly Trap
Dionaea muscipula Ellis
Family: *Droseraceae*

Venus fly trap is an endemic, perennial, insectivorous plant of the southeast coastal plain of North and South Carolina. The roots consist of a few stiff, adventitious hairs that emanate from the very bottom of the bulb. The roots are dark brown and appear alive only at the growing tip, where the color is cream. The bulb itself is really composed of the blanched, layered, swollen bases of the leaf petioles. There is no "core," per se, but rather a composite effect, maintained by the ongoing formation of new, thickened leaf stems from the center. After accomplishing several digestive cycles, the mature, peripheral leaves die off right to the base of the bulb. The leaves also die back as the plant enters winter dormancy. The leaf itself is composed of a wide stem with a rounded dorsal ridge (opposed by a ventral channel) that runs between two flattened wings. These wings shoulder in gracefully just prior to the trap, and the dorsal ridge becomes a neck-like support for the trap, eventually composing the hinge. The hinge is the result of advanced evolution of cell structure–opposing cell surfaces become flaccid or turgid through osmosis, thereby opening or closing of the trap. The trap itself is composed of two reddish-green, symmetrical, flattened hemi-spheres (lamina) rimmed on the outer edge with a reptiliomorphic line of curved teeth. These interlock when the trap is closed. When open, the "trigger-hairs" are also visible, mounted on the fleshy inside surface of the lamina, three to each side. The plant excretes an agreeably sweet nectar from glands located at the base of the teeth. Flies or other insects are attracted, but when they land to drink, they stimulate the trigger hairs. This sends a primitive neurological signal to the hinge, which causes the precipitous closing of the lamina. They close in two phases. In the first step, the trap closes incompletely, thereby allowing small insects to escape through one of the many gaps between the teeth. This is an adaptation designed to conserve digestive energy—if the reward is too small to justify the expenditure of plant resources, then the digestive process is curtailed and the trap again swings open. If the insect is too large to escape, then the unlucky victim in its struggle will continue to stimulate the trigger hairs. The lamina then close upon it, interlocking the teeth and hermetically sealing the edge. Excreted from glands on the surface of the membrane, digestive enzymes then liquefy the proteins of the insect. This nitrogenous energy is absorbed into the plant, and after about six days the trap again opens and the process can repeat.

Plant carnivory has evolved in many parts of the world, but the commonality of all habitats where insectivores live is simply that the soil substrate is nutrient-poor. The insectivorous plant puts little energy into the root, devoting the majority of its resources into (and deriving most of its nutrients from) insect capture and digestion.

The flowering stalk of the Venus fly trap is smooth and round, rising to a height of 6 to 18 inches (~15 to 46 cm). The stem is topped by a cluster of largish, 5-petaled flowers colored white with greenish veins. There are usually 3 to 10 flowers in a cluster. These give way to the seedpod, an ovoid capsule that splits open when ripe. The seeds are numerous, smooth and very black.

Current Range of Venus Fly Trap

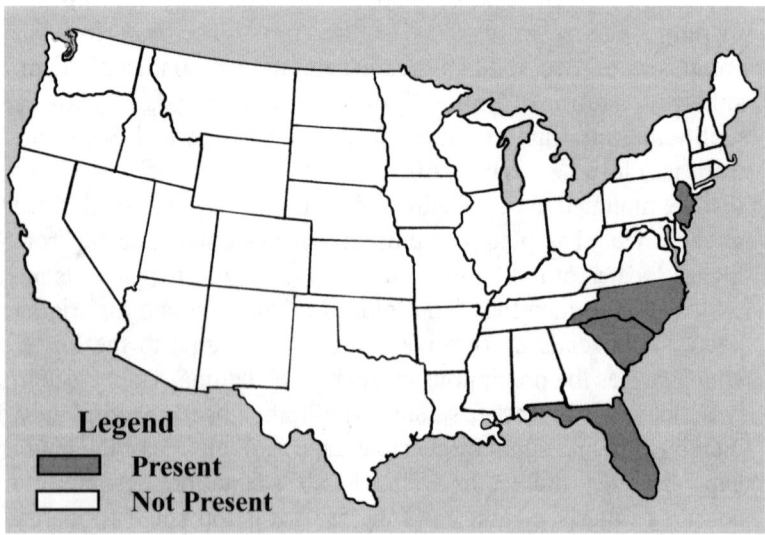

Range, hardiness and adaptability. Venus fly trap is native to a very localized range in the outer coastal plain and sand hills ecological regions within a 100-mile radius of Wilmington, North Carolina. The largest extant concentration, probably comprising 50% of the remaining wild population, is located on Holly Shelter Game Reserve near Wilmington. The plant has been transplanted and naturalized to the wilds of the New Jersey pine barrens and also to the Apalachicola National Forest of the Florida panhandle (Clewell, 1985).

Venus fly trap has a tenuous hold on existence and relies on a very limiting group of exacting environmental conditions to support its survival in the wild. Although acid wetlands outside the native range (even when located in the eastern Piedmont or in the South) might serve as surrogate homes for the plant, a primary conservation objective is to protect and encourage the growth of remaining wild stands in situ. Another relevant objective is to support the rehabilitation of wetlands, thereby winning back the many places within the native range of the plant where it once grew, but is now extirpated.

The plant is relatively easily grown in a cool greenhouse, and many of the plants sold to the novelty trade or sold for extraction are greenhouse-grown. In all cases the original plants must have been taken from the wild. Ideally, propagation would continue without further damaging the wild populations, by utilizing seed, bulb divisions, leaf cuttings and tissue culture from cultivated progeny. Given the right combination of soil and water, the plant may also be successfully grown in a backyard bog (see sundew). This will be effective in mild winter areas only, where wintertime temperatures dip no lower than 40° F (4.4° C).

Ecology and plant community. Venus fly trap prefers a warm, sunny exposure and a constantly moist substrate. In nature, the plant grows in wetlands, generally where a high water table is maintained by seepage of water over an impermeable hardpan (such as clay), usually located within 24 inches (60 cm) of the surface. The plant grows in wet, coarse, acidic, nutrient-poor soils. The pH value ranges between 3.9 to 4.5 (Roberts, 1958).

267

Venus fly trap actually grows best in ecotonal areas—that is, in the zone where one ecological type melts into another. These ecotonal zones exist between, for instance, the longleaf pine savanna and evergreen bogs, or sometimes along the edges of slow streams or seasonally flooded waterways.

These ecotones are kept open by the influence of frequent flash fires, which prevent the encroachment of woody species. The growth of Venus fly trap is actually much stimulated by flash fires, which help assure that the plant gets adequate light. The fires also purify the growing beds, serving to diminish the growth of fungi, which are somewhat of a plague to the soft tissues of the plant. In turn, the burned-over plants clump-up, multiply and spread rapidly after a fire.

These ecotones are also areas of great plant diversity and are a hot spot for other carnivorous plants such as butterworts *(Pinguicula* spp.), pitcher plants *(Sarracenia purpurea* and *S. rubra)* and sundew *(Drosera* spp.). All of these plants are basically pointer plants for each other, and equally dependent on an ever-moist substrate that does not flood.

Other associates of Venus fly trap include bryophytic mosses, canebrake, sedges, grasses such as bushy broom grass *(Andropogon glomeratus)* and rushes such as redpod rush *(Juncus trigonocarpus)* and slender nutrush *(Scleria minor).*

A diverse grouping of semiaquatic and terrestrial herbs such as blue flag *(Iris versicolor),* brahmi *(Bacopa monniera),* eclipta *(Eclipta alba),* death camas *(Zigadanus* spp.), gayfeather *(Liatris spicata),* milkworts *(Polygala* spp.), rough boneset *(Eupatorium pilosum),* savannah meadowbeauty *(Rhexia alifanus),* saw palmetto *(Serrenoa repens),* slender goldenrod *(Solidago stricta),* true unicorn *(Aletris farinosa),* and white pond lily *(Nymphaea odorata)* may often be found in the area.

Life cycle. Venus fly trap flowers in the early summer. The flower is borne on a long stem at a surprising distance above the rosette, possibly to provide a safety zone for beneficial pollinators that might otherwise fall prey to the traps. The flowers soon blacken and whither, revealing the seed capsule, which then splits apart to reveal clumps of tiny, black seeds that persist on the stalk and in time gradually fall away. When they come into contact with the coarse surface of the soil, they are able to work their way in a little, being dense and smooth. This is a perfect situation for germination, where the seed is slightly buried on a friable surface and fed water from below through capillary action within the substrate. Germination occurs in warm soil. The growing rosette of the plant is small at first, but capable of catching insects in the first year of growth. The rosette goes dormant in the winter, and reestablishes itself in the spring, sprouting new traps. The rate of growth is directly proportional to the level of protein intake. In nature, it requires five to seven years for a flytrap to reach flowering age from seed.

The plant is capable of self-division, where a single rosette divides and becomes two. In fact, asexual splitting and clumping is a more significant proliferation tactic than is self-seeding. The plant also frequently self-layers when the dorsal surface of a healthy leaf comes into contact with moist medium and roots-in. In this manner, the plant can spread to form patches regardless of the success or failure of seed germination. The ability to self layer is important, because the very act of producing seed saps much energy from the plants, while division and layering seem to increase vigor and longevity. To my knowledge, the maximum age of Venus fly trap has not yet been established. Given the tendency toward asexual replication, clonal individuals representing centuries-old genotypes are probably still extant.

Cultivation from seed. In keeping with the natural dissemination cycle, the seed may be sown during the late summer all the way through to spring. The soil medium for the seedbed, flat or pot is best composed of equal parts of peat moss and coarse, sharp sand. The method for producing coarse, sharp sand is detailed in the peyote chapter (under "cultivation from seed," page 173). Some growers use 100% peat moss; others make do with equal parts of peat moss and perlite or pumice. Mix the very fine seed with a little sand, and strew it over the surface of the medium. Then cover with a crumbling of coarse peat moss or small pieces of live sphagnum moss and firm in gently. Germination is improved when the temperature remains between 70° and 80° F (21° and 27° C), also by maintaining a high relative humidity (70% to 90%), and by providing bright light. The seeds must be watered by a fine mist from above, or by capillary action from below. A typical method is to immerse the plastic pot in a shallow tray that is then filled with water. Purified water, or soft water from rain, ponds or streams is best. Chlorinated water is poison to the plant. Seed will lie dormant during cold weather, and germinate when conditions are more favorable. Germination usually occurs within 3 to 6 weeks of planting in a warm medium. The plants may be transplanted to 6 inch (15 cm) centers as soon as they develop 3 traps. In the greenhouse, seedlings may reach sexual maturity as early as two years after planting.

Cultivation by division and by cuttings. The "bulb" is really no more than a rosette of thickened stem bases, not unlike the basal portion of a celery plant. This may be divided by removing the plant from the growing medium, removing all dead or dying vegetal debris, then separating the healthy plant into two equal halves. If each division retains a few root hairs, all the better. The divisions may then be replanted at a distance by burying in the root hairs and firming the medium around the base to hold the plant in place.

Cuttings consist of the entire petiole and trap, removed from the plant at the point of juncture, which is just below surface level. Place the cutting dorsal side downward on the moist medium and sprinkle a few coarse pieces of peat moss or sphagnum moss on top of the stem. Gently tamp in. Keep the cutting warm, slightly moist and in filtered light. Bottom heat is helpful at this stage. Within the space of 10 weeks or so, roots will emerge and take purchase in the medium, and a new bud then forms (Slack, 1979).

General care. During the growing season, Venus fly traps will thrive when temperatures range from 70° to 80° F (20° to 27° C), where the relative humidity ranges between 70% and 90%. The plants require little upkeep beyond the maintenance of the soil, moisture and light requirements that have already been discussed. In such a situation, weeds are not usually a problem, but if grasses or other herbaceous plants encroach, they are best removed. A healthy plant usually consists of about five operable traps, with new traps forming at the center of the rosette and old traps dying off at the perimeter. In order to discourage formation of molds, the old leaves need to be removed with a sharp knife or scissors as soon as the traps blacken and die. Aphids can infect indoor flytraps. They suck the juices from the stems and leaves, but suffer a reversal of fate when they wander onto the surface of the trap and are in turn digested by the plant.

Fertilization of Venus fly trap from below is contraindicated. The plants will sequester their own nutrient supply from above in the form of gnats and flies. Some propagators supplement by foliar feeding. A weak protein solution such as very dilute fish emulsion is most commonly employed, given once a week. However, reasonable care must be taken to mist only the leaves, and not the substrate. Other growers close the windows and raise vegan flytraps by foliar-feeding with weak soy milk or the whey left over after making tofu.

Winter dormancy is an essential phase. Plants should be allowed to enter their normal dormancy in the late autumn. Watering is kept to a minimum at this time, in order to discourage rotting. Ideal temperatures for winter dormancy range between 45° and 55° F (7° to 13° C). In mild winter areas, the cold greenhouse is an ideal place to overwinter Venus fly trap, but in severe winter areas the plants will have to be kept indoors.

Medicine. The use of Venus fly trap as an immunostimulant and anticarcinogen was first conceived by a German medical doctor named Helmut Keller. In the year 1973, during a trip to the United States, he chanced upon a Venus fly trap at a flower shop in Maine. He stood transfixed, marvelling at the apparently advanced immune system at work in the plant that allows for the conversion of potentially pathogenic foreign substances into nutrients. He further intuited that the plant extract might stimulate the *human* immune response by assisting in the breakdown of primitive tumor cells. Dr. Keller proceeded to test and support his theory, first by means of chemical analysis and later in clinical trials. He confirmed the presence of a complex chemistry in the plant, which includes naphthoquinone derivatives that hold commonality with other immunostimulating and anticancer herbs (e.g. sundew and pau d'arco *(Tabebuia impetiginosa)*). The plant

271

also contains substantive quantities of flavonoids, phenol carboxylic acids, amino acids and enzymes which may combine in synergy to produce the pharmacological effects. The results of Venus fly trap therapy have reportedly been positive in the treatment of suppressed immunity, cancer and leukemia. Dr. Keller developed several forms of administration, including oral drops, capsules, an inhalant and injectables. He eventually patented a "phytonutrient" made from Venus fly trap juice, which he named Carnivora® (Keller, 2000).

For home use, the fresh plant juice is obtained by grinding the entire Venus fly trap plant, expressing the juice under pressure and immediately adding sufficient grain alcohol to preserve it (Cech, 2000).[1] The preserved plant juice reportedly has very low or no human toxicity, but this must be approached with circumspection. External exposure to the raw juice of the plant will damage the skin, since the proteolytic enzymes fail to differentiate human proteins from insect proteins. The raw juice, if allowed to sit for more than a few minutes without any means of preservation (such as grain alcohol), can become contaminated by poisonous endotoxins. Such a contaminated extract would be deleterious if taken internally and would be decidedly harmful if further manufactured into the injectable form. The presence of endotoxins in injectables is almost certainly responsible for listed side-effects of Venus fly trap therapy, which include elevated body temperature, chills and circulatory damage (Greunwald, ed. 2000). Subcutaneous or intramuscular injection of Venus fly trap juice should never be attempted by laypeople. Professionally manufactured Venus fly trap injectables are administered under the care of qualified physicians, mainly in Germany.

---

[1] For more information on making herbal succi (preserved plant juices), see "Making Plant Medicine" by Richo Cech (Chapter 9, Herbal Succi and Syrups).

Yield. The average weight of a fresh, mature Venus fly trap plant is 3 grams. Therefore, 1 pound of fresh plants would be composed of approximately 150 plants. The water content of the fresh plant averages around 87%. Due to the innate inefficiencies of grinding and expression of juice from fresh plant material, in practice each fresh plant yields approximately 2 ml of juice.

Harvest, processing and storage. The herb is processed in the fresh state as soon as possible after harvest. The entire plant is lifted from the growing medium, picked through to remove dead or dying leaves, then briefly washed in cold water. It is extremely important to avoid use of decayed material due to the potential of contamination with endotoxins. If the plants are to be stored or shipped to a distance, they must not be washed, but instead packed in moist sphagnum moss and kept cool until they can be used. The plants may then be unpacked, picked through, washed, promptly processed and preserved immediately with alcohol. The preserved plant juice lasts for about two years in storage, but all precipitate must be filtered out before use.

Seed. Venus fly trap seed is black, smooth, shiny and tear-shaped. The seeds measure about 1 mm long by 0.6 mm wide, but are slightly irregular in size and shape; 1 gram of seeds contains approximately 7,000 seeds.

Seed collection, processing and storage. The seed of Venus fly trap is easy to collect. However, many growers remove the flowering stalks as soon as they appear, having observed that adult plants become much more robust if flowering and seeding energy is redirected to the formation of new roots and traps. It is a good idea to allow some of the plants to make seed, though, since planting by seed is the best way to assure genetic diversity and stability in cultivated populations. After the stalk matures and begins to dry, the seed capsules break down, but the seeds still adhere in tiny clusters. The seed is hand-stripped from the stalk, spread out on a white sheet to dry for a day or two, picked through or screened to remove foreign debris, then stored in a sealed plastic bag or glass vial in a cool and dry place. The seed retains its viability for at least a year, but best results will be obtained by using recent seed.

Conservation status. Venus fly trap is not listed as a federally endangered species (and probably should be), but it *is* listed by the state of North Carolina as "imperiled" and by the state of South Carolina as "possibly extirpated." International trade in live Venus fly traps is also controlled by CITES, which helps assure that plants sold internationally are derived only from cultivated sources. CITES listing notwithstanding, wild harvest of the plant continues. One investigator noted that "This is one of the most exploited of southeastern plants, large populations being decimated or exterminated for the novelty plant trade" (Kral, 1983). Recent surveys of remaining Venus fly trap populations seem to confirm that the plant is losing its tenuous grasp at a very fast pace. Historically, there were 49 recorded occurrences of the plant in North Carolina which are now considered extirpated. In South Carolina there were 26 such sites. Within the last 15 years, 37 known populations of the plant have been extirpated, indicating a rapid deterioration of habitat. The plant is currently extant in only 10 counties of North Carolina, and one in South Carolina (NatureServe, 2001). Threats to the sustainability of Venus fly trap are fourfold: illegal harvest for the novelty plant trade, illegal harvest for the medicinal herb trade, habitat conversion for forestry or development, and fire suppression.

This Venus fly trap, this intricate, impossible, consummate example of plant evolution, rests at the center of a buzzing swarm of polar opposites. The plant is wonderful, but it eats flies. It likes protein, but hates compost. In nature it lives in noble colonies, but it becomes a freak in the novelty trade: individuated, cupped in styrofoam, capped by a plastic bubble, overstimulated by prodding pencil-point and fed fatal bits of cheese. Humans may think that novelty holds priority over environment, but *frogs* do not agree. Of course, frogs may be better attuned, since they too are fly-eaters. When the wetlands disappear, the communal chorus of the frogs falters and goes silent. Without water, the jellified globules of their eggs dry up like jellyfish on a hot beach. Are we culturally deaf to this message from the frogs? Truly, it is unacceptable that we resignedly prioritize forestry and development (toilet paper and condos) over the preservation of an ancient and irreplaceable environment and all its wetland life forms.

References

Cech, R. 2000. *Making Plant Medicine*. Williams (OR): Horizon Herbs Publishing, 282 pp.

Clewell, A. 1985. *Guide to the Vascular Plants of the Florida Panhandle*. Tallahassee (FL): Florida State University Press, 605 pp.

Godfrey, R. and J. Wooten. 1981. *Aquatic and Wetland Plants of the Southeastern United States: Dicotyledons*. Athens (GA): University of Georgia Press, 933 pp.

Keller, H. 2000. Dr. Helmut Keller is the medical director of Carnivora Research, Inc. in Nordhalben, Germany. His official website is http://www.carnivora.com/carnivora.html

Kral, R. 1983. *A Report on Some Rare, Threatened or Endangered Forest-Related Vascular Plants of the South*. Atlanta (GA): USFS Technical Publication R-8-TP 2, Vol 2, 1305 pp.

NatureServe. 2001. *NatureServe: An Online Encyclopedia of Life Web Application*. Version 1.4. Arlington (VA): Association for Biodiversity Information. www.natureserve.org

Roberts, P. and H. Oosting. 1958. *Responses of Venus Fly Trap (Dionaea muscipula) to Factors Involved in its Endemism*. Ecological Monographs, 28(2), pp. 193-218.

Slack, 1979. *Carnivorous Plants*. London: Ebury Press.

Weakley, A. 1993. *North Carolina Natural Heritage Program List of the Rare Plant Species of North Carolina*. Raleigh (NC): Natural Heritage Program, North Carolina Department of Environment, Health and Natural Resources.

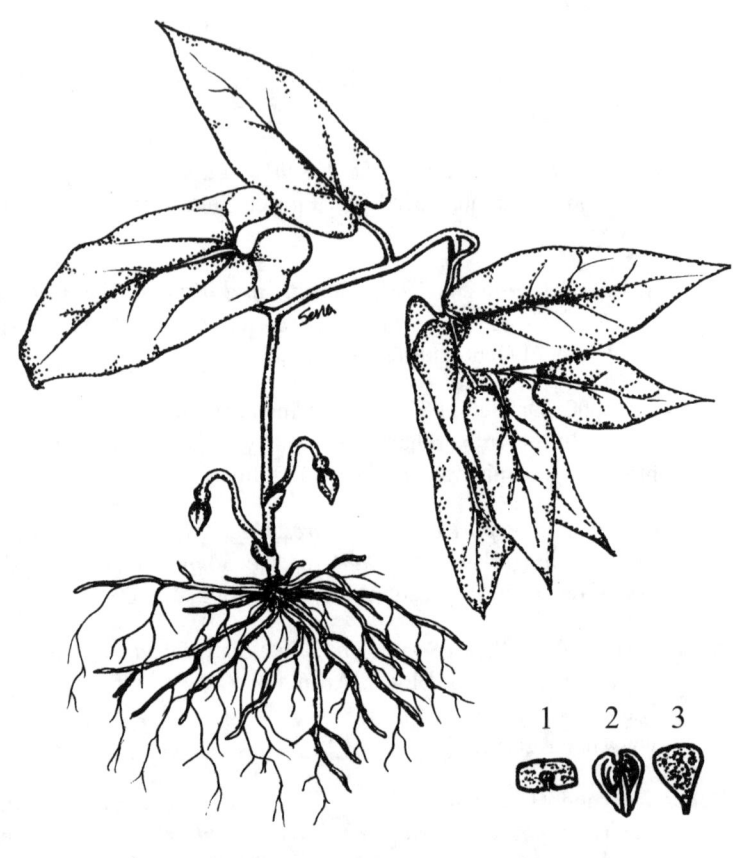

Virginia Snakeroot
Aristolochia serpentaria
root, rhizome and budding plant
three views of enlarged seed:
1) aerial, 2) ventral, 3) dorsal surface

Virginia Snakeroot

Aristolochia serpentaria L.

Family: *Aristolochiaceae*

Virginia snakeroot is a diminutive, crooked, vining, herbaceous perennial of the eastern deciduous forest biome. It is a member of the birthworts, an ancient,[1] diverse and peculiar family of plants represented by 22 species native to North America and about 400 species worldwide, many of them tropical. These are generally woody, climbing vines endowed with unusual flowers shaped like antique tobacco pipes. Several species are referred to by variations on the common name "Dutchman's pipe." Our Virginia snakeroot is the main species used in herbal medicine, although other species are similarly employed (see "other species" section, page 287). The plant once grew in extensive patches, and has been an article of commerce since early colonial times. Since then, this little vine has been hunted and picked nearly to extinction. Regardless of its small size, Virginia snakeroot has never failed to elicit attention, mainly due to the volatile odor of its roots (somewhere between camphor and turpentine) that suggests potent medicinal activity. Along with other members of its genus, Virginia snakeroot is currently under siege by the United States Food and Drug Administration (FDA). The roots contain aristolochic acid, which the FDA claims is a potent carcinogen and nephrotoxin, further charging that intemperate use of the plant has been the cause of kidney failure in some individuals. This information on the taxonomy, conservation status and potential toxicity has been included by way of a preliminary orientation to the complexities of the plant.

---

[1] Indeed, some investigators consider the *Aristolochiaceae* to be "paleoherbs" that were among the first representatives of angiosperms on earth, dating back perhaps to the Cretaceous period. Angiosperms are plants that produce seeds enclosed in a protective vessel. Paleoherbs have uncomplicated flowers, demonstrating a mixture of features pertaining to both monocots and dicots (Wing et al, 1993).

The underground parts of Virginia snakeroot are a root-rhizome structure, known in commerce as "the root." The rhizome is compact and dense, giving off numerous wiry, yellowish roots that spread horizontally and much exceed the bulk of the rhizome and are equally endowed with aromatic qualities. The odor is volatile and pervasive. The crown gives rise to one or more slender, smooth, reddish stems that rise up from the forest floor to a maximum height of about 12 inches (30 cm). The stems are jointed and give a muted zigzag impression. They are branchless vines, producing new leaves and increasing in length only from the growing tip. The graceful, alternate leaves are firmly clasped to the stem by short, tough petioles. These light green and inconspicuous leaves are shaped in the form of an elongated heart. The flower consists of a dull, reddish-purple, tubular calyx, shaped like the letter "S," swollen at the base and at the opening, with a triangular lip. The flower is rarely seen, as it is borne on a stalk that bends down to the earth, generally hiding below the leaves of the plant, also being camouflaged by the duff of the forest floor. The flower gives way to an oblong, 6-celled seed capsule that contains up to 20 seeds (Angeroth, 2001). The profile of the seed is like a triangle with rounded corners. The seeds are shell-like, composed of a hard and durable testa that protects the thin internal endosperm. The ventral surface is deeply concave, sporting a white, upright raphe that stretches across the wide opening. The dorsal surface is convex, colored light brown and covered with distinct white dots that are best observed under slight magnification. Viewed from above, the characteristic hole-and-notch may be observed where it opens into the cavity (see seed illustration p. 276).

Range, hardiness and adaptability. Virginia snakeroot is native to the eastern, southern and midwestern United States. The plant is now an uncommon find in the wild, but was once represented by large patches throughout its range.

Virginia snakeroot is specific in its requirements for a shaded, moderately dry, hardwood forest habitat. Extremely cold winter temperatures are not well-tolerated, and this is one of the factors which limits its distribution in the North. Plants growing within the native range on well-drained, forested slopes, insulated by a thick mulch of leaves and buried under snow, are likely to come through

278

dormancy in very good condition. Gardeners outside the native range of the plant may have success by matching the preferred conditions in the shade garden or in forest plantings. However, gardeners in the far North, the mountains of the West and the Southwest may have difficulty creating the right microsite. The plant has been successfully cultivated in the maritime West.

Current Range of Virginia Snakeroot in the U. S.

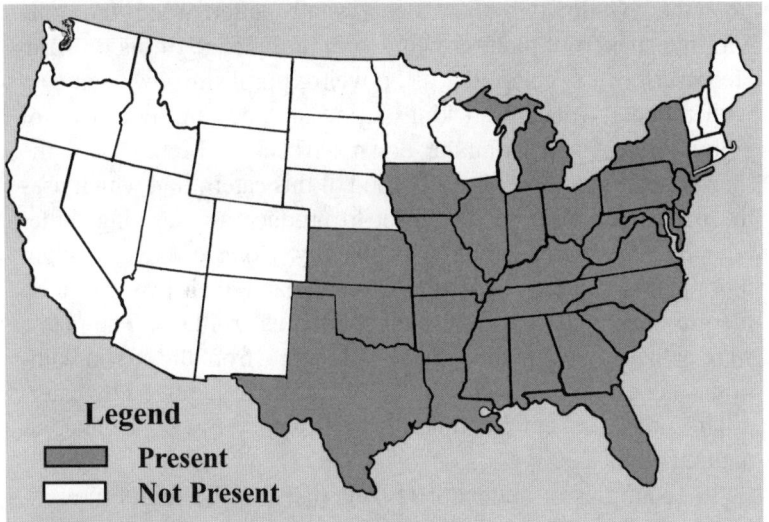

Legend

Present

Not Present

Ecology and plant community. Virginia snakeroot prefers the full to partial shade of a mixed hardwood forest. Full sunlight is not tolerated—this is truly a forest-dependent species.

In nature, the plant lodges in a wide range of soil types, including loam, sand, shale and clay soils. Deep forest loam is preferred. Soils produced by hardwood trees are best. The ideal pH value ranges between 5.5 and 6.5. The plants are most commonly found in soils that are sweetened by limestone detritus or by larger limestone features within the forest.

The plants require good drainage, although they will thrive both in moderately dry forests and in moister areas. In a drought year the Virginia snakeroot often survives better than associated plants. According to Rod Angeroth, in a dry autumn in Iowa "the wild ginger wilted to the ground, but the serpentaria remained upright . . ."

Virginia snakeroot tends to grow in sparse colonies that are maintained by self-seeding and by way of creeping stolons. According to historical accounts, the plant once made monotypic colonies composed of many hundreds of individuals, but in all my trekking through the eastern forests I have never seen more than a few individuals in a colony. Normally if you see one plant, it is likely that there are one or two more close by. Doug Elliot tells a good story about finding the caterpillar of a rare and handsome pipevine swallowtail *(Battus philenor)* butterfly on the lone Virginia snakeroot plant growing wild at the edge of his orchard. He describes the caterpillar as "a weird, purplish-brown sea slug with rubbery tentacles sticking out on all sides and two rows of yellow-orange spots running down its back." Members of the *Aristolochia* genus are the only food of this caterpillar, which uses the potent chemistry of the plant to produce an alarming, bitter odor that repels predators. On this day, Doug discovered eight more plants in the orchard, not by recognizing their leaves, but by the presence of more of the multicolored caterpillars. The plants were actually eaten to the ground, but regrew from the crown within the same year and were not that year further harassed by caterpillars—an excellent example of the tendency toward balance in nature (Elliot, 2000).

Examples of understory plants that may be found in association with Virginia snakeroot include American ginseng *(Panax quinquefolius),* briers *(Smilax* spp.), goldenseal *(Hydrastis canadensis),* skullcap *(Scutellaria* spp.), twin leaf *(Jeffersonia diphylla*) and wild ginger *(Asarum canadense).*

Among the many tree species that make up the eastern mixed hardwood forest, black oak *(Quercus velutinas),* hickory *(Caya* spp.), pawpaw *(Asimina triloba),* sassafras *(Sassafras albidum)* and wild cherry *(Prunus serotina)* are likely to shade Virginia snakeroot. If these plants and trees occur in the woods, it is likely that conditions are right for growing Virginia snakeroot.

In the west, ideal soils are found under mixed alder *(Alnus oregona)* and big leaf maple *(Acer macrophyllum)* forests. Understory plants that are good indicators for black cohosh in the west are false Solomon's seal *(Smilacina racemosa),* Oregon grape *(Mahonia nervosa)* and wild ginger *(Asarum canadense).*

280

Life cycle. The seed of Virginia snakeroot germinates late in the spring, usually during the month of April or May. The plant itself also remains dormant for longer than most woodland plants, and may not become apparent in the forest until early June. The vining habit of the plant makes this late emergence possible, since vines occupy a different spatial niche than other forbs, thereby successfully competing for growing room and light. The flowers appear in the early summer, emitting a fetid odor that attracts ants and beetles to pollinate, also trapping tiny winged insects such as fungus gnats *(Sciarra* spp.). Mature plants may produce as many as 12 or more seed pods. When ripe, the pods open in the space of a few hours, in much the same manner as the blossoming of a lotus flower. The seeds are dispersed by gravity, falling around the base of the plant, and if they are buried by mulch and do not dry out, then they will germinate in the first or second spring after dispersal. Seedlings emerging in the direct vicinity of the parent are self-thinning, so any vector that contributes to scattering the seed to a greater distance (e.g. the movements of small mammals and invertebrates) is significant in furthering the species. Germination is hypogeal, with the formation of the first leaf about 5 weeks after germination (Deno, 1993). The seedlings vine up and produce several new leaves in the first year. Precocious seedlings may flower and produce 1 seedpod in the second year after germination, but it takes 3 to 4 years for the plant to flower and pro-duce seed on a consistent basis (Angeroth, 2001). Older plants may also form localized patches by sending out creeping stolons, often with multiple buds attached. These form new plants that are clones of the mother. Each mature plant produces one or more dormant buds for the next year's growth. In the late summer to early fall, the leaves turn bright yellow. The plant dies back after the first killing frost of autumn. The life span of Virginia snakeroot has not, to my knowledge, been accurately determined, but Rod Angeroth has kept individual plants in cultivation for around 10 years' time. Given the fact that relatives of this plant were among the first of all angiosperms on earth, and given the preservative properties of the root and the preference for moderately dry forest habitat, it would not surprise me in the least to learn that individual Virginia snake-roots live at least as long as the trees that shade them.

Cultivation from seed. In cadence with the natural cycles, the seed is best sown as soon as possible after it ripens, thereby fulfilling the requisite period of warm conditioning followed by overwintering with germination in the late spring. The seed will perish if allowed to dry out. The easiest way to meet the necessary requirements is to sow the newly harvested seed in a prepared bed in the forest, or in a bed or flat in the shade garden or shadehouse. The majority of seeds will germinate in the first spring, with additional germination in the second spring. Seed sown in the shadehouse at Horizon Herbs Seed Farm on 9/25/01 germinated vigorously on 6/1/02, a germination period of 249 days. The germination rate was approximately 60%.

Subjecting the seed to cold storage immediately after harvest will cause extended dormancy. A good procedure for preparing the seed for short-term storage has already been discussed in this book (e.g. chapters on bloodroot, ginseng and trillium). In this method, the newly harvested seed is kept in a mesh bag at the back of the sink for a period of at least three weeks and washed daily with pure water. This leaches germination-inhibiting compounds from the seed, and fulfills the requirement for an initial period of warm conditioning. After pretreating the seed in this manner, it may then be sown immediately or it may be stored in the refrigerator at 40° F (~4° C) in a moist medium (peat moss) in a sealed plastic bag, then sown in the autumn or in the very early spring.

General care. The seedlings may be grown at close spacing (~2 inches = 5 cm) apart for 2 years, until they are sufficiently developed to transplant. Thin or transplant to the final location at a spacing of 6 inches to 1 foot (15 to 30 cm) between plants. Firm the roots down in, with the crown slightly above the surface of the mineral soil, then fill in around the plant with a thick mulch of decomposed leaves or rotted hardwood sawdust. The mulch will also help exclude weeds. In very cold winter areas, the mulch should be applied again in the early winter to cover and protect the plants. Virginia snakeroot does not require fertilization, but the constant breakdown of the thick mulch will provide an ongoing source of vital nutrients. Plants grown from seed require at least 4 years to produce a useable root.

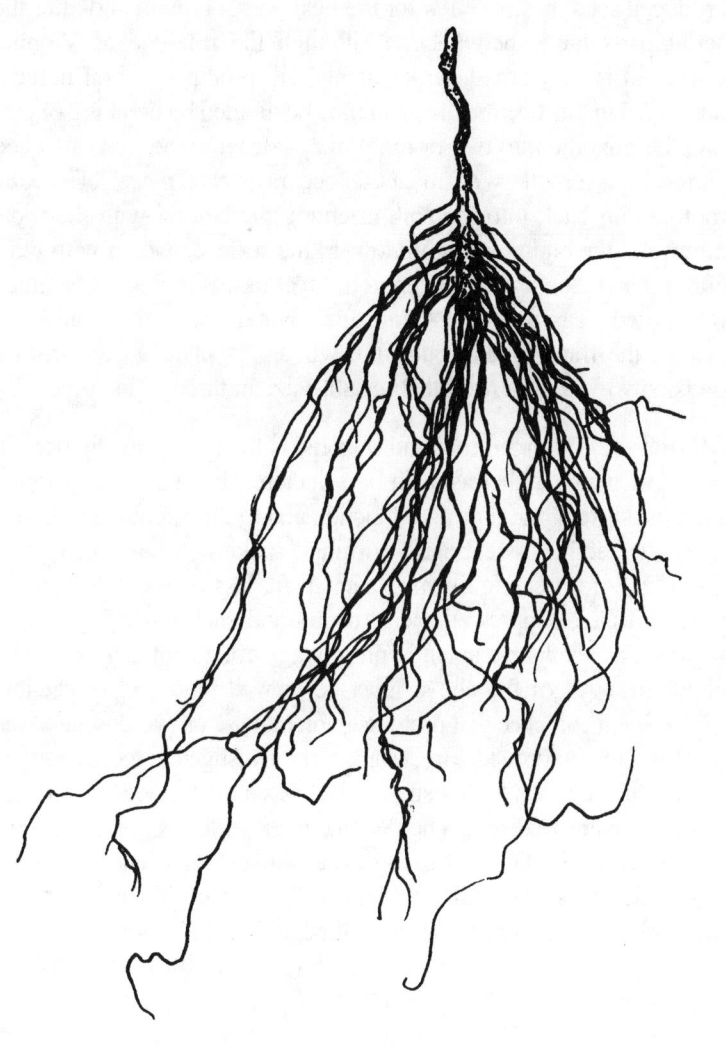

Virginia Snakeroot
Aristolochia serpentaria
two-year-old dormant seedling

283

Cultivation from division of the rhizome. Divisions are best made from mature individuals in the autumn, after the plant has produced seed, has set buds for the next year's growth and after the aerial parts have died back. Although the rhizome of Virginia snakeroot is very small, larger plants will produce several nascent buds. When this occurs, the plant may be divided by breaking or cutting the rhizome into two or more pieces, leaving the roots attached and making sure that a dormant bud occurs on each piece. Nestle the root cutting back into the soil, orienting the cutting with the roots down and the bud pointing up toward the surface. Cover with mineral soil and then provide a generous layer of leaf mulch, bark mulch or rotted sawdust to improve water retention and to protect the transplant through the winter. A plant grown from a division will usually reach harvestable size in three years' time.

Medicine. The dried root and rhizome is the part generally used in herbal medicine, either as a tea or a tincture. It is stimulating to the immune system, the digestive function and to the circulation. It also promotes active sweating. Virginia snakeroot has been used historically for treating fevers, rheumatism, loss of appetite, indigestion, parasites, suppressed menstruation and snakebite; it was once regarded as a valuable agent in promoting strong contractions during childbirth. All of the above must be viewed with circumspection, given recent evidence that prolonged internal use or overdosage of the plant is likely to prove toxic. Many early investigators recommended that the plant be used on a short-term basis and at low dosage. This advice remains relevant. The poultice made of the entire, crushed or masticated fresh plant was used by the Native Americans for treating toothache and snakebite (Moerman, 1986). There is good evidence suggesting that the plant does indeed neutralize the venom of poisonous snakes and spiders, and in fact many species of *Aristolochia* are used as antivenins in disparate cultures (Otero, 1995). The root is also used as an inhalant for treating headache, and the dilute tincture or the tea is used for treating sore throat and canker sores. Although external use may prove harmless, there are certainly other herbs which are more common and are also effective treatments for these disorders. Any herb rich in tannins (e.g. self-heal or white oak bark) may be substituted, and cultivated wild indigo root *(Baptisia tinctoria)* is a specific for treating atonic disorders of the throat.

Yield. An average mature rhizome with rootlets weighs 4 g fresh and dries down to 1 g. The water content of fresh roots ranges between 72% to 76%. There are about 113 fresh roots per pound, and 454 dried roots per pound. Fresh roots weighing 1 pound would dry down to about ¼ pound of dry roots.

Harvest, processing and storage. The plants are best harvested in the autumn, after the plant has disseminated its seed and when the root is at peak medicinal activity. Dig the roots and shake them free of dirt. If shipping fresh roots to a distance, they should be left unwashed and packed in moist peat in order to prevent deterioration. If the roots are bound for dehydration, wash them thoroughly in cold, running water. Dirt tends to cling to the matted rootlets. To dry, spread the roots out on screens in a warm, dark place with positive airflow, turning often. An herb dehydrator is very helpful in drying Virginia snakeroot. Dry for 1 day with low temperature (70° F = 21° C) and high air flow, then turn the temperature higher (90° F = 32° C) and dry it completely. The roots contain volatile oils that will dissipate under excessive heat. To a certain extent, the potent odors arising from the roots as they dry represent a diminution of the stimulating constituents of the root. Once they are thoroughly dry, the roots are best stored in glass jars or sealed plastic bags in lightproof sacks, in a cool, dark and dry location. Stored in this manner, the roots retain their potency for many years.

Seed, seed collection, processing and storage. Virginia snakeroot seed measures approximately 5 mm long by 3 mm wide. There are about 120 seeds in 1 gram of fresh, newly harvested seed. The seed does not withstand dry storage, and must be kept moist during harvest and handling until it is again planted.

This is certainly one of the rarest of seeds, and I hardly ever see it listed among the tens upon tens of seed catalogs and lists that arrive at my post office box in the (sometimes) bustling town of Williams. The plant is rare, and the seed capsule hides below the plant. Ripening and dissemination occur within the space of a day or two. Therefore, the seed collector must maintain an intimate relationship with the plant in order to know *where* the seed is, and *when* it is likely to be ready for harvest; otherwise the seed will most certainly get away.

One somewhat tedious method of seed collection is to tie a little mesh bag around the seedpod, arranged in such a way that the seed will fall into it when ripe (Angeroth, 2001). Another method is to cut a slit in a sheet and pull the plant and the unripe seedpods through this aperture, then tuck it in all around. The seed will fall on the sheet and can eventually be funneled into a container. Another method is to pick the gravid pod itself, and keep it in a warm and humid environment until it splits apart of its own volition and spills the ripe seed. It is difficult to determine the best day to pick the pod, and this method may result in wastage. Good luck!

The seed of Virginia snakeroot is best processed with the "mesh bag" technique (discussed previously under "cultivation from seed"). Live seed may be separated from dead seed by flotation—viable seed sinks and poor seed floats. Stored in a moist medium in the refrigerator, the seed may remain viable for up to two years, but best results will be obtained by planting recent seed.

Conservation status. It is perhaps a bit ironic that the active chemistry of Virginia snakeroot, originally produced by the plant as a protective mechanism, should prove in the end to be its undoing. If its roots and foliage were bland to the taste, the plant would have never found its way into international commerce, nor would it be so avidly chomped by the pipevine swallowtail caterpillar. Despite its small size, the inconspicuous flowering and the leaves that somehow melt into the mottled forest floor, Virginia snakeroot still garners its share of attention. The plant is listed in Connecticut, Illinois, Iowa and Michigan as a "threatened" species and is considered "rare" in both Maryland and Delaware.

In the year 1787, Thomas Jefferson penned a kind of historical milestone entitled "Notes on the State of Virginia." He described the fantastic resources of land, water, wildlife and trees of that early time, as well as such wonders as spontaneous water fountains and geysers of natural gas. Medicinal plant resources were also reported. In fact, 15 medicinal plants were mentioned—among them our Virginia snakeroot. Jefferson's document is worthwhile reading, providing an accurate and impressive rendition of what we once had, as well as an indication of how much we have truly lost.

Other species indigenous to the U.S. Among the many species in the *Aristolochia* genus, the presence of aristolochic acid is a commonality. This indicates a general similarity of medicinal activity, as well as a shared disadvantage of potential toxicity.

The pipevine *(Aristolochia macrophylla)* is a perennial vine native to rich, moist woodlands in the mountains of eastern North America. The leaves of this plant are broadly heart-shaped and may measure as large as 10 inches (25 cm) in length. The root of this plant was once considered to be a weak, but serviceable, substitute for Virginia snakeroot.

The wooly Dutchman's pipe *(Aristolochia tomentosa)* is a tall, climbing vine with downy branches that occurs at lower elevations, mainly in the southern United States and most commonly in the state of Louisiana. The activity of this plant was once considered to be nearly identical to that of Virginia snakeroot (Felter and Lloyd, 1898).

Texas Dutchman's pipe *(Aristolochia reticulata)* is native to the southwestern United States. It is another hairy species that once bore the strictly cowboy name of "Red River snakeroot." Historically, this plant was easier to find than Virginia snakeroot and also yielded more medicine on a per-plant basis. Therefore, it became widely used in medicine, and was considered an official species (Felter and Lloyd, 1898).

Indian Root *(Aristolochia watsonii)* is a trailing or climbing vine of the southwestern United States, Mexico and Baja. It is a desert plant, with brown-green leaves shaped like arrowheads and a purple flower that resembles the ear of a mouse. The plant produces seed capsules about the size and shape of a pecan, containing stacked rows of jet black, triangular seeds. Indian root evolved a completely different root structure from other members of its genus—a deeply excavating taproot—that allows it to survive in the open sun in the desert. The native (and current) uses of the plant are quite similar to those assigned to other species in the *Aristolochiaceae,* although Indian root lacks the stimulating, volatile oils that characterize Virginia snakeroot (Moore, 1989).

References

Angeroth, R. 2001. Personal communication. Rod is an accomplished grower of a few rare and unusual forest-dependent plants. He lives near the Missouri River, in the Loess Hills of western Iowa. This is a peculiar ecology formed by the prehistorical deposition of large quantities of river silt by wind. The Loess Hills are a hot spot for forest-dependent herbs, with representation of many significant species (e.g. American ginseng, goldenseal and our Virginia snakeroot). Rod served as a generous and knowledgeable consultant to this chapter, contributing to the plant description and giving technical information for the sections on life cycle, cultivation from seed and seed collecting, cleaning, storage and longevity.

Deno, N. 1993. *Seed Germination Theory and Practice, Second Edition.* State College (PA): Pennsylvania State University.

Elliot, D. 2000. *Virginia Snakeroot,* in Gladstar (ed.), *Planting the Future: Saving our Medicinal Herbs.* Rochester (VT): Healing Arts Press, p. 80.

Felter, H. and J. Lloyd. 1898 (Reprinted 1985). *King's American Dispensatory.* Portland (OR): Eclectic Medical Publishing, Vol. 1 & 2, 743 pp.

Moerman, D. 1986. *Medicinal Plants of Native America.* Ann Arbor (MI): University of Michigan Dept. of Anthropology, Vol. 1, 534 pp.

Moore, M. 1989. *Medicinal Plants of the Desert and Canyon West.* Santa Fe (NM): Museum of New Mexico Press, 183 pp.

Otero, R. et al. 1995. *Ability of Six Latin American Antivenins to Neutralize the Venom of Mapana Equis (Bothrops atrox) from Antioquia and Choco (Colombia).* Toxicon 33(6), pp. 809-815.

Wing, S. et al. 1993. *Implications of an Exceptional Fossil Flora for Late Cretaceous Vegetation.* Nature 363, pp. 342-344.

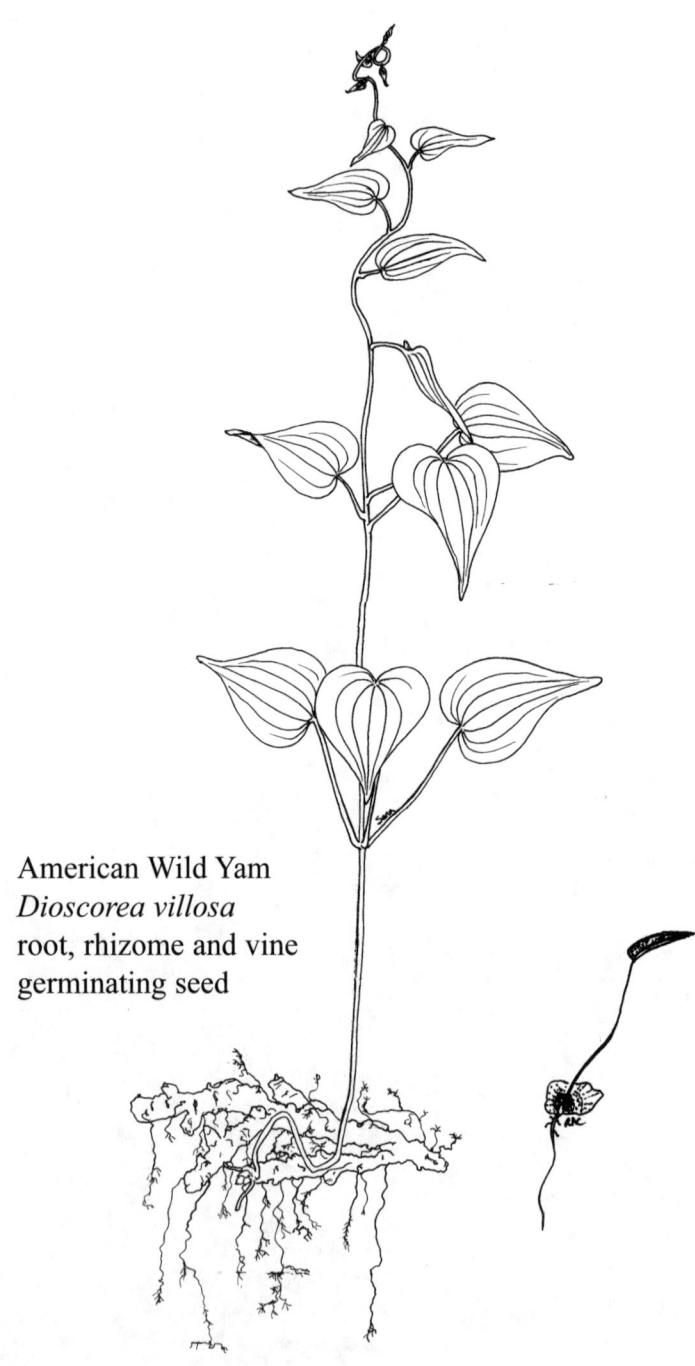

American Wild Yam
Dioscorea villosa
root, rhizome and vine
germinating seed

290

Wild Yam, American

Dioscorea villosa and *D. quaternata*

Family: *Dioscoraceae*

American wild yam is a perennial, dioecious, climbing vine of the deep forest or forest edge, found throughout the southern, central and eastern United States. Two main species are used indigenously in herbal medicine, in commerce almost always identified as wild yam *(Dioscorea villosa)*, but often consisting of the dried rhizome of fourleaf yam (*Dioscorea quaternata*). There is little difference in the medicinal potency of the two, and they are considered medicinally interchangeable. The plants are similar, to be sure, but there are definite differences between them, both in terms of morphology and preferred habitat.

Wild yam *(Dioscorea villosa)* has a contorted, pencil-thin rhizome that runs parallel with the surface of the soil. The rhizome is internally white and externally a mottled brown, punctuated on the dorsal surface with circular stem scars remaining from the growth of previous years. The rhizome also shows smaller, raised scars caused by the deterioration of root fibers. The texture of the rhizome is cartilaginous and somewhat brittle when fresh, becoming hard and immutable as bone once dried. The rhizome branches freely along its length, elongating healthily from the soft, whitened tips that nose through the soil, eventually creating an interlaced web. Hair-like feeder roots emanate from the rhizome, dense below and sparser above. The feeder roots consist of single, long filaments bristling with short, alternating rootlets. The feeder roots are soft when fresh, but become coarse and wiry upon dehydration. The top of the rhizome gives rise to one or many round, smooth, green, vining stems that bear multitudes of prominently veined, heart-shaped leaves. The leaves often occur in a single whorl at the base of the plant. Progressing upward, the leaves attach alternately to the stem, diminishing in size as they approach the leading tendril. The vines rise up, sometimes self-entwining into thickened bundles, taking purchase wherever possible on other plants, bushes and trees. Wild yam can easily reach a height of 20 feet (6 m). Male plants produce loose, drooping spikes of inconspicuous, greenish-yellow flowers that dry up after pollination. Female plants, when sufficiently mature and in a good year, produce drooping masses of three-winged fruits that are held individually upright by means of a short, hook-shaped stalk. When the fruit dries, it turns from bright green to a papery brown. Upon opening, the silvery, mother-of-pearl interior is revealed. Each pod contains up to two seeds per chamber, totalling six seeds per pod under ideal conditions. The seeds are thin wafers, chocolate brown in color and winged for transport.

Fourleaf yam (*Dioscorea quaternata*) has a contorted rhizome that is knuckled on the back (like a fist) and attains the thickness of a large thumb. Although the rhizome will run through the upper layer of the soil, it is not as aggressive as *D. villosa* and it tends to remain more in place. The rhizome of fourleaf yam is scaly on the surface and colored a dark brown. It is punctuated on the dorsal surface with circular stem scars or the woody stumps of previous stems. Internally, the rhizome is textured similarly to *D. villosa,* being cartilaginous and somewhat brittle when fresh and becoming hard and bony once dried. Coarse feeder roots emanate from the rhizome, above and below. These roots are sparser, smoother and noticeably thicker than those of *D.villosa* (~0.7 mm as opposed to ~0.3 mm), becoming extremely tough and wiry upon dehydration. The top of the rhizome gives rise to one or several round, smooth, green, vining stems that bear wide, prominently veined, heart-shaped leaves. The leaves are substantially larger than those of *D. villosa,* usually occurring as two sets of four-leaved whorls at the base of the plant. Under ideal conditions the plant progresses upward into a vine, with leaves attaching alternately to the stem, overlapping like the scales of a fish. However, many plants, especially those found in the deep woods, do not vine at all, giving rise to only a single stem supporting a whorl of leaves. The pods and seeds of *D. quaternata* are larger than those of *D. villosa.*

Range, hardiness and adaptability. American wild yam currently ranges throughout the southern, central and eastern United States with the exception of the northern states of New England. The Rocky Mountains form a barrier that has prohibited its spread into the West. The plant grows most prolifically in the southern portions of its range.

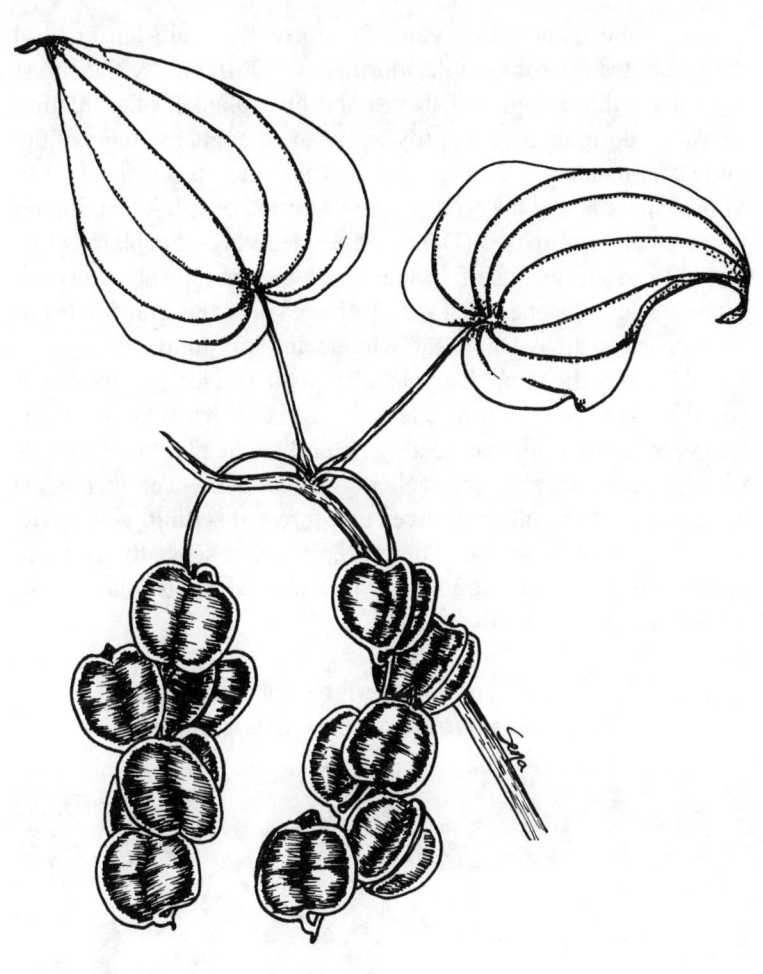

American Wild Yam
Dioscorea quaternata
leaves and green seedpods

American wild yam is perfectly cold-hardy and demonstrates a strong winter dormancy. Buffered by the forest trees, by a thick mulch of leaves and by a blanket of insulating snow, the dormant roots readily withstand the bitter winters of the midwestern states. Another sign that the plant is accustomed to a cold winter is that the seeds require a period of cold-conditioning for optimal germination (Deno, 1993). However, the plant is just as likely to sustain itself in the forest by sending out creeping rhizomes to a distance as it is to self-seed, and this contributes to its survival in areas where the winters are very mild.

During the growth cycle, the plant thrives in moist, hot conditions in the semishade of a mixed hardwood forest. Growers in the South can readily naturalize the plant in the hardwood forest and expect excellent yields. However in the far North, even if the plant survives in a forested setting, yields will be disappointingly small. Therefore, it makes sense to grow the plant outdoors in the South, and in a shaded, moist and humid greenhouse in the North.

Current Range of American Wild Yam
(*Dioscorea villosa* and *D. quaternata*)

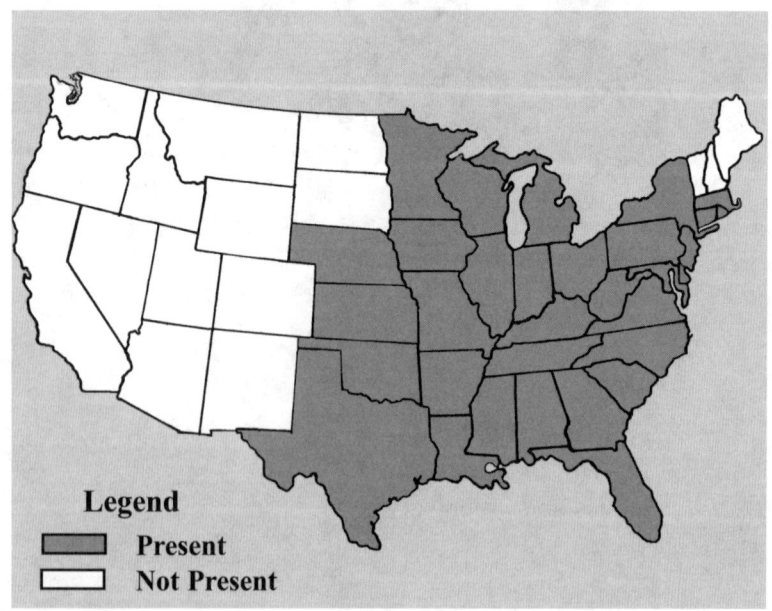

Legend

◼ Present
☐ Not Present

Ecology and plant community. American wild yam prefers the partial shade of a mixed hardwood forest. *Dioscorea villosa* grows best at the edge of the forest where it receives partial sun. *D. quaternata* tends to grow in the deep forest, where it receives only dappled light. The larger size of the leaves of *D. quaternata* may be an adaptation designed to increase photosynthetic efficiency in shady areas.

The wide distribution of the plant is also an indication of adaptability to diverse soil types, which may include loam, clay and shale. The ideal pH value ranges between 5 and 6. Heavy soils are not a challenge to the plant, which prospers equally well in light loam and in heavy clay. Both of these soils tend to hold the moisture throughout the summer. Sandy soils protected from dehydration by a deep mulch of organic debris are fine for growing wild yam, but the roots will die in sandy soils that dry out during the summer.

Adequate rainfall is another prerequisite to healthy growth, flowering and root production. In a drought year the plants will struggle, flower sparsely or not at all and slip into an early dormancy. Conversely, a summer of plentiful water will much increase root production and speed development of the vine while supporting healthy flowering and seed production.

Plants that associate with wild stands of American wild yam are those forest-dependent herbs that are tolerant of partial sun. Black cohosh *(Cimicifuga racemosa)* and mayapple *(Podophyllum peltatum)* are good examples. Spice bush *(Lindera benzoin)* is a woody shrub species that is an indicator plant for rich soil and may often be found in close association with American wild yam. Among the many tree species that make up the eastern mixed hardwood forest, tulip poplar *(Liriodendron tulipfera)* and pawpaw *(Asimina triloba)* are likely to shade and perhaps serve as a natural trellis for wild yam.

In the western states, ideal ground for growing wild yam may be found in the alder-maple forest. Look for soil pockets resulting from long term deposition of carbonaceous debris and soil, and avoid areas where there is a lot of sand or cobble. Plants that indicate good wild yam growing ground in the West include sword fern *(Polystichum munitum),* Oregon Grape *(Mahonia nervosa)* and trillium *(Trillium* spp.).

Life cycle. Reproduction of American wild yam by seed requires both male and female plants, which then pollinate with the wind. Flowering occurs during the summer, and the seed is disseminated in the autumn and in the winter. The three-winged pod breaks in pieces, spilling the seeds that float and turn on the air, often landing at some distance from the parent. If the seed is covered by debris or by soil, then there is a good chance that it will germinate as the ground warms in the spring. A certain percentage of the seed will not germinate until the second spring, an adaptation designed to widen the reproductive window for the plant. This is especially significant because seed production is dependent on ideal conditions of light, fertility and water that do not occur every year.

Germination is hypogeal. The seedling consists of a single true leaf in the first year, giving rise in the late summer to another stem and more leaves, becoming in successive years a twining vine that seeks light and elbow room by climbing above the herbage of the forest floor. Vines in general are good survivors, opportunistically using other plants for support. They utilize a unique niche in the forest not occupied by forbs, bushes and trees. This allows them to optimize their resources. In nature, the plant takes about four years from seed to produce a full-sized root and to reach sexual maturity. Reproduction by seed is important because it assures the availability of both male and female plants.

The plant spreads vigorously by way of the creeping rhizome, often producing vines that appear to be from separate plants, but are actually connected. Old portions of the rhizome may die off, while the leading tips remain healthy and viable. In this manner, the plant may travel for a great distance at the edge of the forest, forming a genetically identical community. To my knowledge, the maximum age for wild yam has not been established. The rhizome does not make growth rings, and counting stem scars is not a reliable method of determining the age of a plant that may produce scores of stems in a single growing season. The tissues of the rhizome are extremely resilient and rot-resistant. I have personally tracked seed plants in my own gardens for at least 15 years. They show no signs of deterioration. On the basis of all this, I would not be surprised to learn that the plants survive and prosper for hundreds of years.

Cultivation from seed. In accordance with the natural cycles, the recent, dried seed of American wild yam is best sown in shaded beds or flats in the fall, midwinter or very early spring, after which it germinates in the late spring in warm soil. For example, recent seed of *Dioscorea villosa* was sown on 11/27/01 in deep flats in the shadehouse at Horizon Herbs Seed Farm. The seeds germinated synchronously, each producing a single true leaf on 5/3/02, a germination period of 157 days. Similarly, *D. quaternata* sown on 11/3/01 germinated on 5/12/02, a germination period of 190 days.

When sowing in nursery beds in the shade garden or in the forest, prepare a fine seedbed and sow the seeds in shallow furrows, then cover with mineral soil, followed by a light mulch of decomposed leaves or rotted sawdust. Given the potential for a low germination rate, it makes sense to plant the seed densely.

My experiments show a range of germination from 40% to 70% for seed sown in the fall. Dry-stored seed sown in warm soils in the spring (without cold-conditioning) will not germinate until the second spring.

The new seedlings form a pea-like nugget (a bulbous rhizome) in the first year. They can be easily separated at this early stage without damage to the roots. They may be transplanted immediately to pots or left in the flat and grown at close spacing for a year, then transplanted into larger pots or to the final location, with a desired final spacing of 2 feet (60 cm) between plants. Raising plants from seed requires about four years from planting the seed to the harvest of a mature root.

Cultivation from root cuttings. This is by far the easiest way to propagate wild yam. In the autumn, simply dig the parent plant and break or snip the rhizome into sections. Or, dig only the peripheral running rhizomes and leave the central crown undisturbed. It will regrow. A good cutting consists of from 2 to 4 inches (5 to 10 cm) of running rhizome with associated root fibers still intact in a ball of soil. Replant the cutting in the desired location, nestling it about 1 inch (2.54 cm) deep in mineral soil and covering with mulch. New vines arise from the upper surface of the rhizome. Plants grown from cuttings require from two to three years to attain sexual maturity and a full-sized root.

General care. Wild yam is a heavy feeder. Plants grown in five-gallon pots in the greenhouse will literally consume the majority of the potting soil within a year or two, after which they require repotting with new soil. Plants grown in the shade garden may be fertilized in the spring with a dressing of composted manure or organic compost, which will greatly improve growth of the vine as well as flowering, seeding and root production. Plants grown in the forest tend to develop more slowly, and may be allowed to naturalize. After the autumn leaffall, it makes sense to rake large quantities of leaves onto the yam beds, which will then compost down and nourish the emerging plants in the spring. Make sure to provide a trellis, or allow the vines to climb on associated plants and trees.

Medicine. The dried rhizome with associated rootlets (the root) is the part used. Ingestion of the fresh root may cause gastric irritation, nausea and/or emesis. Reasonable dosages of the dried root (in tincture form or as a decoction) are a dependable tonic and antispasmodic for smooth muscles and organs, including the gastrointestinal tract, ovaries and uterus. The indications are: colic (a paroxysm of acute abdominal pain), hiccups, gastrointestinal irritation, pain caused by gallstones, painful menstrual cramps, cramps during ovulation, nausea during pregnancy, neuralgia and nerve spasm. The efficacy of wild yam for treating premenstrual syndrome (PMS), hot flashes and other symptoms associated with menopause is due to the antispasmodic and tonic effects, not because the herb is a "progesterone precursor." There is no known physiological pathway that converts the saponins of wild yam into progesterone. Instead, the human body uses endogenous *cholesterol* as a steroidal hormone precursor in order to produce progesterone.

Yield. Representative 2-year-old plants that had been grown in the greenhouse from cuttings were dug and weighed. On the basis of these samples, the average fresh weight of *Dioscorea villosa* roots was determined to be 105 grams. The average fresh weight of *D. quaternata* roots was 205 grams. The water content of the roots of both species ranged from 62% to 66%. A pound of fresh root would therefore contain from 2 to 5 plants. A pound of dried roots would contain from 6 to 12 plants. The yield is extremely variable. Wild-harvested fresh roots weighing a pound or more are common.

Harvest, processing and storage. American wild yam root is best dug in the fall, after the plant has fixed primary and secondary constituents for the long winter dormancy. Dig with a garden fork or with a shovel. The roots of *D. quaternata* are usually pretty easy to get up, because they are dense and localized. The roots of *D. villosa* are slower to dig, because they are thin and tend to run out to a greater distance. Shake the roots free of dirt, then transport them to the nearest stream or garden hose. Watch for off-colored, dead or moldy sections of rhizome and discard these right away. Although the saponins are water-soluble, the tissues of the root are so hard that even extended washing in cold, clear water will not deplete the medicine. After the roots are clean, they are best snipped into pieces while still fresh and cartilaginous. The preferred size of the pieces depends on the efficiency of the milling apparatus. A heavy duty hammermill can, with difficulty, digest whole roots and eventually reduce them to powder. Wear ear protection. A smaller grinder (such as a kitchen blender or coffee grinder) will grind only thin pieces. If no method of grinding is available, then the roots may be sliced into very thin flakes while still fresh, and the pieces dried. Once dried, these slices can then be extracted as-is, without grinding.

Wild yam root pieces are subject to mold formation in the drying process. Therefore, it is important to dehydrate them in a very warm place with adequate ventilation, and to turn them regularly until they are dry. Take care not to allow the roots to take on moisture at night, or they can easily mold and be ruined. An herb dehydrator is very useful in drying wild yam. Dry for 1 day at low temperature (70° F = 21° C) and high air flow, then turn up the temperature to 110° F (43° C) and dry them for at least 2 more days, or until they are dehydrated all the way through.

Store dried wild yam roots or root pieces in sealed plastic bags or glass jars, out of the light. Properly dried roots will retain their potency for a year (despite their hardness, they are subject to deterioration in storage). Once the dried roots are ground up, they oxidize more quickly and the powder is best used immediately.

Seed, seed collection, processing and storage. Wild yam seed is chocolate brown, with a flattened central germ plasm surrounded by a thin, irregular wing. Wrinkles radiate from the periphery of the central germ plasm through the membranous wing to the outer margin. The overall appearance is a little like a fried egg, although the color would be wrong. The central germ plasm measures about 5 mm, while the entire width of the seed is about 2 cm. There are about 80 seeds in a gram.

The three-chambered seed pod is green when unripe, and brown when fully ripe. Because the seed matures late in the season when precipitation and cold weather combine to encourage sodden, moldy conditions, it can be challenging to pick the pods at just the right time for optimal seed maturity. Pick too early and the seed is unripe; pick too late and the seed is likely to have flown from the pod or molded within the pod.

The ripe pods are stripped from the vine and taken home for further processing; they are best dried in a warm, airy place, where the temperature does not exceed 90° F (32° C). Once they are thoroughly dry, the pods are spilled out on a table and pulled apart by hand. Chaff and damaged seed goes in one pile, while good seed goes in another.

Wild yam seed is best stored in a glass jar or in a sealed plastic bag, in a cool and dry place. Expected life span is about 1 year, but best results will be obtained by using seed from the recent harvest.

Conservation status. At this writing, the Federal Department of Fish and Wildlife is considering American wild yam for a CITES Appendix II classification *(Federal Register/*Vol 66, No. 113/ Tuesday, June 12, 2001). Such a classification would prohibit export of wild yam plants and dried roots. However, since the plant is utilized mainly within the United States, a CITES classification would have little impact on the sustainability of the plant. Also, it is unclear whether such legislation would group all species of American wild yam together, or whether there would be some attempt made to differentiate the various taxa. This would seem to be an impossible task, since there is little or no attempt made to identify the species or variety of plants being dug and sold on a commercial level.

The current harvest of wild yam (all species) from the American forests ranges between 58,000 and 62,000 (dry) pounds per year (McGuffin, 2001), which equates to the loss of approximately 745,000 plants. The plant is still a fairly common find in many parts of its range, although it can be quite rare in peripheral areas. Although harvest for medicinal use may deplete populations in some areas, the main challenge facing this forest-dependent plant is most certainly the loss of essential habitat.

Other species. There are three species of wild yam native to the continental United States. *Dioscorea villosa* and *D. quaternata* have been discussed at length. The third is Florida wild yam *(D. floridana),* which has a sparse distribution within a limited range that includes the coastal plain of South Carolina, Georgia and Florida (Wunderlin, 1996). The plant is listed as a species of "special concern" in Georgia. Wild harvesters do not necessarily differentiate this plant from the more common species of American wild yam, and no doubt the root of Florida wild yam occasionally passes as *"Dioscorea villosa"* in commercial shipments.

The hairy-stem wild yam *(Dioscorea villosa* var. *hirticaulis)* is one of the several accepted varieties of American wild yam (USDA PLANTS database, 2001). The hairy-stem wild yam is probably the original source of the "true wild yam" mentioned in *King's Dispensatory* (Felter and Lloyd, 1898). According to Felter and Lloyd's historical documentation, these "true rhizomae" were already becoming "very scarce" by the year 1850. The hairy-stem wild yam is now listed as "imperiled" in New Jersey, "rare and endangered" in Maryland and a species of "special concern" in Georgia.

Mexican yam *(Dioscorea mexicana)* is native to Mexico. The vine has a glabrous stem that exudes a clear, viscous nectar at each node. This sweet substance is highly prized by ants, which will travel long distances to partake of it. The plant is characterized by its glistening, flattened, semiaerial bulb that is decorated with handsome tortoiseshell-like markings. The bulb of the mature plant measures up to 1 meter in diameter. In the early 1940s, Russel Earl Marker of Penn State University identified Mexican yam as a rich source of the saponin constituent

301

known as diosgenin. Professor Marker subsequently developed a revolutionary and efficient process that employed *D. mexicana* as a raw material to synthesize the human hormone progesterone. This research eventually resulted in the manufacture of the first birth control pills, also contributing to the development of cortisone and other steroidal drugs.

There are at least a score of *Dioscorea species* native to Mexico. Of these, *Dioscorea floribunda* has proven most useful as a rich source of saponins (Dixit, 1987). This plant is now being grown on a commercial level (mainly in India) to supply the pharmaceutical industry with diosgenin, but most synthetic progesterone is currently produced from a much more abundant and inexpensive plant, the soybean.

References

Deno, N. 1993. *Seed Germination Theory and Practice.* State College (PA): Pennsylvania State University.

Dixit, B. S. et al. 1987. *Analysis of Diosgenin Content in Some Selected Clones of Dioscorea floribunda.* Journal of Economic and Taxonomic Botany, 10(2), pp. 313-316.

Felter, H. and J. Lloyd. 1898 (Reprinted 1985). *King's American Dispensatory.* Portland (OR): Eclectic Medical Publishing, Vol. 1 & 2, 743 pp.

McGuffin, M. 2001. *AHPA's Tonnage Survey Results.* United Plant Savers Bulletin

USDA, NRCS. 2001. *The PLANTS Database, version 3.1* (http://plants.usda.gov). National Plant Data Center, Baton Rouge, LA 70874-4490 USA.

Wunderlin, R.P. 1996. *Atlas of Florida Vascular Plants.* Institute for Systematic Botany, Tampa (FL): University of South Florida.

Afterword
(by the author)

I wrote this book from beginning to end, literally. Somewhere around the writing of the chapter on trillium, a feeling of restlessness grew within me. This restlessness was synchronous with the onset of spring, heralded by the Siskiyou fritillaria *(Liliaceae)* that poked through the leaf mulch in the bottoms— I mean the creek bottoms on our farm in Williams, Oregon. One morning in April, I sat in my office in the seed house, improbably hunkered over a humming computer, surrounded by cascading reference books, magnifying glasses, scientific rulers, half-desiccated roots and piles of seeds. Birdsongs pierced through the shrouded window, reminding me of the spring I was missing. I pushed back the keyboard. Suddenly finding myself outdoors, I knew in an instant that I would be outside for the rest of the day. Clouds billowed down from the peaks away and above, buffeting-in spatters of rain from the coast. Meanwhile, warm winds wafted up from the sun-heated lowlands, the two fronts of weather creating an ever-changing display in the sky against the mountains. Before I knew it, I was in the bottoms, eagerly raking up leaves from the trails onto the beds and fitting half-rotten logs as people-bumpers around the growing areas. Intermittently, I challenged myself by transporting rocks. These waterworn boulders were lodged in the creek, having rolled downstream during the height of the winter rains. A few of them were bound to become part of a stone wall I was planning to build to define a new garden area out by the goat shed. There I was, calf-deep in crashing mountain creek water, choosing out and hefting up a medium-sized boulder, feeling its awesome weight increase as it broke the surface. But lift it I could, and I was already finding a place for the rock in the wall that was taking shape in my mind. Hands half-slipping on the cold, wet stone, I raised it first onto my thigh, examining it thoroughly, brushing away and returning back to the water all clinging creatures— *Crustacea* and sand-clad periwinkles. Grasping the rock with what I hoped was unshakable determination, I made my way solidly out of the creek, feet barely lifting in shoes that felt as heavy as iron and spouted water with each step. Leaning back slightly, waddling around a few sword ferns, I felt like a woman pregnant with twins. I staggered down my newly defined paths between the awakening beds (bloodroot and Jack-in-the-pulpit) and veered uphill. About halfway up the crude board-and-dirt steps on the bank, I thought my heart would jump out of my chest, and waited for a second at a tiny landing, the rock balanced on one thigh. But the rock was heavy enough to sap my strength even during rest, and so I continued up, trying to avoid making too many histrionical ejaculations. With a last surge of effort, I trudged over the top of the hill and clunked the stone down on the bed of my waiting Toyota pickup, which then sagged appreciably. I fell exhausted on my back, next to the rock, chest heaving involuntarily. But after a few breaths, my pulse slowed. Lying there, looking again at the clouds that were now partially obscured by the unfurling leaves on the maple trees above, I considered how the journey of making this new book was like hauling rocks from the creek—a lot of work for a small and heavy thing.

****

One late evening in July I was weeding among the corn plants out in the garden. In the western sky, a portentious, red-clouded sunset slowly gave way to a sparkling crescent moon. In the eastern sky, gathering storm clouds shuttered the glowing stars, sending a grumble of thunder across the mountainside. My hands felt their way between the turgid cornstalks, fingers pushing through a light crust into the still-warm depths of the soil. The roots of the manure-fed crab grass stretched as I pulled, then came free with a satisfying, muted sound of tearing. I shook out the dirt and tossed the weeds on the path behind me. Pushing the newly loosened soil back around the corn plants, I left in my dark wake a perfect row, free to grow and buttressed against the wind. A frog tuned up in the nearby pond. I stopped weeding, gazed again at the moon and realized that it is through nurturing the soil and growing plants that we humans can return to the earth a little of what we owe. I found myself at that moment in balance with all life and happy to be alive. Those of us who have the opportunity to garden are truly blessed. May we all find ourselves in the garden, and dedicate our work to the benefit of all beings.

306

Plant Index

Please note: Numbers given in **bold** indicate the page or pages where the plant species or genus is characterized in detail.

309

312

The beautiful and accurate botanical drawings that grace
this book flowed from the steady pen of Sena Cech.
When she is not hunkered down in the woods with the
flowers, she travels internationally, speaking many
languages and spinning fire. Sena also illustrated
"Making Plant Medicine" and is the author of
"Kidzerbs, a Kid's Guide to Growing Medicinal Plants."

Richo Cech started his professional work as an archaeolo-
gist and ethnobotonist in East Africa. Upon his return to
the United States in 1978, he began cultivating and saving
the seed of medicinal plants. Over the years, this growing
collection has become the basis for Horizon Herbs, LLC,
dedicated to "Sowing seeds worldwide for the benefit of
people, plants and the planet." Richo teaches and lectures
internationally. He is the author of the widely acclaimed
and quoted "Horizon Herbs Growing Guide and Catalog"
and "Making Plant Medicine." Richo lives with his family
on their herb seed farm in Williams, Oregon.

NOTES

NOTES

NOTES

NOTES

NOTES